TIFFANY SILVER

page 115 - #150 Renaissance

TIFFANY SILVER

by Charles H. Carpenter, Jr.

with Mary Grace Carpenter

DODD, MEAD & COMPANY   NEW YORK

First published as a Dodd, Mead Quality Paperback in 1984

Published by Dodd, Mead & Company, Inc.
79 Madison Avenue, New York, N.Y. 10016
Distributed in Canada by
McClelland and Stewart Limited, Toronto
Manufactured in the United States of America
Designed by Sidney Feinberg

Library of Congress Cataloging in Publication Data

Carpenter, Charles Hope, date
    Tiffany silver.
    Bibliography: p.
    Includes index.
    1. Tiffany and Company, New York.   2. Silverwork—
United States—History 19th century. 3. Silverwork—
United States—History 20th century. I. Carpenter,
Mary Grace, joint author. II. Title.
NK7198.T5C37   739.2'3'77471   78—12273
ISBN 0—396—08338—2 (pbk.)

Dedicated to our parents:

Grace Abercrombie Winnett
Mark Clarkson Winnett
Ila Atwood Carpenter
Charles Hope Carpenter (1889–1975)

Contents

Acknowledgments ix

Introduction by Henry B. Platt, President, Tiffany & Co. xiii

Foreword xv

1 Changing Views on Victorianism 1

2 The Early Years: 1837–1867 6

3 The Leading Silversmiths 24

4 The Sumptuous Table—1: Hollow Ware 51

5 The Sumptuous Table—2: Flatware 90

6 Silver Out of the Dining Room 124

7 Presentation Silver 140

8 Presentation Swords and Guns 154

9 Yachting and Other Sporting Trophies 169

10 The Japanese and Other Exotic Influences 180

11 Electroplated Silver 212

12 The Making of Tiffany Silver 222

13 Tiffany Marks 243

14 The Twentieth Century—A Postscript 262

A Note on the Care of Silver 273

Notes 277

Tiffany Source Material 283

Bibliography 285

Index 289

Acknowledgments

It would have been impossible to write this book without the cooperation and help of Tiffany & Co. When we originally approached Mr. Walter Hoving, Tiffany's Board Chairman, we asked for assistance and access to their files, while making it clear that we would write the book in our way and that all the final decisions would be entirely our own. We were given carte blanche. Tiffany's files (they are vast) were opened to us, and many people in the organization helped and advised us, and yet no one told us what to include or what not to include in the book. Duane Garrison coordinated our activities and opened doors. La Bar Hoagland's files on Tiffany marks and flatware patterns and his general assistance were invaluable. Henry B. Platt, President of Tiffany's, George O'Brien, Oscar Riedener, John Brown, and Edward Wawrynek contributed ideas and insights which appear in the book.

We spent many hours at the Tiffany plant in New Jersey studying the plant records, the library and working drawings, and silvermaking processes. Albert Grosskreutz was our mentor, advisor, and chief critic. Al's good-humored assistance and staunch belief in our project were very important to us. Many others at the plant were helpful: Louis A. Jensen, Edward Leavy, Gero Grohs, Deborah F. Cochran, Felix Linfante, and Joseph Levendusky.

We feel very fortunate to have had the advice and assistance of Donald L. Fennimore of The Henry Francis du Pont Winterthur Museum several times during the writing of this book. Donald read most of the manuscript with care and perception, making a number of valuable suggestions.

We wish to thank others who critically reviewed parts of the manuscript: Albert Grosskreutz and La Bar Hoagland of Tiffany & Co.; J. Herbert Gebelein of Gebelein Silversmiths, Boston; Colta Ives of The Metropolitan Museaum of Art; and Sohei Hohri of The New York Yacht Club.

We also wish to thank these people from the following institutions: Albany Institute of History and Art: Christine Averill, Norman S. Rice; Anglo-American Art Museum, Baton Rouge, Louisiana: H. Parrott Bacat; Art Institute of Chicago: Milo M. Naeve; Art Museum, University of California, Berkeley: Mark Rosenthal; Baltimore Museum of Art: William Voss Elder III, Mrs. M. B. Mumford; Barnum Museum, Bridgeport, Connecticut: Kenneth B. Holmes; Bethnal Green Museum, London, England: Elizabeth M. Aslin, Caroline G. Goodfellow; The Brooklyn Museum: Celestina Ucciferri; The Cleveland Museum of Art: Sherman E. Lee, Henry Hawley; Fairfield University Library: Elizabeth G. Coombs; The Hagley Museum, Wilmington, Delaware: Maureen O'Brien Quimby; The Hearst Mining Building, University of California, Berkeley: Judy Roberts; The Henry Francis du Pont Winterthur Museum: Alice K. B. Cooney, Mary Piendak, Deborah Waters; The Lockwood Mathews Mansion Museum, Norwalk, Connecticut: Barbara Ellison, Mrs. David B. Findlay, Jr., Carol Sutherland; Middleborough (Mass.) Historical Society: Mrs. Lawrence B. Romaine; The Metropolitan Museum of Art: Yasuko Betchaku, Marilyn Johnson Bordes, Mary Doherty, Sue M. Hazlitt, Diane Solomon, K. Tsujimoto; The Morse Gallery of Art, Winter Park, Florida: Hugh F. McKean; Museum of Art, Carnegie Institute, Pittsburgh: David Owsley; Museum of the City of New York: Margaret Stearns; Museum of Contemporary Crafts, New York City: Joanne Polster; Museum of Fine Arts, Boston: Wendy Cooper; The National Gallery of Art, Washington: J. Carter Brown; The National Museum of Ireland, Dublin: John Teahan; The New-York Historical Society, New York City: Mary Black, Robert G. Goelet, Mary Alice Kennedy; New York State Museum, Albany: G. Carroll Lindsay, J. L. Scherer; The New York Yacht Club: Julian K. Roosevelt; The Newark Museum: Phillip H. Curtis; Norwalk Historical Commission, Norwalk, Connecticut: Ralph C. Bloom; Office of Architect of the Capitol, Washington: Florian Thayn; The Philadelphia Museum of Art: Jane Claney; Preservation Society of Newport County, Rhode Island: John Cherol; The Roosevelt-Vanderbilt Historical Sites,

Hyde Park, N.Y.: Katherine B. Menz; The Smithsonian Institution: Craddock Goins, Margaret Brown Klapthor, Donald Kloster, Rodris Roth; Sotheby Parke Bernet: Kevin L. Tierney; Smith & Wesson: Roy Jinks; The Tennis Hall of Fame, Newport, Rhode Island: Mrs. Robert H. Haire, Robert S. Day; Union League Club, New York: Guy St. Clair; United States Naval Academy Museum, Annapolis: James W. Cheevers, William W. Jeffries; United States Patent Office: Barbara A. Evans; University of Nevada, Reno, Nevada: Kenneth J. Carpenter; University Club, New York: Thomas Boylan, James J. Carpra; Victoria and Albert Museum, London, England: Shirley Bury; West Point Museum, West Point: Robert Fisch, Michael J. McAfee; The White House, Washington: Betty Monkman.

We wish also to thank the following individuals: Mr. and Mrs. William Ball, Jr., Mrs. Irving Berlin, John Nicholas Brown, Mr. and Mrs. William C. Burt, Robert Carrick, Annette K. Diehl, Victor du Pont, Jr., Janice DuVal, Mr. and Mrs. Frank K. Edwards, Mr. and Mrs. Cruger D. G. Fowler, Mrs. Clarence E. Galston, Wendell D. Garrett, Sir William Gladstone, Flora Miller Irving, Mrs. Junius Jones, Allen Klots, Robert Koch, Clay Lancaster, William T. Lusk, Mr. and Mrs. John W. Mackay, Alfred Mayer, Mr. and Mrs. Karl E. Miller, Robert Mitchell, Mr. and Mrs. C. F. Murray, Andrew Nelson, Myron Orlovsky, S. Phelps Platt, George Reed, Dr. and Mrs. Edward H. Richardson, Mr. and Mrs. William D. Roosevelt, Maud Sargent, Barbara Briggs Seiler, Christopher Webster, Dr. Allen C. Weinert, Ellen Thomsen Weiss, Bruce Wood.

We particularly want to thank Arthur Vitols of Helga Photo Studios and Leland A. Cook of Tiffany & Co. who, together, were responsible for about half the photographs in the book. Other cooperating photographers not connected with museums were Clinton E. Clark, John Hopf, Terry McGinnis, Colin C. McRae, John Mills, Robert Mitchell, and Duane Suter.

Finally we want to thank our friends, Harry and Valdemar Hilbert, who suggested that we write this book and who encouraged and helped us in many ways.

MARY GRACE AND CHARLES CARPENTER

NOTE: Parts of Chapters 3, 4, and 9 were published in *The Magazine Antiques.*

Introduction

My interest in this book can hardly be called totally objective as it is in many ways a history of my family and the principles of quality as laid down by my great-great-grandfather, Charles L. Tiffany, founder of Tiffany & Co.

However, I do believe that Charles Carpenter, in this book on Tiffany nineteenth-century silver, has contributed greatly to our knowledge of American mastery of the decorative arts. Of particular interest is the heretofore little known influence of Edward C. Moore, under whose design leadership Tiffany became the world's preeminent manufacturer of silver articles. Indeed, Mr. Carpenter's research proves that Moore was far more important than any of us realized and that he was one of the most important forces in the formulation of the international Art Nouveau movement.

While Tiffany silver is Mr. Carpenter's main theme, he has skillfully woven it into the fabric of the nineteenth century. We are informed of social and working conditions. Telling anecdotes bring the world of the nineteenth century alive and illuminate our design inheritance and debt to the last century.

HENRY B. PLATT
President
Tiffany & Co.

Foreword

THE PRIMARY emphasis of this book is on the silver made and sold by Tiffany & Co. in the last half of the nineteenth century plus a brief postscript chapter on Tiffany silver of the twentieth century. We have also included in Chapter 5 twentieth-century flatware patterns. We felt it was important to show *all* of Tiffany's flatware patterns from the beginnings in about 1850 to the present day since many nineteenth-century flatware patterns continue to be made in the twentieth century.

On the other hand it was logical to end our study of Tiffany's silverware forms other than flatware essentially at the turn of the century. Victorianism died quickly. There was a marked stylistic change in these forms which took place around 1900. This is, of course, an oversimplification since examples of Victorianism continued to be made in the twentieth century. However, based on a careful study of the working drawings in Tiffany's files, and the study of the many surviving pieces of Tiffany silverware of this period, the evidence is clear that, particularly in hollow ware, a marked stylistic change *did* take place at the turn of the century.

The nineteenth century silver of Tiffany is fascinating and exciting in its range and quality. This is the part of the Tiffany story we feel will be most interesting to our readers. A more detailed study of the twentieth century silver can come later.

We trace the growth of Tiffany & Co.'s silver business from its beginnings in the middle of the nineteenth century to its world eminence by the end of the century. This book is *not* a history of Tiffany & Co., nor of its jewelry, nor of the fascinating objects other than silverware the company has made and sold in the fourteen decades of its existence. An account of the company itself has been well told in Joseph Purtell's *The Tiffany Touch* (New York: Random House, 1971).

We give full credit to the great Tiffany designers such as Paulding Farnham, James Whitehouse, Charles T. Grosjean, and particularly Edward C. Moore, the original driving force behind Tiffany's success in silver. We also discuss the place in the Tiffany story of Louis Comfort Tiffany. Although he was one of the great designers of his time and his glass has found a permanent place in art history, his influence on the silver made by Tiffany & Co. is shadowy. He was a director of Tiffany for many years, but only a relatively few pieces of Tiffany & Co. silver can be traced to his influence. Louis Comfort Tiffany's glass and decorating business which later became Tiffany Studios was entirely independent of Tiffany & Co., although Tiffany & Co. and Tiffany Studios did share exhibition spaces at several world's fairs around the turn of the century.

We give considerable attention in this book to the stylistic influences that went into the design of Tiffany silver. These influences range from the silver of Tiffany's American and European contemporaries, to earlier silver, classical objects of all kinds as well as Near and Far Eastern art. This was always a matter of *influences,* not of copying. Edward C. Moore and his Tiffany designers were exposed to an ever increasing range of world arts which they felt free to use in their own work. They were always conscious of their sources but were not slaves to them. In the same way Louis Comfort Tiffany used Persian glass as a source and inspiration for his own Favrile glass. The abstract painter Ad Reinhardt said "All art comes out of art." This has always been true in the whole history of art, and certainly in the history of the decorative arts.

The conventional wisdom of the twentieth century labels Victorian art eclectic. It is, of course, inescapable that there were many artifacts produced during the Victorian era that did have unassimilated borrowings from earlier times and cultures. But the best of Victoriana transcended its sources to create what was essentially a new style, Victorian. We all know there is a look that is characteristically Victorian. And the further the era recedes into the past, the clearer the look becomes. Of course, Victorian was neither a static nor a completely homogeneous style. There are concurrent stylistic variations in all periods and cultures.

Generally speaking, the style of Tiffany silver changed continually during the period covered by this book. But there were exceptions. For example, such flatware patterns as *Japanese,* now called *Audubon,* and *Olympian,* which were introduced in the 1870s, are still being made today, a century later.

Basically Tiffany silver has always been conservative. Even when the designs were most innovative as with the Japanese-influenced silver of the 1870s, or the *Lap Over Edge* flatware patterns, the actual pieces of silver were seldom extreme. The Tiffany designers understood their sources and knew how to work with them, i.e., they approached their work basically in an academic manner. Conversely, the extreme and radically interpreted objects made by others clearly displayed a lack of understanding of the "antique styles" with which they were working. Tiffany almost never indulged in what we think of as the excesses of Victorianism. The silver was always well crafted, often heavier in gauge than that of their competitors, and in tune with the good taste of its time.

We say something in this book of the people who bought and used the silver and of the social history of the times that produced it. Victorian America was an age of silver. The metal, silver itself, became more and more plentiful after the Civil War and the price declined. The production of silver mined in the United States grew from thirty-nine thousand ounces in 1850 to almost sixty million ounces in 1900, while the price declined from $1.32 per ounce in 1850 to sixty-one cents per ounce in 1900.

The increasing availability of silver after 1850 was certainly a major factor in the greatly increased production of silverware in the United States, but there were also social reasons for the great popularity of silver in the last half of the nineteenth century. Silver had long been a status symbol and it became preeminently so for the Victorians. It became almost *the* accepted way of showing affluence at a time when there was a rapid expansion in wealth by large numbers of people, not only in New York but all over America. There was a vast increase in the numbers of middle- and upper-class households along with a marked increase in social activity and entertaining of all kinds where quantities of silver were conspicuously used and displayed.

The style of interior decoration was a factor. Dark and overcrowded Victorian rooms needed the gay glitter of silver and were enhanced by it. And finally there was the very practical consideration of the Victorians having sufficient servant help in the house to keep silver always polished. Even when the ubiquitous coal fires spewed corrosive sulfur gases in the air, a weekly cleaning of the household silver kept it gleaming.

As for the silver objects shown in this book, we must admit we are only showing the tip of a rather sizable iceberg. Tiffany's silver production was large. At the peak of its output in the 1870s and 1880s Tiffany employed over five hundred people in their silvermaking plant on Prince Street in New York, and a considerable number of workmen were employed in New Jersey making electroplated wares.

We have studied thousands of pieces of silver in the preparation of this book and the choice of objects to be illustrated was not easy. We have attempted to illustrate a fair representation of the range of objects and styles of Tiffany silver from the smaller and more modest examples that any collector could expect to find to the grand presentation pieces and the fabulous dinner services of the era. It is not always a neat and orderly story. There are, for example, certain odd pieces of Tiffany silver that simply do not fit any categories. But these offbeat, sometimes whimsical pieces such as the box in Figure 185, the portable stove in Figure 289, and the jelly jar with its clever lid device in Figure 316, are part of the story too.

We have consciously favored objects belonging to museums and public institutions, even though many are, unfortunately, in storage rather than on display. Most museums have far too many objects to show at any one time, and late nineteenth-century silver has in general not been fully appreciated until fairly recently. Private collectors have been generous and we know that there are many other fine pieces in private collections that could have been illustrated. But we had to make a choice.

We have included a few gold objects since they were made by Tiffany silversmiths using the same techniques as for silver (remember that in the eighteenth century silvermakers were usually called goldsmiths).

Chapters 12 and 13 deal with the making of silver and Tiffany marks. We give a layman's description of how Tiffany made their silver in the nineteenth century, illustrated by using magazine pictures of the 1870s from drawings actually made in Tiffany's plant. The chapter on marks is rather extensive, but we felt in this area we should err on the side of completeness. We have included over forty-five Tiffany marks and variations and list all of Tiffany's pattern numbers so that objects can be identified and dated with some degree of accuracy.

Finally, we want to say a word about the photographs in the book. We went to great lengths to obtain the finest and most interesting photographs available. Silver is notoriously hard to photograph. Even seasoned professional photographers sometimes have difficulty in producing a clean, clear pictorial record of a piece of silver that has no disturbing highlights or reflections. We do want to thank all of the photographers who cooperated in this book for their skill and knowledge and patience.

We have used a few photographs that have been previously published. Some of the better known pieces of Tiffany silver have been shown in one or more books, but our own story would have been grossly incomplete without these very pieces. So we include them without further apology.

A note on the illustration captions

Figure numbers of captions are indicated by the number set off to the left of the caption. Dimensions, when available, are given both in inches (in.) and centimeters (cm.). The mark numbers refer to the listing of marks in Chapter 13. The numbers after the mark number in parentheses are the numbers on the mark—the pattern and order numbers of the piece. The last line in the caption indicates the present owner.

1. Changing Views on Victorianism

QUEEN VICTORIA's name so dominated the last half of the nineteenth century that the period of her reign is called Victorian, even in America. Queen Victoria's reign began in 1837, the year Tiffany & Co. was founded, and continued to 1901, the year before Charles Tiffany, the company's founder, died. Thus the turn of the century was the end of an era for Tiffany & Co. as well as the Western World.

The Victorian era made a sharp break with its past in architecture and the arts, particularly the decorative arts. It was an era of tremendous expansion. In America we "conquered the West" and built whole industries such as petroleum and chemicals and steel from scratch. For example, in 1867 the United States produced less than twenty thousand tons of steel. By 1900 steel production had increased to ten million tons—a five hundred fold increase. We crisscrossed America with railroads. In Tiffany's first year, 1837, America operated 1500 miles of railroads. By 1900 we were operating 193,000 miles.

The arts grew and expanded. In the decorative arts it was an era of joyous unrestraint, of vast energies, an era where new tastes replaced old ones at a fast clip. The past was eagerly scoured for ideas for furniture, for silver, for clothing, and for houses. Rooms and walls of houses were crowded. And the floors—in the 1890s they even put grizzly bear and polar bear rugs on top of Oriental rugs. Ornament was everywhere. Simple old pieces of silver looked too plain for Victorian taste. It is not uncommon to see eighteenth-century silver that has had its plain surfaces repoussé with profuse overall ornamentation by a Victorian silversmith.

A writer in *The Connoisseur* clearly expressed the

contemporary mid-Victorian preference for ornamentation:

The essential quality of our silverware of today is its decorativeness. It is made for ornament and it is highly ornamental. Yet, if we go back some twenty years, we shall come upon ornamental silver made in this country that was not ornamental to any degree. Last year the Coney Island Jockey Club showed a grand silver trophy which has passed nominally from hand to hand for years, but is to be definitely the property of any owner whose horse wins a certain race two consecutive years. In 1883 it was won by Fred Gebhard, with his famous horse Eole. In 1884 Eole's fore legs were ailing, and the trophy passed to the Dwyer stable. Years back the piece of silver was made by the house of Tiffany, of New York, for some Kentucky or Tennessee race association, and it was considered in its day a splendid and unparalleled piece of the silversmith's art. Last year, when it was exhibited, every tyro declared it to be queer. It was queer. There was good, honest work about it, and there was modelling indicative of intelligence and good workmanship. But it was not decorative. The comprehension of what is decorative, and the intuitive sense of what is artistic, possessed by modern New York society, made a huge gulf between it and that old trophy.[1]

The lush exuberance of high Victoriana has tended to embarrass the twentieth century. On the other hand, the less sophisticated arts of the nineteenth century—the quilts, the weathervanes, the slipware jugs, the baskets, the folk paintings, the country furniture—are chic and fashionable. But the more sophisticated arts of the time— the paintings, the architecture, the furniture, the silver— have only recently begun to be taken seriously. The renaissance of nineteenth-century paintings led the way. The prices of paintings by such artists as Fitz Hugh Lane, Albert Bierstadt, and Martin Johnson Heade, the once neglected nineteenth-century academic painters, have skyrocketed. Museums scramble for their paintings and feature them in their exhibitions.

The rejection of Victoriana started at the very beginning of the twentieth century. All eras tend to reject the taste of the immediate past, but in retrospect the break with the Victorian era was sharper than most. Writers, critics, architects, and artisans of many kinds turned their backs on the nineteenth century and the design of almost everything that touched our lives began to change and simplify, often drastically. Artists and architects were in the forefront of the new. The cubists and fauvists

2

changed the way a picture looked. The architects—Frank Lloyd Wright and others in America, Le Corbusier, and particularly the artists and architects of the German Bauhaus in Europe—created a whole new world. The result: severe bare-bones architecture (the International style), austere furniture, and "modern" decorative objects. By the middle of the twentieth century these ideas ruled the world. The Austrian architect, Adolf Loos, said "ban all ornament and decoration." And it was almost banned for a while. A 1920s or 1930s "pure" interior would have had plain walls, plain carpeted floors (Oriental carpets were out), severely plain furniture, a piece of sculpture (an Arp would have been perfect), and a painting or two—preferably a Léger, or a Picasso, or a Braque.

Of course, in such a severe visual world the fancy, sometimes wild, decorative arts of the Victorian era *were* out of place. A lot of Victorian furniture went to the Goodwill; no respectable antique dealer wanted it. People sawed the carpenter Gothic "gimcracks" off their Victorian houses, and loads of heavy ornate Victorian silver were sold and melted down for their metal content. It was pretty well agreed that the Victorian era was an artistic aberration that should be forgotten. And for a while it was pretty much in oblivion. The leading museums practically banned it. The great Henry Francis du Pont Winterthur Museum ends its collections at 1840. Most books ignored it, and leading dealers and collectors would not touch things of the period.

Mr. William T. Lusk, former president of Tiffany & Co., told an amusing story about a piece of their own earlier silver. The New York University Club had a turn-of-the-century silver backgammon trophy which they brought to the Tiffany store for minor repair in the 1930s. Mr. A. L. Barney, who at the time was Tiffany's design director, showed the rather ornate backgammon trophy to John C. Moore, Tiffany's president, who was aghast. He thought the trophy was awful. In fact Mr. Moore was reputed to have said, "I was so ashamed of it. To think that Tiffany could have made such a monstrosity." He immediately suggested that Tiffany should offer to redesign the cup so as to get rid of the horrible Victorian look. After consultation and discussion with the University Club, the old backgammon trophy was streamlined and modernized. Unfortunately there are no "before" photographs of the piece, but the modernized version is still in the possession of the club (Fig. 1) and

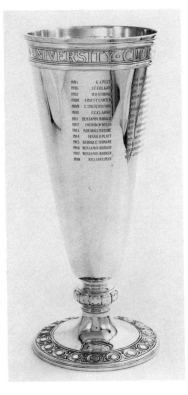

1 The University Club's backgammon tournament trophy engraved with the annual winners from 1905 to 1975. The base is decorated with a band of backgammon discs above which is a band of dice alternating fours and ones. This is a 1930s modernized version of an older "Victorian monstrosity." Height: 15 1/2 in. (39.4 cm.). *(University Club, New York City).*

each year the name of the club's new backgammon champion is added. We can only guess what the original version looked like. Mr. Lusk assured us that it was a "Victorian monstrosity."

But times are changing. Serious attention is being given to Victorian arts. The Victorian Society in America has a fast growing and enthusiastic membership. Books on the architecture and the decorative arts of the time are being published. In the field of American silver, Katharine Morrison McClinton's pioneering book *Collecting American 19th Century Silver* (New York: Charles Scribner's Sons, 1968) emphasized the last half of the nineteenth century and dealt sympathetically with this "late" silver. Several museums have recently shown various facets of nineteenth-century decorative arts. But the real breakthrough was the Metropolitan Museum of Arts' great exhibition of *Nineteenth Century America* in 1970 celebrating the hundredth anniversary of the museum's founding. This sumptuous, beautifully installed, wideranging exhibition was a landmark. For the first time, it seemed, a major cultural institution in America really took the nineteenth century, particularly the last half, seriously. The exhibition was documented by two scholarly, attractively illustrated catalogs, one on paintings and sculptures and the other on furniture and other decorative arts. The furniture and other decorative objects of the nineteenth century were carefully orchestrated in handsome and colorful room settings with paintings and sculpture of the era. The silver, much of it from the Met's own collections, was carefully displayed in well-lit isolation, enabling one to really study the individual exhibits (Fig. 2). Objects, particularly more highly decorated ones, always look better when they are displayed in this way. But of course the piece must have the quality to withstand this sort of concentrated inspection.

The Metropolitan Museum of Art has for some time owned some of the finest and best-known pieces of Tiffany silver: the Bryant Vase, possibly the most famous piece of American silver of the nineteenth century, the opulent Magnolia Vase which was Tiffany's chief offering at the 1893 Columbian Exhibition in Chicago, and the Adams Gold Vase, that incredible tour de force of the goldsmith's art. The Metropolitan and Tiffany have had a close association from the early days of the museum. Charles Tiffany, the founder of Tiffany & Co., was on the Board of Trustees of the Metropolitan and

Edward C. Moore, head of Tiffany's silver department for many years in the nineteenth century, left his vast collection of classical and Oriental art to the Metropolitan in 1891.

Certainly we can now at this point in time examine the nineteenth-century silver of Tiffany with care and something like true love. It is a highly fascinating body of decorative art. We believe the best of it will endure, will be collected, and will enter its rightful place in the history of the arts.

2 Installation photograph of the Magnolia Vase *(left)* and the Viking Punch Bowl *(right)* in The Metropolitan Museum of Art's exhibit "19th Century America," which celebrated their hundredth anniversary in 1970.

2. The Early Years: 1837-1867

CHARLES LEWIS TIFFANY, founder of the house of Tiffany & Co., was born in Danielsonville, Connecticut on February 15, 1812. He was a sixth generation New Englander. His father, Comfort Tiffany, was a successful mill owner, who, when Charles was fifteen years old, built a new cotton mill on the Quinebaug River, called the Brooklyn Manufacturing Co. While he was building the mill Tiffany opened a small country store in Danielsonville and put his son in full charge. Charles ran the store, kept the books, and went to New York on buying trips. The store prospered and expanded and it soon became obvious that Charles Tiffany had a promising business career ahead of him.

Boys grew up quickly in those days. Most went to work at fourteen or fifteen. It was not unusual for twelve year olds to go to sea as cabin boys, and many whaling ships in the first part of the nineteenth century were captained by Masters in their early twenties.

When Charles Tiffany was twenty-five years old he made his big decision. He knew from his buying trips to New York that great opportunities were there. He was determined to make his future in the fast growing city. His friend and neighbor, John B. Young, had gone to New York six months earlier to work in a stationery and fancy goods store. The two young men wanted to open their own store in New York and were able to do so with a loan of a thousand dollars from Charles's father. Their first store—only fifteen feet wide—at 259 Broadway was considered rather far uptown at the time. But the expansion of the city soon made the area fashionable and the store flourished.

The opening of Tiffany & Young on September 18, 1837 came at a hazardous and uncertain time in the history of New York. The city was in a deep recession which was to last two years. The panic of 1837 had been a serious blow to the whole economy of the United States and had been particularly devastating in New York. Businesses had failed by the hundreds and the unemployed walked the streets. The businesses that survived had a hard time. It would have appeared to have been a most inauspicious time to start up a luxury goods business. But Tiffany and Young were successful from the beginning. They had the kind of drive and energy and taste that filled their store with interesting merchandise affluent New Yorkers wanted to buy. So, in those "worst of times" they prospered.

At first Tiffany & Young was a stationery and fancy goods store. The fancy goods were mostly imported luxury items including Chinese ceramics and small furniture, Oriental papier-mâché and terra-cotta ware; umbrellas, canes, and "curiosities of every description" (Fig. 3).

In 1841 a new partner was admitted to the firm, Mr. J. L. Ellis, the firm name becoming Tiffany, Young & Ellis. It was also in 1841 that a member of the firm, Mr. Young, made the firm's first buying trip to Europe. The importing business of the firm had grown so fast that a firsthand knowledge of European markets was vital. Young's profitable visit was the beginning of close mercantile ties with Europe which Tiffany was to maintain over the years. It was to lead to a store in Paris (1850) and later one in London (1868).

In 1845 Tiffany, Young & Ellis issued their first catalog. This was the forerunner of Tiffany's famous *Blue Books,* their annual catalogs. The 1845 catalog was, however, a one-time event since they did not issue another until 1877. After 1877 they became annual publications.

The 30-page 1845 catalog of Tiffany, Young & Ellis listed only a relatively few silver items and no silver flatware or hollow ware as such. The silver items in the catalog included:

Silver thimbles
Tea boxes with silver tea implements
Silver card cases
Silver pens and pencils
Silver handled parasols
Silver snuff boxes
Vinaigrettes

3 Tiffany & Young printed label, about 1841. Found pasted in interior of ladies dressing case.

These silver items were almost incidentals, indicating with certainty that in 1845 Tiffany, Young and Ellis were not yet really dealing in silver. They did sell a marvelous array of items ranging from stationery and porcelains to glass, bronzes, toilet articles, gloves, fancy French furniture, Chinese goods, American Indian goods (moccasins, etc.), papier mâché, cutlery, games, and French jewelry. One odd item in the catalog was "Quaker (Shaker) Goods." This could have been Shaker boxes or textiles.

It was a little later, about 1848, that Tiffany began to focus on the two lines which were to be the basis for their worldwide reputation: silver and precious stones. George Frederic Heydt in his little book on Tiffany & Co., tells the story of how fast and decisive action almost instantly propelled Tiffany into the diamond market:

The political disturbances of 1848 in Paris offered many opportunities for shrewd investments. In the panic that followed, diamonds declined about fifty percent. Mr. Tiffany and his partner, Mr. J. B. Young, were quick to grasp the situation, and immediately decided to invest all the available resources of the firm in these precious gems. Mr. Young, accompanied by Mr. Thomas Crane Banks, who conducted the jewelry department for the house, had just arrived in Paris, prepared to make large purchases of jewelry and European novelties; but instead of searching for the latter, they directed their whole attention and resources to the purchase of diamonds. In spite of suffering arrest as suspects, and encountering numerous other unpleasant experiences in the panic-stricken city, they yet fulfilled their mission so successfully as to raise the firm Tiffany, Young & Ellis to the front rank of diamond merchants.[1]

The beginnings of Tiffany's silverware business is not as precisely documented as its entry into the diamond market. It probably started in 1847 or 1848. As noted above, the 1845 sales catalog indicated that Tiffany was not dealing in silverware as such at that time. Heydt states that the move of Tiffany, Young & Ellis to larger quarters at 271 Broadway in 1847 allowed them to expand into the silverware business. In 1848 the firm employed a young German immigrant named Gustav Herter as a silver designer. Herter, who afterward became well known as a decorator and furniture designer in New York, worked for Tiffany, Young & Ellis until 1851 when he left to become a cabinetmaker at 48 Mercer Street. One would guess that Herter's position simply became redundant when the firm made their arrangement (discussed below) with John C. Moore.

During the 1847–1851 period Tiffany, Young & Ellis retailed silver from a number of New York silvermakers. These included John C. Moore, Henry Hebbard and the partnerships of Moore & Hebbard, Gale & Hughes, and Wood & Hughes. Usually the pieces of silver would bear both the marks of the maker and Tiffany, Young & Ellis. We also cannot rule out the possibility that Tiffany, Young & Ellis could have retailed silver from England and France during this period since the store had good connections in both countries.

Tiffany's silver had already become well known in 1850. When P. T. Barnum brought Jenny Lind, the Swedish Nightingale, to New York in that year one of the first places she visited was Tiffany's. She ordered a silver tankard for the captain of the ship that had brought her over. The tankard was a thoroughly nautical creation with a handle of a mermaid rising out of the sea and a Triton emerging from the cover. Part of the decoration was a rainbow, which the singer had seen on the voyage.

The splendidly rococo teapot and lampstand in Figure 4 is an interesting example of Tiffany, Young & Ellis silver of the 1848–1851 period. This magnificently crafted object has a handle and spout of twig and leaf design that was very popular in the 1850s. A similar but slightly coarser design was used by Wood & Hughes in the late 1850s, and related designs were used by Hayden & Whilden, Charleston, 1855–1863 and by Laforme Brothers, Boston, 1850–1855.[2] An unusual feature of the teapot is the chinoiserie decoration. Chinoiserie is not often encountered in American silver of this period; it is beautifully handled here. On the front is a lady with parasol in her garden and a man in a peaked Chinese hat fishing from a bridge; on the rear is another lady beside a flower bush balanced by a Chinese falconer with his falcon. The background is chased with tiny circles and dots which glow and sparkle in reflected light. The figural finial is not unrelated to that of the hot water kettle in Figure 23 which the Moore company made for Tiffany in 1854. However, the background chasing and the rococo decorations of the two pieces are quite different. The teapot is marked only "Tiffany, Young & Ellis."

In Chapter 10, we show a water pitcher (Fig. 249)

9

4 Teapot on lampstand made ca. 1850, chinoiserie decorations with twiglike handle and figural finial, monogrammed and dated "JAN 24," the stand raised on four openwork scroll supports. Height: 12 3/8 in. (31.c cm.). Weight: 51 ozs. 10 dwts. Mark: TIFFANY, YOUNG & ELLIS. (*Private Collection*).

with similar chinoiserie decorations and background which has the identical mark. Both pieces were obviously made by the same maker at about the same time, but are not part of the same service. (The monograms are different.) The teapot is dated "Jan 24" on the monogram indicating it was a silver anniversary or presentation piece of some kind and was probably not part of a tea set.

John C. Moore and Edward C. Moore

The greatly increased demand for silverware, both household silver and presentation pieces, led Charles Tiffany and his partners to the decision that they should control their own silver-manufacturing shop. John C. Moore was their choice to run that portion of their establishment. Moore, who made silverware for Ball, Black & Co. and others, was certainly one of the best silversmiths in New York. The arrangement made in 1851 was for Moore to manufacture exclusively for Tiffany, Young &

Ellis. However, Tiffany continued to retail the silverware of other makers besides Moore. Moore made only hollow ware for the company during this period, the flatware coming from other makers.

The move to employ Moore was a brilliant decision. Within a very few years—by the middle of the 1850s— Tiffany was recognized as the leading silverware house in New York. Tiffany's silver sales expanded rapidly, soon necessitating a considerable expansion of Moore's shop. In 1851 the Moore shop was small, with only a handful of employees. By the end of the decade he employed hundreds.

Soon after Tiffany and Moore made their arrangement in 1851, John C. Moore retired from the business, turning over its leadership to his twenty-four-year-old son, Edward C. Moore. Obviously Charles Tiffany and his partners knew of this arrangement and approved of it. They knew they were getting a first-rate man.

Edward Chandler Moore (Fig. 5) was born in New York City in 1827. He learned his trade as a silversmith in his father's shop and became his partner in 1848 when he was twenty-one years old. At the time the Moore company joined forces with Tiffany, Edward was a seasoned silversmith with a decade of experience. This was the beginning of an association that was to last for forty years during which time Edward Moore was the guiding genius of Tiffany's silverware business. His talents as a designer and as an executive were unquestionably the chief reason for Tiffany's swift rise in the silverware business and for their international leadership in the latter part of the nineteenth century. Charles Tiffany, always the entrepreneurial leader, chose his men well, and certainly Edward C. Moore was one of the most astute choices of his long and successful career.

The rapid growth of the Moore shop in the 1850s brought on changes that were duplicated in other growing silversmithing businesses in America and in Europe. In the small shops the silversmiths did all types of silversmithing from designing, to making the silver, to finishing. The larger shops were forced to resort to a division of labor whereby each of the steps in silvermaking were performed by specialists, such as designers, spinners, engravers, finishers, etc. This assembly-line type of production meant that in most cases the finished piece of silver was no longer the work of one man as it might have been in a small eighteenth-century shop. This did

5 Photograph of Edward C. Moore dated January 1879.

11

not necessarily mean a decline in quality (we discuss this in some detail in Chapter 12, "The Making of Tiffany Silver"). Full-time engravers and finishers and so on obviously could and did become highly expert in their specialty, uniformly producing work of the highest quality.

The key was the business manager and the designer. Edward C. Moore was both. He was one of a new breed of men who fitted perfectly into a new industrial society. He had the knowledge and the background-training in all phases of silversmithing to manage Tiffany's silverware business, and he had the sensitivity and eye of an artist to lead their design activities.

An early sketchbook of Edward C. Moore has survived which gives us some idea of his design abilities and interests. It also indicates some of the design sources of Tiffany silver of the 1850s and the 1860s.

The sketchbook, which contains thirty-seven pages of pencil drawings, was made in the summer of 1855 when Moore was in Paris. Figure 6 shows the inside cover,

6

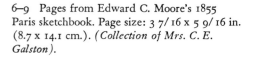

indicating the sketchbook was started on July 26, 1855 and that Moore made his headquarters at Tiffany's Paris store, Tiffany & Reed at 79 Rue Richelieu.

The book has drawings of objects in the Louvre, the Luxembourg, and the 1855 Paris Exposition. No doubt the exposition was the main reason for Moore's Paris visit. There he could study what was new in European silver. He also studied classical objects in museums, not only silver and other metals, but ceramics as well. At the exposition he sketched a number of pieces of Sèvres porcelain.

6–9 Pages from Edward C. Moore's 1855 Paris sketchbook. Page size: 3 7/16 x 5 9/16 in. (8.7 x 14.1 cm.). (*Collection of Mrs. C. E. Galston*).

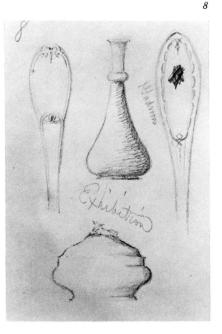

7

The full, sensuous but simple forms in Figure 7 are reflected in such pieces as the vegetable dish from the du Pont service in Figure 21. Figure 8 is particularly interesting and important for the flatware patterns sketched. The one on the left is related to Tiffany's first flatware pattern issued in 1869 named *Tiffany*. There is no record that Moore ever made any flatware for Tiffany before 1869, even though John C. Moore did obtain a flatware design patent in 1847.

The last drawing in the notebook (Fig. 9) of a tomato and a handle in the form of a vegetable and leaf shows Moore's considerable talents as an artist.

The sketchbook shows clearly Moore's interest in the silver and ceramics of his contemporaries and in classical art. There is no hint of his interest in Oriental art which was later to become his passion both as a collector and as a designer. Moore's great collection of Oriental art and its influence on Tiffany silver will be discussed in the next chapter.

In 1853 Charles Tiffany gained complete control of the

8

9

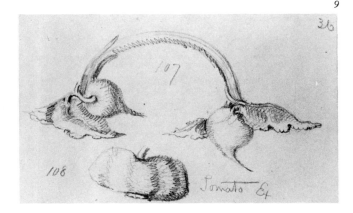

firm. His partners, Young and Ellis, retired and the name of the firm became Tiffany & Co. The increasing business required another move of the store to 550 Broadway, between Spring and Prince streets, where it was to remain until 1870.

Charles Tiffany was not only a merchant of great energy and taste, he was also a master publicist. The selling of bits of the first Atlantic cable lines seems a far cry from the silver of Edward C. Moore, but Tiffany's brilliant coup in 1858 gave the store enormous publicity and undoubtedly led to the sale of a lot of Moore's silver.

Cyrus Field made four unsuccessful attempts in 1857–58 to lay the first Atlantic cable from Europe to North America in ships provided by the English and American governments. Finally, the cable was completed by Field in August 1858. The well-publicized event created tremendous excitement in New York. Seeing an opportunity, Tiffany made a deal with Field to buy twenty miles of cable recovered from one of the unsuccessful attempts. An ad from *Frank Leslie's Weekly* (September 11, 1858) announced the great event:

MISCELLANEOUS.

TIFFANY & CO.,

No. 550 Broadway, New York,

announce that they have secured the entire balance of the

ATLANTIC TELEGRAPH SUBMARINE CABLE,

Now on board the

U. S. Steam Frigate Niagara.

In order to place it within the reach of all classes, and that every family in the United States may possess a specimen of this wonderful mechanical curiosity, they propose to cut the Cable into pieces of four inches in length, and mount them neatly with brass ferules.

Each piece will be accompanied with a copyrighted fac-simile certificate of

CYRUS W. FIELD, Esq.,

that it is cut from the genuine Cable. Twenty miles of it have been actually submerged and taken up from the bottom of the Ocean. This will be first sold in precisely the condition in which the great Cable now lies in the bed of the Atlantic.

Orders will be received from dealers and others for not less than 100 pieces at a time, at $25 per hundred. Retail price, 50 cents each.

Each order must be accompanied by the money, in funds current in New York, as it will not be possible to open accounts. A register will be kept of the orders as they are received, which will be filled in turn without favor or partiality.

A large portion of the specimens will be ready, it is expected, for delivery within a week.

New York, August 21st, 1858. 144-146

CENIN'S LADIES' AND CHILDREN'S

In addition to these souvenirs, Tiffany created a whole line of Atlantic cable items incorporating pieces of the famous cable: paperweights, canes, umbrellas, whip handles, watch charms, and "coils for ornamenting parlors and offices." When the items were put on sale in Tiffany's, the crowds were so great that policemen were required to keep order.

Tiffany received additional publicity from the Atlantic cable when New York City commissioned them to make a medal and gold box for presentation to Field. The marvelous little gold box engraved with the cable-laying ships, the arms of New York, and various symbols of the event (Fig. 10) was of course exhibited in Tiffany's window before it was presented.

The fact that the Atlantic cable ceased working soon after it was finished and was not really successful until 1866 made little difference to Tiffany and other New Yorkers. Field was the conquering hero and was the toast of New York. And Tiffany was in the center of the whole affair.

Silver of the 1850s

Tiffany's silver of the 1850s was relatively conservative and traditional. There were classical pieces made that were closely related to early nineteenth- and late eighteenth-century forms. The Classical Revival in America still lingered on in the 1850s, both in the decorative arts and architecture. Some of the great Greek Revival southern plantation houses were built in the period just before the Civil War, and there was a continued interest in Empire furniture and silver. Tiffany's Classical Revival silver pieces were characterized by full, simple forms with decoration often limited to Greek key or beaded borders. An occasional piece such as the sugar bowl in Figure 11 had no surface decoration. The simple form and the soaring handles give this small piece a graceful monumentality which makes it seem larger than it really is (height: 4¾ in.). This sugar bowl is unusual for Tiffany silver of this period in that it is completely handmade instead of being spun on a lathe which is more typical of the period.

The sauce boat (Fig. 12) with its graceful, sweeping forms combines the Greek borders with beadings as does the vegetable dish in Figures 13 and 14. The sauce-boat form goes back to the American silver designs of the

10

11

10 Gold box, hinged lid edged with miniature cable. The top is engraved with the arms of New York and an ocean scene showing ships laying the Atlantic cable, inscribed, "THE CITY OF NEW YORK TO CYRUS W. FIELD." All sides are engraved with scenes symbolic of the laying of the Atlantic cable. The arms of Great Britain are on the bottom. Inside the lid is engraved the inscription, "THE CITY OF NEW YORK TO CYRUS W FIELD/ COMMEMORATING HIS SKILL, FORTITUDE AND PERSEVERANCE/ IN ORIGINATING AND COMPLETING/ THE FIRST ENTERPRISE FOR AN OCEAN TELEGRAPH/ SUCCESSFULLY ACCOMPLISHED ON THE 5TH AUGUST, 1858./ UNITING EUROPE AND AMERICA." The box has no maker's mark. Size: 1 1/2 x 4 1/2 x 2 3/4 in. (3.8 x 11.4 x 7 cm.). (On loan to The Smithsonian Institution from The Metropolitan Museum of Art).

11 Sugar bowl with cover made by Bogert for Tiffany & Co. about 1865. The body and base of this piece are hand-raised. The finial echoes the shape of the bowl. Height: 4 3/4 in. (12.1 cm.). Mark: NO. 13 (2569). (Private Collection).

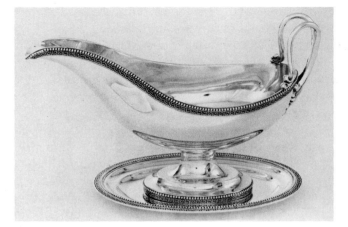

12 Sauce boat (long) with stand made by Moore for Tiffany ca. 1857. Applied handle with acanthus leaf, beading, and Greek key borders. Both engraved with monogram MBP. Length of sauce boat: 9 in. (22.8 cm.). Length of stand: 6 5/8 in. (16.8 cm.). Marks: sauce boat NO. 10 (686/5403), stand NO. 10 (588/5403). (*Private Collection*).

early nineteenth century which in turn hark back to Adam designs of the eighteenth century. The curve of the sauce-boat handle ending in an acanthus leaf casting is similar in concept to a handle of a silver wine jug made by the English silversmiths Boulton & Fathergill in 1776.[3]

The vegetable dish in Figures 13 and 14 is a classical design that was made over a long period of time. This eminently utilitarian piece has a removable handle so that the top can be used as a serving dish when turned over. Figure 14 shows the bottom and top used as separate dishes. Note that the Greek key and beaded border rim is on the *bottom* of the top edge so that it matches the trim of the bottom part when turned over. This vegetable dish dates from about 1855. The sauce tureen in Figure 15 is slightly more ornate but it is still characteristically classical in shape.

13

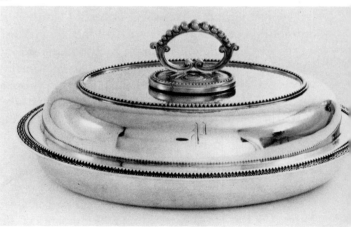

13 Vegetable dish with cover, beading and Greek key borders. Made by Moore for Tiffany about 1855. Length: 11 in. (28 cm.). Mark: NO. 10(356/9674). (*Private Collection*).

14 Vegetable dish in Fig. 13 with cover and turnkey handle, showing how dish and cover make two matching serving dishes when used separately.

The small jug in Figure 16 with its rococo feet and restrained repoussé ornamentation and rustic finial with bird is related to eighteenth-century French silver. Rococo and Classical Revival were the two dominant stylistic influences of the 1850s.

The large centerpiece, "The Four Seasons," in Figure 17 is classical sculpture whose concept goes back to the sixteenth century. The base and figures of this piece are silverplated bronze while the gold-lined seventeen-inch bowl on top is sterling. Although the inscription on the piece is dated 1851, the Tiffany mark (No. 6) on the bowl suggests that the piece probably was made a couple of years later. This centerpiece was shown in Tiffany's exhibit in the Main Exhibition Building at the Philadelphia Centennial in 1876.

The oval tray in Figure 18 shows the typical Renaissance-type decoration which was popular in the 1850s and 1860s.

Children's silver was a popular item with Tiffany from the beginning. Cups and saucers (Fig. 19) along with spoons and forks were typical birthday gifts for children.

The Tiffany, Young & Ellis water pitcher in Figure 20 shows a useful form that has been popular in the United States since the Revolutionary War. The water pitcher, filled with ice water or lemonade, was a staple in American homes. Tiffany made many variations of the water pitcher over its whole history, and a number are illustrated in this book.

The handsome eleven-piece service in Figure 21 was presented to Admiral Samuel Francis du Pont in 1853 for his services as general superintendent of the Exhibi-

15

16

14

15 Sauce tureen with cover, beading, and Greek key borders. Egg molding between base and body. The bases of the side handles are chased acanthus leaves. Made by Moore for Tiffany about 1855. Height: 8 in. (20.3 cm.). Mark: NO. 11 (634/2130). *(Private Collection)*.

16 Hot water jug, pheasant on slanted stump finial, covered lip, fancy base with open sides resting on four scrolled leaves, pear-shaped sides, repoussé chased shield on each side between floral extensions, "water" scratched on bottom. Made about 1855. Height: 7 in. (17.8 cm.). Mark: TIFFANY & CO. *(Gebelein Silversmiths)*.

17

18

19

20

17 Centerpiece, "The Four Seasons." Given to William Watts Sherman on his retirement from the Albany City Bank. Although the inscription is dated 1851 we believe the piece was made about 1853. The sculptured cast bronze electroplated base is unmarked. The 17-inch gold-lined sterling tray sitting on top of the piece is marked "TIFFANY & CO. / 271 Broadway / JCM." Height: 23 1/2 in (59.7 cm.). (*The Preservation Society of Newport County, Rhode Island*).

18 Oval tray on four scroll feet. Applied rope border, hand-engraved well or bottom. Made by Moore for Tiffany in 1854–55. Height: 1 3/16 in. (3 cm.). Width: 15 in. (38.1 cm.). Mark: NO. 9 (191/1126). (*Private Collection*).

19 Octagon-shaped child's cup and saucer, engraved and chased decorations. Made by Moore for Tiffany, Young & Ellis about 1852. Height of cup: 2 7/8 in. (9.8 cm.). Mark: NO. 1. (*The New-York Historical Society, New York City*).

20 Water pitcher with double C-scroll handle, body repoussé chased and panels engraved with abstract pineapple patterns. Made by Moore for Tiffany, Young & Ellis, around 1850–52. Height: 9 5/8 in. (24.4 cm.). Mark: NO. 1 (13). (*Burt Collection*).

21

tion of the Industry of All Nations at the Crystal Palace in New York. Admiral du Pont was a grandson of Eluthère Irénée du Pont de Nemours and married his first cousin Sophie Madeleine du Pont. He had a distinguished half-century career with the American Navy, retiring at the end of the Civil War. In 1853 he was one of three U.S. Naval officers assigned by the government to the New York World's Fair. Admiral du Pont had the title of superintendent of the Crystal Palace. The huge glass building which dominated the fair was in Bryant Park, behind the present-day New York Public Library at Fifth Avenue and Forty-second Street. The Crystal Palace was gutted by fire in 1856.

Figure 22 shows a detail of the top of the tureen cover of the du Pont service. The rustic handle is similar to those seen on eighteenth-century French silver. Some of the most elegant of the French silver tureens had twig or vegetable handles.

The James E. Birch Gold Rush Silver

In the Hearst Mining Building of the University of California at Berkeley is a most interesting and historically important collection of Tiffany silver. This is the silver made by Moore for Tiffany in about 1855 for James E. Birch, a highly successful California pioneer. Birch, originally from Swansea, Massachusetts, was twenty-two when he arrived in California, where he went into the stagecoach business with a partner, Frank S. Stevens. They quickly expanded their stagecoach lines and at one

21 Service presented to Admiral Samuel Francis du Pont for his services as superintendent of the Crystal Palace at the 1853 New York World's Fair. The service consists of a tureen with cover, a pair of covered serving dishes on feet with lamps, a pair of vegetable dishes, a pair of sauce boats and stands, and two open salts. Mark: NO. 5 (356). *(Collection of Victor du Pont, Jr.).*

22 Detail of handle casting on lid of tureen of du Pont service in Fig. 21. The two side handles of the tureen are similar rustic castings.

22

time their coaches covered fifteen hundred miles per day. Birch made a quick "fortune," and went back to Massachusetts, where he married. Later he returned to California where he sold all his business interests preparatory to going East for good. He shipped his money ahead in the form of gold bars. He later sailed to Panama, and after crossing the isthmus, he boarded the steamer *Central America* for New York.

When the vessel was off the coast of the Carolinas, it rode into a tremendous hurricane. On September 12, 1857 it sank, and Birch along with over four hundred of his fellow passengers perished. The news of this great disaster filled New York newspapers for two weeks after the event. Birch was listed amongst the missing as "James E. Birch (U.S.M. Comm.) Fall River."

Some time after this, Frank Stevens, Birch's partner, went East to visit Birch's wife and his godson, Frank Stevens Birch. Later Stevens and Birch's widow were married.

There are two dozen pieces of the Birch silver at Berkeley, of which we show four of the most important examples.

The kettle and stand in Figure 23 has a finial of a miner panning gold, and the cartouche encloses a miner digging with a shovel. His tent is in the background. The Birch hot water kettle is similar in size and design to a kettle John C. Moore made for Ball, Tompkins and Black in 1850 to honor Marshall Lefferts. The Lefferts piece is now in the Metropolitan Museum of Art where it was shown in the 1970 100th Anniversary Exhibition (No. 141). The Birch piece is more restrained in its chased repoussé decoration than the Lefferts piece, although it is still romantically rococo. These magnificent hot water kettles with stands were impractically large whereas post–Civil War examples were made considerably smaller and more compact.

The covered vegetable dish in Figure 24 has a bear-shaped finial and handles in the form of bears' heads. The strong, relatively simple chasing gives this piece a feeling of great power and compact strength. The soup tureen in Figure 25 has a carefully detailed stagecoach finial and two scenes depicting early California on each side of the lid. The tureen also has the cast bear's head handles. The large tray in Figure 26 has four scenes of early California engraved in rococo cartouches. Two of the scenes are of Sutter's Mill and Sutter's Fort, one

23 Hot water kettle of the James E. Birch service made by Moore for Tiffany about 1855. The finial on top is a miner panning gold. There is another miner with shovel in the rococo cartouche. All plain areas are chased to give a mat background to the repoussé work. Height: 17 1/2 in. (44.4 cm.). Mark: NO. 9. (*Hearst Mining Building, University of California, Berkeley*).

of a stagecoach and one of San Francisco Bay. Figure 27 shows the San Francisco waterfront scene in detail with its sailing ships, covered wagon, houses, and rather peculiarly proportioned trees. The Birch initials, J.E.B., are engraved in the center of the tray.

The Civil War

The coming of the Civil War put a crimp in Tiffany's silver business. Foreseeing the need for military wares, Charles Tiffany converted the store into a depot of military supplies. They sold French rifles, army shoes, army and navy swords, and military equipment of every kind. In 1861 the following advertisement appeared in *Frank Leslie's Weekly:*

TO ARMY AND NAVY OFFICERS. Tiffany & Co., 550-552 Broadway, have in store, and are receiving by every steamer, swords "warranted to cut wrought iron," from Solinger Passants. Cap ornaments and other embroideries from Paris. Gold Epaulettes and Navy Laces, etc. from London. Orders by mail promptly filled, and goods forwarded to all ports of the Loyal States.

During the draft riots of 1863 mobs were on their way uptown smashing store windows and looting stores. When it was thought they were headed towards the area where Tiffany was located, Charles Tiffany barricaded the doors to his store and he and his employees waited for them armed with hand grenades and guns from the store's stock. Fortunately, the police stopped the mob a couple of blocks away.

During that dreary, bloody war an event happened in New York in 1863 that provided the North with a bit of

25

24 Vegetable dish with cover of Birch service, one of a pair. Cast bear finial and bear's head handles. In the cartouche below the finial is a miner's tent with mountains in the background. Height: 7 1/2 in. (19.1 cm.). Width: 9 in. (22.9 cm.). Mark: NO. 9 (672). *(Hearst Mining Building, University of California, Berkeley).*

25 Tureen with cover of Birch service. The finial is a realistically modeled stagecoach. In the cartouche on the top is an animated scene of a stagecoach and four horses crashing along. Cast bear's head handles. Height: 12 in. (30.5 cm.). Width 14 1/2 in. (36.8 cm.). Mark: No. 9 (659). *(Hearst Mining Building, University of California, Berkeley).*

26 Tea tray of the Birch service engraved with early California scenes—Sutter's Mill, Sutter's Fort, a stagecoach and four, and a San Francisco waterfront scene (detail in Fig. 27). Bull's-eye border and beaded handles. Length: 30 1/2 in. (77.5 cm.). Mark: NO. 9 (122/657). *(Hearst Mining Building, University of California, Berkeley).*

26

27 Detail of Birch tray in Fig. 26 showing San Francisco waterfront scene.

much needed distraction: Tom Thumb's wedding. "General" Tom Thumb, the two-foot eleven-inch protégé of P. T. Barnum, was twenty-five years old when he married Lavinia Warren, a pretty little two-foot eight-inch girl from Middleborough, Massachusetts. Lavinia, who was born Mercy Bump, was twenty-one years old when she married Tom Thumb in Grace Church in New York on February 10, 1863. The wedding was an extraordinary event. Everyone wanted to go. The church was filled with two thousand guests, including the Astors, the Vanderbilts, and the Roosevelts. The streets around Grace Church were jammed with spectators trying to get a glimpse of the two little people. President Lincoln couldn't make it but a few days later he received General Tom and his bride at the White House.

Tiffany was involved from the beginning. As soon as they heard about the coming event they had a tiny silver filigree horse-drawn chariot made for the couple (Fig. 28). This was displayed in the Tiffany window before the wedding, attracting widespread attention. The silver chariot was originally set with rubies and the eyes of the horse were garnets. But later, when Tom and Lavinia retired to Middleborough they saw leaner times. Tom had squandered most of their fortune made from the P. T. Barnum days. He sold the rubies and the garnets from the horse and chariot and had them replaced with paste imitations.

The end of the Civil War was also the end of an era for Tiffany & Co. The making of gold- and silver-handled presentation swords (Chapter 8) would continue for a while, but other wartime items were gladly set aside.

People were ready for new things. Charles Tiffany, the business leader, and Edward C. Moore, the artist and silversmith, were soon to make Tiffany & Co. the greatest silverware house in the world.

28 Silver filigree horse and chariot made by Tiffany & Co. for Tom Thumb's wedding in 1863. The eyes of the horse were originally garnets, and rubies were set in the coach. These were later sold by Tom Thumb when he came on hard times and were replaced by paste imitations. Length: 7 in. (17.8 cm.). Height: 2 1/8 in. (5.4 cm.). *(Middleborough Historical Museum, Middleboro [sic], Massachusetts).*

3. The Leading Silversmiths

CHARLES TIFFANY met the period of peace after the Civil War with his usual energy and ebullience. He had ambitious plans for his silver department. Tiffany & Co. was already famous in America for the quality of its silver, so the firm was now directed towards international markets. Tiffany's already had a toehold in Europe in the Paris store, and they had been dealing in all kinds of goods from Europe and the Orient since the beginning, so a post–Civil War international expansion was a natural move. And Charles Tiffany knew that fame and success abroad would be important to his New York business.

Tiffany used the vehicle that was one of the nineteenth century's most efficient methods for getting goods known and sold: the international expositions. The first of these was Prince Albert's Exposition in London in 1851 with its great glass and steel Crystal Palace. Although New York had its first big exposition in 1853, it was the Paris Exposition in 1855 that really demonstrated to the Tiffany management the commercial, promotional, and artistic ideas that could be generated by such an event. Edward C. Moore spent several weeks in Paris in 1855, visiting the exposition several times, as was discussed in the previous chapter. It was clear that in the post–Civil War period the big international expositions would be of critical importance to a firm of Tiffany's ambitions. These expositions, particularly the ones in Paris, the style center of the Western world, where to be of inestimable value in providing a showcase for Tiffany silver. The European expositions were not only great shows, they were also events of considerable commercial importance. Large numbers of actual sales were made at the expositions and crowds of people who would never have seen the inside of a Tiffany store were exposed to Tiffany silver. This straightforward commercial aspect of the European expositions was somewhat different from American expositions where exhibits such as Tiffany's were more promotional affairs, "pointing with pride."

Tiffany's first showing was at the 1867 Paris Exposition. The firm's exhibit was relatively small and modest by European standards since they showed only regular items from their stock such as tea and coffee sets and water pitchers. Among pieces included in the exhibit was the "Mooresque" creamer in Figure 67, now owned by the Philadelphia Museum of Art, and a chased tea and coffee service similar to the one in Figure 202.

The exhibit was a success. Tiffany received a prize for their silverwares and some very favorable press comments. *The London Art Journal* (November 1867) in a review of the Paris Exposition singled Tiffany out for praise:

They [speaking of Tiffany's silverwares] are all designed and executed by American artists, and are not surpassed by any articles of the kind in the Exhibition. The designs are of the best order, introducing neither too much or too little ornament, while they all bear evidence of good workmanship. The establishment of Messrs. Tiffany is the largest in the new world: it is of great importance, therefore, that they should minister to pure taste in America; they are doing so, if we may judge from their contribution, our only regret is that they have not sent more; it is, however, something to show what America is producing and estimating. These exhibits hold their own besides the best of England and France.

The "Society for the Encouragement of Arts, Manufactures and Commerce," an English association dating back to the eighteenth century, sent more than a hundred observers to the Paris fair, and their massive 700-page report had a number of favorable references to the Tiffany exhibit. One Frank J. Jackson, "designer and art-teacher" wrote of the Tiffany exhibit:

Compared with works of a similar kind, exhibited by other nations, they seem to be perfect of their class, having no rivals. While other exhibits rest principally upon rare and costly works, elaborated to the highest degree, this little display of the Americans rests upon humble work, proving that ordinary articles may be exalted and invested with a dignity that will entitle them to rank with the proudest achievements of industrial art.[1]

The *New York Herald* pointed out that the firm of Elkington, the Birmingham silverware manufacturers,

25

paid Tiffany the highest compliment by buying a half-dozen pieces from the Tiffany exhibit. They had tried to buy the entire exhibit but could not. It is said that Elkington quickly offered for sale copies of the Tiffany wares.[2] Thus, influences began to go *back* to Europe from America.

Tiffany advertisements made a big thing of the publicity they received from the Paris Exposition. Their ads headlined the award as the

ONLY AWARD EVER MADE BY A FOREIGN COUNTRY

TO

AMERICAN MANUFACTURER OF SILVERWARE

The Merger of Moore's Silver-Manufacturing Operations into Tiffany

In 1868 Tiffany had grown to the point where incorporation was logical. On May 1, Tiffany & Co. was incorporated with Charles L. Tiffany as president and treasurer. At the same time Edward C. Moore sold his silversmithing business on Prince Street to Tiffany for $55,000 plus sixty-one shares of Tiffany stock, becoming general manager of the company's silverware operations. It should be pointed out that the merger of Moore's business into Tiffany & Co. was made without any change in the operations at the Prince Street works which, for all practical purposes, had been an integral part of Tiffany & Co. since 1851. The Tiffany plant records of the 1865–1875 period give no hint or mention of the changeover. The change, insofar as the plant was concerned, was obviously only an organizational formality.

This marked the beginning of Tiffany's greatest period in silver. Plans were underway for a new, larger store to be located on Union Square, and the move was made to expand the silvermaking plant on Prince Street.

There was a great flurry of design activity. The decision was made to go into sterling flatware manufacture. In 1869 the first flatware pattern, *Tiffany,* was introduced. Four patterns were introduced in 1870, two in 1871, and two more in 1872 (see Chapter 5). In addition, the 1870s saw the introduction of new forms and new decorative styles that not only made Tiffany the leading silver house of the world, it also made them the genuine leader in the introduction of new styles.

We believe the period from right after the Civil War

to the late 1880s was the most important and innovative period in the whole history of Tiffany silver. This was the period when the great flatware patterns, such as *Vine, Lap Over Edge, Japanese (Audubon),* and *Olympian* were introduced. It was the period when silver decorated in the Japanese taste, which was to be an important precursor of Art Nouveau, was introduced. It was the period in which some of the great presentation pieces, such as the Bryant Vase, were made. And finally it was a period when a whole flood of handsome and useful water pitchers, tea and coffee services, and other household silver was made. Many of the designs created during this period continued to be used later, even into the twentieth century, with such early flatware patterns as *Japanese (Audubon)* and *Olympian* introduced in the 1870s still being produced today (1978).

The Edward C. Moore Collection

The collection of Oriental art formed by Edward C. Moore in the post–Civil War years was to have a profound effect on the design of Tiffany silver. Containing some twenty-five hundred objects, it was given to the Metropolitan Museum of Art in 1891 after Moore's death. In the early part of the twentieth century the collection was shown in one room at the Metropolitan, but today the objects have been dispersed to the relevant departments of the museum. The new Islamic Galleries of the Met have many pieces of Moore's Near-Eastern metal works on exhibit (1978). Moore's taste has withstood the test of time. He collected objects of the highest quality in great numbers. It was an extraordinarily avant-garde collection for its time. A mere listing of the kind of objects in the collection is impressive:

Metalware
        Japanese—eighteenth and nineteenth century
        Persian
        Syrian and Mesopotamian
        Indian
Ceramics
        Thirteenth- to eighteenth-century Persian
        Syrian
        Turkish
        Chinese—Sung to nineteenth century
        Siamese
        Hispano-Mooresque

Etruscan
Classic Greek Pottery

Textiles

Hundreds of Japanese, Chinese, Indian, Persian, and Caucasian silks, brocades, and costumes

Lacquers

Japanese, Chinese, and Persian

Armor

A large collection of Japanese sword guards (tsuba)
Japanese Daggers and Swords
Persian Daggers, Swords, and Armor
Guns

In addition there were Japanese and Chinese baskets, Japanese ivories and netsuki, Indian and Persian jewelry, pre-Columbian gold, snuff bottles, and a large collection of Persian, Egyptian, Roman, and Syrian glass.

A comparison of the objects in Moore's collection with his 1855 Paris sketchbook shows a remarkable growth in the breadth of his artistic interests. The 1855 sketchbook is relatively conventional in its outlook, showing European art of that time and the past—no hint of the Orient.

The influence of Moore's collection on Tiffany's silver designs will be noted in a number of places in this book. For example, we feel that the simple full shapes of Tiffany's water pitchers (Figs. 95 and 309) derive from such pieces as the fifteenth-century Persian brass jug in Figure 29. The several versions of these Tiffany water pitchers are among the most beautiful examples of Tiffany silver. The water pitchers made a big impression in the 1867 and 1878 Paris Expositions, being simpler and more straightforward in design than the ones being made in Europe at the time.

Even the handle of the Persian jug in Figure 29 has echoes in Tiffany silver (The Morgan Cup, Fig. 242). The openwork decoration on the bottom of the jug handle is not unrelated to the Philadelphia creamer handle in Figure 67.

Moore's design interests of the post–Civil War period are clearly indicated in a second sketchbook from Tiffany's files.

Edward C. Moore Sketchbook II

The Tiffany & Co. files have an important early sketchbook of Edward C. Moore's that is filled with design

29 Islamic engraved brass jug inlaid with silver and gold and traces of black paste. Iranian, late fifteenth century. Height: 5 1/2 in. (14.1 cm.). (*The Metropolitan Museum of Art, New York. Bequest, Edward C. Moore, 1891*).

ideas that appeared later in Tiffany silver. Although the sixty-three (9¼ x 12¼ in.) pages of pencil sketches (two of the pages are partially watercolored) are not signed, a careful comparison with Moore's 1855 sketchbook discussed in the previous chapter indicates Moore's hand everywhere. Both sketchbooks have quick, summary, undeveloped sketch ideas as well as neat, carefully finished drawings. It is difficult to tell whether the Sketchbook II sketches are *all* by Edward C. Moore, but the visual evidence of both the handwriting and the drawings points strongly to his hand. The first dates in Moore's Sketchbook II are November 1865. The latest dates are 1869 and 1873. The 1873 date is puzzling since it is part of a crude sketch in red crayon on a page of pencil drawings. The red crayon date is in a handwriting style that is different from everything else in the sketchbook, just as the red crayon sketch is also unrelated to anything else in the notebook. It is as if someone in the Tiffany shop grabbed an old notebook and used a blank space to quickly demonstrate a design idea.

Based on the dates in the sketchbook and the dates of the silver derived from these sketch ideas, we would date the second Moore sketchbook from 1865 to the early 1870s with many or most of the sketches having been made in the 1860s.

Figure 30 shows a page of nautical drawings. The drawing of a buoy (marked 5) is almost surrealistic since the anchor ball is on the water while the buoy appears to float in the air like a balloon. This was a period when Tiffany was beginning to make a large number of yachting trophies, some of which are illustrated in Chapter 9.

About a third of Moore's Sketchbook II deals with Japanese influences. Two pages are illustrated in chapter 10, because of their relevance to Tiffany's silver in the Japanese style. Figure 31 shows two sensitive drawings with a typical Oriental flavor. On the left is a section of a slim, tall nineteenth-century Japanese vase. The right-hand drawing in Figure 31 is a naturalistic floral arrangement including several plant species and a piquant bird.

The sketchbooks of Edward C. Moore, along with a careful study of objects from his collection plus contemporary accounts, show clearly how Moore radically changed the dominant direction of Tiffany silver in the post–Civil War period, the period in which, as we have previously noted, Tiffany silver made its greatest advances. In Chapter 10 (The Japanese and Other Exotic

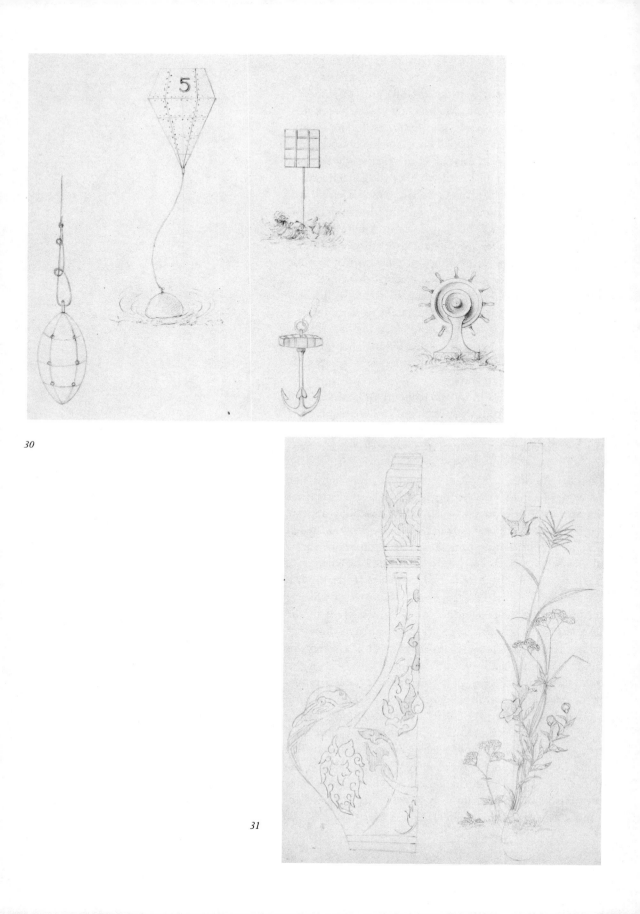

30

31

Influences), these all-pervasive influences from the Orient and their relationships to Moore's silver are discussed at length.

We should never forget, however, that the Tiffany organization involved a variety of individuals who made significant contributions. A number of talented designers were employed by the company, which is clearly apparent from the wide diversity of silver made during Moore's time. Moore's designers were given full credit for the work that they did. For example, James H. Whitehouse was given widespread publicity in 1876 as the designer of the Bryant Vase (Fig. 33), while Moore, his boss, kept discreetly in the background.

Moore was not only a designer of genius, he was also a perceptive and first-rate manager. He introduced a training program in the silver works that was a model for the whole American silverware industry. He traveled extensively abroad and it was on early trips to Paris that he made a special study (with G. T. Reed, the resident partner of Paris's Tiffany & Co.) of the working of local technical schools supported by the city of Paris. This is where he saw the system of drawing and modeling from nature as part of the training of apprentices which he introduced into Tiffany's training program.

Moore received honors in the Paris Exposition of 1878, and at the 1889 Paris Exposition he was made a Chevalier of the Legion of Honor of France.

Samuel Bing, the collector, writer, and dealer, whose Paris shop, L'Art Nouveau, gave the Art Nouveau movement its official title, was a longtime friend and admirer of Edward C. Moore. He singled Moore out as an outstanding artist (along with John La Farge and Louis Comfort Tiffany), saying they were men "whom the old continent would have been proud to possess."[3]

In speaking of the surprise generated by seeing at the 1878 Exposition "several examples of metal work of the most extraordinary quality," Bing noted: "This sudden resurgence was due to the clairvoyance of a man whose country should forever enshrine him in grateful memory; Edward C. Moore, artistic director of the famous Tiffany & Co was one of the first to comprehend the real value of the treasures just emerging from the Orient."[4]

Moore, who was honored and hailed in his time, had a prodigiously productive career with Tiffany. But his position has tended to be obscured by time and there is a tendency among present-day writers to downgrade or not know of Moore's achievements. There has even been a tendency to attribute certain pieces of Tiffany silver to names that are better known today, such as Louis Comfort Tiffany. Moore did no horn-blowing for himself during his lifetime. He was too busy and it wasn't his style. This reticence of Moore's was noted in a piece that appeared in 1891, just after his death, titled "Edward C. Moore, Tiffany & Co., A Prince of Silversmiths":

The late Edward C. Moore was easily the foremost silversmith in the United States. It is largely due to his skill and industry that American silverware has reached a degree of perfection that makes it celebrated all over the world. He practically developed a new industry here: but modest and retiring, almost morbidly adverse to publicity of any kind, he passed through life without assuming in the eyes of the general public the credit he so well deserved. In the words of his warm friend, M.S.P. Avery, the world will never fully know the loss it met in the death of Mr. Moore, and what he did for the industrial arts will never be fully told.[5]

Three years after his death a group of his friends commissioned a bronze head of Moore by the American sculptor Charles Calverley for presentation to the Metropolitan Museum of Art (Fig. 32). Its inscription reads:

Edward C. Moore
Born August 30th, 1827. Died August 24, 1891
SILVERSMITH,
ARTIST,
COLLECTOR,
A TRIBUTE FROM FRIENDS
1894

The Bryant Vase

In 1875 a group of prominent New Yorkers including J. P. Morgan, Theodore Roosevelt (father of Teddy), and Franklin H. Delano, along with leading citizens from Boston, Philadelphia, and other cities, formed a Bryant testimonial committee to honor the eightieth birthday of William Cullen Bryant. The poet and newspaper editor enjoyed a level of fame and almost universal acclaim that few poets ever achieve.

The committee decided "that a commemorative vase, of appropriate original design and choice workmanship, would be the best form of tribute, especially since Mr. Bryant did not need any material aid."[6] A subscription of five thousand dollars was completed and the "field of

32   Bronze bust of Edward C. Moore by the American sculptor Charles Calverley. Height: 20 in. (50.8 cm.). *(The Metropolitan Museum of Art, Gift of C. T. Cook and others, 1894).*

competition was thrown open to the whole craft of silver-smiths." Five leading firms submitted the final designs: Black, Starr & Frost; the Gorham Manufacturing Co. of Providence, Rhode Island; Starr & Marcus; Tiffany & Co.; and the Whiting Manufacturing Co.

Tiffany, with a design by James H. Whitehouse, won (Fig. 33). Whitehouse said this about his design:

When the Bryant Testimonial was first mentioned to me, my thoughts at once flew to the country—to the crossing of the boughs of trees, to the plants and flowers, and to a general contemplation of Nature; and these, together with a certain Homeric influence, produced in my mind the germ of the design—the form of a Greek vase, with the most beautiful American flowers growing round and entwining themselves gracefully about it, each breathing its own particular story as it grew.[7]

33 The Bryant Vase, given to the poet and editor William Cullen Bryant in honor of his eightieth birthday. The vase, designed by James H. Whitehouse, is marked "TIFFANY & CO. UNION SQUARE NEW YORK," "DESIGN PATENT MAY 1875," and "TIFFANY & CO. MAKERS." Height: 33 3/8 in. (84.8 cm.). (*The Metropolitan Museum of Art, Gift of William Cullen Bryant, 1877*).

33

The vase was presented to the poet on June 20, 1876 at Chickering Hall in New York. The elaborate, stately ceremony before an elite crowd started with organ music by George William Warren. Then there was a formal presentation of the vase to the committee by Charles Tiffany and his associates of Tiffany & Co. After more music by Mr. Warren, the vase was presented to Mr. Bryant by the chairman of the committee, Samuel Osgood. Osgood made a proper speech expressing the love and affection of the American people for the venerable poet and finally Mr. Bryant spoke, simply and straightforwardly. His speech ended with a eulogy for the makers of the vase and some prophetic remarks on the fleeting fame of poets:

And now a word, concerning the superb vase which is before me, the work of artists who are the worthy successors of Benvenuto Cellini, and eminent in their department. It has been greatly admired by those who have seen it, and deserves their admiration. This vase I may call a product of genius, both in the design and the execution; for who would suppose that any skill of the artist could connect with such a subject as he had before him images so happily conceived, so full of expression, and so well combining expression with grace? My friends, we authors cultivate a shortlived reputation; one generation of us pushes another from the state; the very language in which we write becomes a jargon, and we cease to be read; but a work like this is always beautiful, always admired. Age has no power over its charm. Hereafter some one may say, "This beautiful vase was made in honor of a certain American poet, whose name it bears, but whose writings are forgotten. It is remarkable that so much pain should have been taken to illustrate the life and writings of one whose works are so completely unknown at the present day." Thus, gentlemen artists, I shall be indebted to you for causing the memory of my name to outlast that of my writings.[8]

Bryant was right in his predictions which, incidentally, probably struck his contemporaries as an act of contrition. His poetry is little read but the Bryant Vase has endured. It was Tiffany & Co.'s chef d'oeuvre at the Centennial Exposition in Philadelphia. In 1877 Bryant gave the vase to the Metropolitan Museum of Art in New York. It was one of the features of the Met's one hundredth anniversary exhibit in 1970 and was shown at the Smithsonian Institution's great bicentennial show in Washington in 1976.

The Bryant Vase is probably the most important piece of American silver of Victorian America, for both its artistic and its historic importance. It is very much a piece of its time. It is completely covered with ornament; it has its storytelling medallions; and it is filled with symbolic notes. The iconography of the Bryant Vase was worked out very precisely. A Tiffany publication in connection with the Philadelphia Centennial Exposition gave a detailed explanation:

The heavier lines of the fretwork are derived from the apple branch, which suggests that while Mr. Bryant's writings are beautiful, they also bear a moral; as the apple tree blooms with a beautiful flower in the spring, and in the autumn bears fruit. Poetry is symbolized by the Eglantine, and Immortality by the Amaranth, which is said never to lose its fragrance, and these are blended with the lines formed of the apple branch.

The Primrose, for early youth, and Ivy for age, form a border directly above the handles. Encircling the neck at the narrowest part, the immortal line: "Truth crushed to earth shall rise again," is rendered verbatim, the beginning and end being separated by a representation of the Fringed Gentian, which Mr. Bryant remembers in one of his poems as always pointing to heaven. Eras in the Poet's life are illustrated by a series of bas-reliefs. In the first, as a child, looking up with veneration at a bust of Homer, to which his father points as a model.

The second shows him in the woods, reclining in a meditative attitude, under the trees.

Between the first and second of these medallion pictures, is a portrait of the Poet, laurel crowned.

Above this, the lyre for Mr. Bryant's verse, and beneath, the most primitive printing press, for his connection for over half a century with the New York Evening Post.

In a smaller medallion is the Waterfowl, used by Mr. Bryant as an emblem of faith, and introduced for that reason as the key note of his writings. The ornament around the lower part of the vase is of the Indian Corn, with single band of Cotton leaves, and at the foot is the Water Lily, emblematic of eloquence, for Mr. Bryant's oratory. The two great American staples are introduced to complete the ornamentation of the handles, the stalk, leaf, and grain of the Indian Corn on the inside, and the ripened boll of the Cotton on the outside. On the base which supports the vase, is the lyre for verse, which with the broken shackles point to Mr. Bryant's services in the cause of Emancipation.

From a formal point of view the Bryant Vase is extraordinary. The overall design is tight and sculptural; the precise rows of cornstalks on the lower part of the vase force the eye up to the medallions which are the center of attention; the interlaced fretwork locks the free-flowing flower background into place. The cornstalks with birds in the handles are tightly confined by the strong returning handle outline. The overall effect is one of great energy kept under iron-tight control. It reflects the kind of discipline that good art and good poetry always have.

The Philadelphia Centennial Exhibition

Tiffany & Co. made a major effort for the Centennial Exhibition. Their exhibit was located at the main crossing in the center of the Main Exhibition Building.

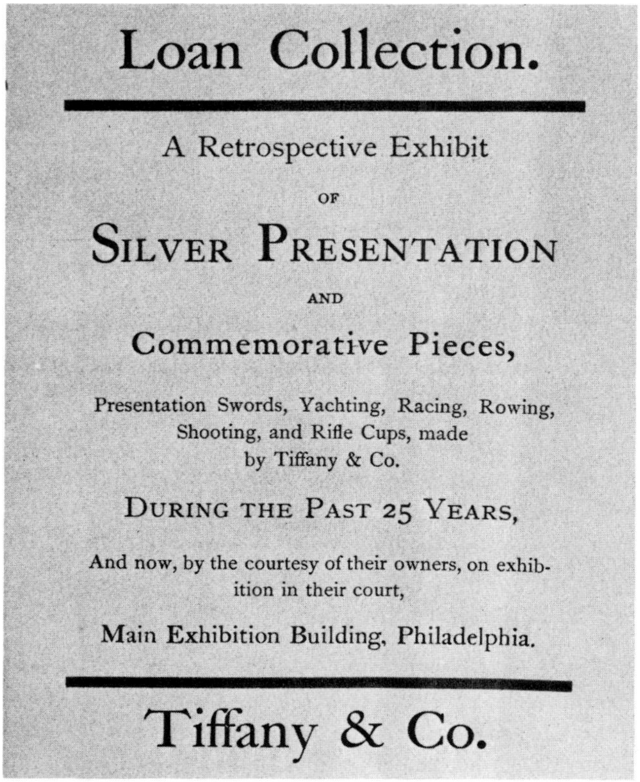

Loan Collection.

A Retrospective Exhibit

OF

SILVER PRESENTATION

AND

Commemorative Pieces,

Presentation Swords, Yachting, Racing, Rowing, Shooting, and Rifle Cups, made by Tiffany & Co.

DURING THE PAST 25 YEARS,

And now, by the courtesy of their owners, on exhibition in their court,

Main Exhibition Building, Philadelphia.

Tiffany & Co.

A large loan show was organized, with about a hundred and twenty-five pieces of silver on exhibit. Almost half of these were yachting trophies, four of which we illustrate in Chapter 9 (Figs. 234, 235, 237, and 238). There was the Bryant Vase plus sixteen other major presentation pieces including "The Four Seasons" Center-piece (Fig. 17). There were presentation swords, rifle prizes, pigeon shooting cups, and racing cups. Mrs. Le Grand Lockwood loaned her silver wedding centerpiece; William Astor, a punch bowl; C. A. Lamont, a tea set and fruit bowl; John B. Heckscher, a cigar stand; and Lorenzo Delmonico, a wine sleigh.

In addition to the loans there was silver for sale including a "Group of Silver Articles, Chromatically decorated by inlaying with copper, gold, and niello enamel—the first examples produced here." One of the copper-decorated silver pieces, the stunning pitcher in Plate I, was purchased from the Tiffany exhibit at the Centennial Exhibition for the Boston Museum of Fine Arts. This was the first piece of Tiffany silver that we know of to go into a museum, and it was also one of the first objects acquired by the Boston Museum.

The 1876 Centennial Exhibition was an unqualified success for Tiffany. They received the gold medal and special awards for jewelry, watches, silverware, and silver inlaid with niello and copper. They received much favorable publicity and their continuing position as the leading silversmiths in America was unchallenged.

The Paris Exposition of 1878

Tiffany's blockbuster exhibit at the 1878 Paris Universal Exposition was a sensation. Compared to their modest, low-key exhibit in London in 1867, Tiffany's Paris showing was a major effort. Their large silver exhibit featured two highlights: (1) The Mackay service, the opulent 1,250-piece dinner and dessert service for twenty-four, which we discuss at some length in Chapters 4 and 5, and (2) a remarkable collection of silver in the Japanese style. The Mackay service, which was awesome in its size and workmanship, got a mixed press. Some writers praised it while others felt it was ostentatious. But the crowds of people swarming through the Tiffany exhibit loved it.

The "Japanese" silver was something else. The critics liked it and universally praised it. And it sold extraordinarily well. The list of buyers (which Tiffany made available for publication) was a veritable Who's Who ranging from the Prince of Wales, Baron Gustav de Rothschild, the Japanese government, to museums of Vienna, Berlin, Stuttgart, and Dublin. The small bell in

34 Bell with etched Oriental bird with fantastic plume feathers, fern fronds, and cherry blossoms on handle. Length: 3 5/16 in. (8.4 cm.). Mark: NO. 19 (4793/9307). (*National Museum of Ireland*).

35 Testimonial presentation piece made by Tiffany in 1887 for William E. Gladstone from his American admirers. Height: 36 5/8 in. (93 cm.). Mark: TIFFANY & CO STERLING/N.Y. (*Sir William Gladstone, Hawarden Castle*).

Figure 34 was purchased by the National Museum of Ireland in Dublin directly from the Paris Exposition.

The fact that great museums in America and Europe were acquiring examples of Tiffany silver in the 1870s certainly underscores the exalted position the firm's wares enjoyed at the time. They were indeed the leading silversmiths of the world.

Tiffany also received official recognition for their contribution to the 1878 Exposition in the form of the *Grand Prix* for silverware, a gold medal for jewelry, plus six other medals. Charles Tiffany was made a Chevalier of the Legion of Honor of France, and from the Czar of Russia he received the Gold Medal *Praemia Digno*.

In the months following the exposition Tiffany & Co. received appointments as imperial and royal jewelers, gold- and silversmiths to almost every crowned head in

36 Detail of Gladstone Testimonial in Fig. 35.

Europe. This added the royal stamp of approval to that of the critics and the public.

Tiffany did not make direct use of their royal appointments in their advertisements or in their store. Nevertheless they made the fact well known through publicity releases to the newspapers.

The designing and making of presentation pieces was from the beginning an important and newsworthy part of Tiffany's silver business. There was one presentation piece that not only got a lot of newspaper publicity but also caused a bit of an international flap: the Gladstone Testimonial.

The fight of William Gladstone, the great English prime minister, to obtain Home Rule for Ireland had gained him wide sympathy in the United States and a huge number of enemies in Great Britain, including Queen Victoria. Gladstone's first attempt to get Home Rule through Parliament failed in the summer of 1886 and as a result his government was forced out of office. This only strengthened the feeling of Americans, particularly those of Irish origin, for the Grand Old Man of English politics. Joseph Pulitzer, the owner of the New York *World,* in the fall of 1886 organized a campaign to raise funds for a testimonial award for Gladstone. Through the newspaper over ten thousand people contributed to the testimonial fund, and Tiffany received the commission to make a suitable piece of presentation silver.

The presentation was made on July 9th, 1887 at Hollis Hall, a 250-acre estate belonging to the Earl of Aberdeen, on the outskirts of London. Mrs. Gladstone had invited a large number of guests to a garden party for the occasion. The box containing the massive testimonial, which had arrived the day before, had not been opened. Mrs. Gladstone called for the keys to the box, and Gladstone himself helped remove the three-foot high piece. He examined it carefully and asked a number of questions about Messrs. Tiffany "saying he had heard that they were the best silversmiths in the world."[9]

The newspaper account said Gladstone colored with pleasure when he discovered the words DOUBLE FIRST on the piece. This referred to the Double Firsts he had received on his final examinations in Classics and Mathematics from Oxford fifty-six years earlier, in 1831. The Tiffany designer had researched his subject well.

The presentation speech was made by Joseph Pulitzer, who had gone to England for the occasion accompanied by his wife, Congressman Perry Belmont of New York, Congressman Collins of Boston, and other distinguished Americans. Gladstone began with a graceful response and then proceeded with a speech that caused an uproar in the British press. He said it was all right for Americans to send money to Ireland and to receive their poor immigrants in America, but that when Americans back Ireland's fight for liberty the English press "indignantly expostulate and complain to the world that you are interfering with British Institutions." Thus Gladstone publicly welcomed American support for his unpopular stand on Irish home rule.

The *London Times* attacked both Gladstone and Pulitzer ("Savage attack on Grand Old Man and his American Friends," said the *New York World*). The *Pall Mall Gazette* defended Pulitzer. It took a couple of weeks for the uproar to die down.

The Testimonial itself (Figs. 35–36) is a relatively restrained, dignified example of Victorian silver sculpture. The heroic bust of the Grand Old Man sits solidly on a two-tiered base while Liberty in her star-studded gown praises him with steady eyes. The inscription made it clear that his American friends wanted Home Rule for Ireland even if it had been turned down in Parliament.

The 1889 Paris Exposition

Tiffany & Co. had a large and important exhibit at the Paris Exposition in 1889 befitting their preeminent position. A group of impressive objects of silver were shown plus a fabulous exhibit of precious stones. Tea and coffee services, vases, inkstands, hand mirrors, and other objects were shown, many in an Islamic style dubbed Saracenic. There were also specimens in the Japanese style, some of which were inlaid with gems.

American Indian designs first appeared at the 1889 Exposition in quantity. There were pieces which featured colored silver alloys and enameled goods, many of which were designed by George P. Farnham and John T. Curran. This kind of excessively opulent work of silver reached a pinnacle in the Magnolia Vase (Fig. 37) shown at the World's Columbian Exposition in Chicago in 1893.

From an artistic point of view Tiffany's samplings in the 1889 Paris Exposition showed a far wider number of styles and was more eclectic than the pieces shown eleven years earlier in Paris. For this reason it did not have the critical impact that the 1878 Exposition had and exerted less influence on other silversmiths than the earlier showing. Nevertheless it was a success for Tiffany's and it kept their reputation solid.

37 The Magnolia Vase, enamel and gold insets on silver, "Toltec" handles, naturalistic enamelled and repoussé flowers and plant forms, and Art Nouveau swirls on the base. Designed by John T. Curran. Height: 31 in. (78.8 cm.). Mark: NO. 21 (11168/3137) plus mark of World's Columbian Exposition. (*The Metropolitan Museum of Art*).

Tiffany continued to have major exhibits in worlds' fairs and exhibitions into the twentieth century. The Magnolia Vase and the Viking Bowl were shown in Chicago in 1893 along with large displays of household silver, trophies, and presentation pieces. Tiffany had special marks for silver made for the 1893 Columbian Exposition in Chicago, the 1900 Exposition Universelle, Paris, and the 1901 Pan-American Exposition in Buffalo (see Chapter 13, p. 252).

During the latter part of the nineteenth century Tiffany made a couple of oddities that created widespread publicity: the gold chamberpot Diamond Jim Brady had made for Lillian Russell and a silver bicycle (Fig. 38) also made for Miss Russell as a gift from her admirers. The gold chamberpot with an eye on the bottom was, as Joseph Purtell points out, a gift for Miss Russell that may never have been matched for vulgarity.

Lillian Russell's silver bicycle wasn't unique, since bicycles were listed in the 1897 Tiffany *Blue Book*. An amusing, tongue-in-cheek story appeared in a San Francisco newspaper December 9, 1895, announcing the coming of Tiffany's new line:

ELEVATING THE BICYCLE

A long felt want in the Bicycle line is about to be supplied in New York. Society cannot refrain from biking, but it has been recognized as a grievance that it is practically impossible to buy a bicycle costing over $125.00. This gives the sport an air of cheapness that galls the souls of the exclusive who

38 Silver bicycle designed by Tiffany & Co. for Lillian Russell. It was a gift to the actress from her admirers.

can afford to buy diamonds and Dukes for their daughters. The heiress of the House of Astorbilt takes a spin in the park on her wheel, and there is nothing to distinguish her from a typewriter out for a holiday, and a holiday may have the advantage in point of attractiveness.

At last Tiffany has come to the rescue. As a starter he has designed a bicycle, decorated in silver and ivory.

The handlebars, pedal bars and pedals, the bars holding the seat, and the rivet and bolt heads have been heavily plated with silver. The handlebars are of carved ivory, partly encased in chased silver. All the joints of the frame are encased in solid silver, etched and chased in repoussé style. On the saddle are dainty silver ornaments, with shell-scroll work in the style of Louis Quinze. To go with this is a searchlight lantern which will be ornamented with chased silver. The entire work in silver was done by hand.

This is a gentleman's wheel. The lady's wheel to match is to be much more elaborate. "The frame will be entirely covered with chased silver, while the lantern will probably be further decorated with precious stones."

These machines are to be the entering wedge of luxury. Before the opening of the next season, purchasers will have their choice of machines, for which designs are now being prepared, with ornamentation of gold and gems. Mounted on a wheel of this description, there is every reason to believe that a rider can secure general recognition of the public that he has money to burn, whatever his deficiencies in gray matter. Society is looking forward to the new bikes with enthusiasm. They are also hopefully regarded by the enterprising fraternity of bicycle thieves.[10]

We end this informal outline of the history of Tiffany silver in the nineteenth century with the showing of a child's bowl and dish that is symbolic of the ending of an era and the beginning of another (Fig. 39). The bowl and dish were given by Charles L. Tiffany to his great-grandson, William T. Lusk, on March 10, 1901 when the founder of the firm was eighty-nine years old. He died in 1902. His great-grandson, Mr. Lusk, went on to become president of Tiffany's in the 1950s.

Certainly Charles L. Tiffany was one of the great marketing men of his time. His unerring sense of timing, his genius for picking the right men for his organization, and his energy all went into the building of Tiffany & Co. His days with Tiffany & Co. coincided with Queen Victoria's reign in England (1837–1901) and cover the period with which we are essentially concerned in this book.

39 Bowl and plate with the inscription, "WIL-
LIAM T. LUSK/ FROM HIS GREAT GRANDFATHER/
CHARLES L. TIFFANY/ MARCH 30TH 1901." Height
of bowl: 3 in. (7.6 cm.). Mark: NO. 27 (9619/
8731). (Courtesy of Mrs. William T. Lusk).

40 Claret jug with hinged lid. Engraved on
base "F. S. BANGS/ 1887." Height: 11 1/16 in.
(28.1 cm.). Mark: NO. 20 (5981/6223), also
"2 1/2 P'TS." (Museum of the City of New
York, Gift of Miss Mary Whitney Bangs).

39

40

Art Nouveau Silver and Louis Comfort Tiffany

Tiffany & Co. made relatively little silver that could be
classified as Art Nouveau, and most of the examples in
this style were actually made *before* the 1895–1910 period
when the Art Nouveau movement was at its height.
Silver hollow ware in the Japanese style of the 1870s,
some of the yachting and presentation pieces of the 1880s,
and the *Japanese, Vine,* and *Lap Over Edge* flatware
were truly precursors of Art Nouveau.

A few handsome examples of Tiffany silver of the
1880s and 1890s have an Art Nouveau feeling but usually
in a most restrained and reserved manner. There is practically no counterpart in Tiffany silver to the Martelé
silver of the Gorham Company with its typical sensuous
twisting, flowering, and flowing lines and forms. Gorham's Martelé expressed a sensibility that obviously had
little appeal to Tiffany & Co.

Figure 40 shows a silver claret jug with free-flowing
wave forms with a definite Art Nouveau feeling. The
handsome chafing dish with ivory handle in Figure 41
made in 1891 has wavelike design elements similar to
those of the claret jug, but the overall design of the
chafing dish is more formal, more ordered. The strong
wave elements of the center band are repeated on a
smaller scale on the band on the lid and again on both
the finial of the lid and the legs of the stand. The chafing
dish is made of six different parts: a stand, alcohol lamp,

44

41 Chafing dish with ivory handle made about 1891 from an 1889 design. Height: 10 3/8 in. (26.3 cm.). Width through handle: 15 in. (38.1 cm.). Mark on skillet, water pan, and lamp: NO. 21 (10201/9569). (Private Collection).

42 Vase encrusted with pearls made by Tiffany & Co. about 1893. Height: 7 in. (17.8 cm.). Mark: NO. 20 plus mark for World's Columbian Exposition. (Kunstgewerbemuseum, Berlin).

43 Punch bowl—trophy with inscription "THE GOELET PRIZE FOR SLOOPS 1889/ WON BY TITANIA/ FROM/ BEDOUIN, GRACIE." Height: 12 in. (30.5 cm.). Mark: TIFFANY & CO./ 10221 M 0510/ STERLING SILVER. (Museum of the City of New York).

41

42

a support plate, water pan, skillet, and lid. The pieces of this chafing dish are beautifully engineered, fitting together with precision. This is a fine example of a useful, well-made object whose design still retains its freshness.

The vase in the Kunstgewerbemuseum in Berlin shown in Figure 42 is mainstream Art Nouveau with its whirling organic form encrusted with pearls. The Goelet Prize for Sloops, 1889, in Figure 43 has an ebullient

43

exuberance that only occasionally showed itself in Tiffany silver. The organic, flowing lettering, which seems very Art Nouveau to us, had its origins in the stylized cal-

44 Finger bowl and stand, heavily chased with swirls and pierced with scrolling foliage, gilt interior, made about 1893, and exhibited at the World's Columbian Exposition in Chicago. Designed by John T. Curran. Diameter of bowl: 5 1/4 in. (13.3 cm.). Diameter of stand: 9 3/8 in. (23.8 cm.). *(Sotheby Parke Bernet).*

ligraphy on Persian metal works in the Edward Moore collection.

The finger bowl with stand in Figure 44 with busy swirling wavelike decorations is another of the relatively few pieces of Tiffany silver that fits into the Art Nouveau category. It was exhibited at the 1893 Columbian Exposition in Chicago. The finger bowl was designed by John T. Curran who was granted a design patent on it in 1894.

Because of the leading position of Louis Comfort Tiffany in the whole Art Nouveau movement, it is intriguing (and frustrating) to study his place in the story of Tiffany & Co. silver. He was the eldest son of Charles L. Tiffany and was born in 1848. He never had any real interest in his father's company. He very early made the decision to be an artist, and wanted nothing to do with the business world of Tiffany & Co. He was a friend and admirer of Edward C. Moore, and Moore's early interest in Oriental art was shared with him.

During the busy years of the 1880s and 1890s, Louis Comfort Tiffany was establishing his reputation as a decorator and designer of stained-glass windows and the inventor of Favrile glass. In the 1890s he was on the board of directors of his father's firm and after his father's death in 1902 he became a vice-president of the company, no doubt in recognition of his holdings of Tiffany stock. In 1902 he was also made "artistic director" of Tiffany's and certainly had a voice in what was made and sold by the company. It is impossible from presently available Tiffany records to document his influence during these years but it could have been considerable. A curious footnote on Louis Comfort's activities at Tiffany & Co. is shown in Figure 180 where he ordered the tip of a souvenir spoon deleted. In the "Exposition Universelle" in Paris in 1900 the exhibits of Tiffany & Co. and Louis C. Tiffany's Tiffany Studios were side by side. During the early part of the twentieth century Favrile glass was sold at Tiffany's where a separate "artistic jewelry" department was established as an outlet for Louis Comfort's designs. The department was not profitable and was discontinued in 1916.

One might be tempted to attribute to Louis Comfort's hand the type of designs shown in Figures 40 through 43 but there is no basis for such an attribution. The use of jewels encrusted in silver as in the Magnolia Vase and the Berlin Vase could have been suggested by him.

Louis Comfort Tiffany and his Tiffany Studios made *very* little silver. Indeed at the present time (1978) less than two dozen pieces of silver can be surely ascribed to him, all of which were custom-designed pieces made early in the twentieth century. Louis Comfort Tiffany's Tiffany Studios silver is quite different from Tiffany & Co.'s regular lines. The pieces were all handmade and tend to be more exotic in their feeling. The three-handled cup in Figure 45 set with emeralds and turquoise has a handmade, arts and crafts look that is more related to the Tiffany hand-hammered silver inlaid with copper and gold in the Japanese style of the 1870s than it is to its contemporary Tiffany & Co. silver of the first decade of the twentieth century. We feel that the chunky silver and Favrile-glass inkwell in Figure 46 was probably a Tiffany Studios' design even though the silver top is marked "Tiffany & Co., Makers."

The Tiffany Studios six-piece tea and coffee service in Figure 47 made ca. 1910 is likewise more related to Tiffany Studios bronze objects than it is to the silver of Tiffany and Co. The service illustrates graphically Louis Comfort Tiffany's love of flowers, in this case the yellow wild flower, yarrow, which was a favorite for dried flower arrangements. The massing of the floral motifs on the squat, earth-hugging forms is characteristic of his work.

45 Three-handled silver cup set with emeralds and turquoise. Made by Tiffany Studios about 1905. Height: 8 in. (20.3 cm.). Mark: TIFFANY STUDIOS/ NEW YORK/ STERLING/ 925/1000/ 4787. (*The Metropolitan Museum of Art*).

46 Silver and glass inkwell made by Tiffany & Co. about 1905. The six-lobed Favrile glass has a pattern of wavy striations of iridescent blue. Height: 4 1/2 in. (11.4 cm.). Mark on top: TIFFANY & CO., MAKERS, STERLING SILVER. Mark on bottom: 08468. (*Newark Museum*).

45

46

47

47 Six-piece tea and coffee service made by Tiffany Studios about 1910 for Emily Frances Whitney whose initials EFW are engraved on each piece. The plain flat panels of the service (there are sixteen panels on each piece) are hand-hammered and the yarrow flower decorations are repoussé. Heights: kettle and stand 12 3/4 in. (32.4 cm.); coffeepot 7 1/2 in. (19 cm.); teapot 7 in. (17.8 cm.); sugar bowl 5 3/4 in. (14.6 cm.); creamer 4 in. (10.1 cm.); waste bowl 3 1/4 in. (8.2 cm.). Mark on each piece: STERLING / 925/ 1000 / TIFFANY STUDIOS / NEW YORK / 1842. (See Fig. 49.) (Private Collection).

The lines of beading in the repousséd parts of the tea and coffee service (see Fig. 48) give a geometric ordering to the design in a manner similar to the beading on the cup in Figure 45.

The hot water kettle of the Tiffany Studios service shows some of Louis Comfort Tiffany's design approaches. He has simplified the kettle stand giving the kettle a clean-cut appearance. The kettle stands of the 1870s had been quite ornate (see Fig. 73). The arms of the 1870s' stands which hold the kettle add a confusing decorative element which Louis Comfort Tiffany completely eliminated. It will be noted that he used two locking pins which hold the kettle to the stand. The removal of the back pin allows the kettle to be tipped on the stand for pouring. By removing both pins the kettle can be used independently. A similar device had been used by Edward C. Moore on hot water kettles in the 1850s as shown in Figure 23.

Louis Comfort did not like shiny metal objects.[11] The dense, finely detailed repoussé work on the hot water kettle (Fig. 48) not only has a decorative function but it also cuts down on light reflectivity. Even the plain panels of the body and the spout of the kettle are not mirror bright but are mottled by traces of the hammer marks on the interior. Contrast this with the plain surfaces of the chafing dish in Figure 41, which are smooth, brilliantly polished, and reflective. The Tiffany Studios set has a softer glow due to the partial breaking-up of light patterns by the hand-hammered surfaces. Louis Comfort Tiffany's treatment of the floral elements is interesting. We are shown the yarrow flowers from top, bottom, and side views tied together with Art Nouveau branches. This cubist approach to design was in the air in 1910 when the then daring experiments of Picasso and Braque were making waves in the art world.

The service was commissioned by Harry Payne Whitney and his wife, Gertrude Vanderbilt Whitney (the founder of New York's Whitney Museum of American Art), for a niece, Emily Frances Whitney, who married Allan Lindsay Briggs in 1910. There is a massive 203-ounce tea tray for the service that has the same monogram "E.F.W." as the pieces of the Tiffany Studios tea

48 Detail of repoussé decorations on kettle in Fig. 47.

49 Mark on creamer in Fig. 47.

service, but the tray (not illustrated) was made by Tiffany & Co. The service was also accompanied by the round Tiffany & Co. waiter in Figure 319 with a similar monogram. The engraved flower forms of the waiter show the tops and bottoms of flowers in a manner related to the Tiffany Studios service although the actual details of the two are quite different. We do not know where or by whom the service was actually made. It could have been made at the Tiffany & Co. plant but no account of the service can be found in their records. And it could have been made in the Tiffany Studios' shop, but *their* plant records of this period seem to have been lost.

Louis Comfort's relative avoidance of silver as an art material may have had a psychological implication—perhaps one that is almost *too* obvious. His father and his father's firm were world famous for their silverware, and it would have only been natural for him to want to make it on his own as an artist—in another field. So he painted pictures and made stained-glass windows and Favrile glass but practically no silver. That he could design first-rate silver objects is shown by the few examples Tiffany Studios did make, but he seems to have chosen to make very little of it. As a decorator he appeared to avoid silver. A careful examination of photographs of the interiors he designed shows little silverware, even in the dining rooms. There was practically no silver used decoratively in Laurelton Hall, Louis Comfort's Long Island house. There was only a four-piece silver tea service on the sideboard in the dining room. And the tea tray that was behind it on the sideboard was of hammered copper.

We can sum up by saying that Edward C. Moore and his collection were early influences on Louis Comfort Tiffany's art. Later, Louis Comfort was to have, at the most, only a peripheral influence on the silver of Tiffany & Co.

4. The Sumptuous Table—1: Hollow Ware

The Victorian era was truly an age of silver. Probably more silver was used in the average well-to-do household than any time in history. Up to the time of the Civil War silver was not plentiful in the United States and relatively little silver was mined here. Then, in about 1860, the mines of California and Nevada began to yield their treasures. In 1860 116,000 ounces of silver were mined in the U. S. In 1861 production jumped thirteen fold to 1.5 million ounces. By 1900 U. S. production of silver had increased to 57 million ounces. During these four decades the price of silver declined steadily from $1.35 per ounce to 61 cents per ounce.[1] Silver not only became cheaper and more plentiful during these years, it also became a central debating point of national policy. One of the most famous speeches of the time was William Jennings Bryan's ("The Boy Orator of the Platte") "Cross of Gold" speech before the 1896 Democratic convention. This passionate and dramatic address against the gold standard in favor of silver almost literally blew the roof off the convention. Silver was on everyone's mind as it had been for some time in this country.

Silver had been part of the nation's consciousness since the 1850s and 1860s when the opening of the western gold and silver mines was a matter of great national interest and pride. Silverware for the home became highly fashionable. In this period of incredible expansion in the United States, thousands and thousands of the new well-to-do and the new rich found silver not only a wonderful status symbol but also amongst the most satisfying of useful objects. Of course, much of the silver was used in the dining room, and from our vantage point in the twentieth century we know that it was truly the era of the sumptuous table.

In this chapter we survey the hollow ware used in the dining room—tea and coffee services, compotes and centerpieces, candlesticks and candelabra, trays and water pitchers and punch bowls—all the many silver forms that the Victorians were so fond of and which were so intertwined with their social life. In chapter 5 we discuss flatware—knives, spoons, forks, and the myriad forms of serving pieces.

Although quantities of silver flatware and hollow ware were used in dining and silver was displayed on the dining table, on the sideboard, on mantels, and on serving tables, the idea of displaying silver was not invented by the Victorians. The custom dates back to colonial times in America, and even to Roman times in Europe. Silver has always represented wealth and position, but Victorians did bring the custom to a climax. They displayed more silver and used more silver than ever before. Tea and coffee services were larger, more serving dishes were made of silver, and huge quantities of silver flatware were used and often stored in the dining room.

We illustrate two nineteenth-century dining rooms which show two different but not entirely unrelated lifestyles. The first is the dining room of the Lockwood House in Norwalk, Connecticut, one of the great mansions of nineteenth-century America; the second is the surprisingly restrained and sedate dining room of P. T. Barnum in Bridgeport, Connecticut.

The Lockwood Mansion, which was designed by Detlef Lienau, was four years in its building, having been started in 1864 and finished in 1868. Costing a reputed $1,100,000, it was a forerunner of the great stone mansions of New York and Newport.

The New York *Sun* in an article on October 2, 1869 noted this about the mansion:

LE GRAND LOCKWOODS RESIDENCE
THE MOST MAGNIFICENT COUNTRY SEAT IN AMERICA

Passengers over the New Haven railroad have noticed a magnificent structure on the outskirts of Norwalk. . . . It might be two country seats of English noblemen rolled into one, or it might be a palace of Ismail Pasha. It is the country residence of Le Grand Lockwood, chief partner of the firm of Lockwood and Co., bankers and brokers. . . .

The 1869 article later continues lyrically:

It is a wonder of architecture. . . . Its bright walks sparkle in the sun, towers and spires blend gracefully with its slated roof, and fairy rays of gilt kindle its crest with glory.

Le Grand Lockwood, who was from an old Norwalk family, made most of his money from dealings in railroad securities. Among others, he had controlling interest in the Danbury and Norwalk Railroad which skirted his Norwalk property. He walked from his sixty-room house to the conveniently located station stop on his own property for his daily commute to New York.

The silver medallion in Figure 50 of Le Grand Lockwood and his wife Ann Louisa Benedict Lockwood was made for their twenty-fifth wedding anniversary, the year before they moved into their Norwalk house. Although the medallion doesn't appear to be signed or marked, we attribute it to Tiffany & Co., both because of its similarity to known Tiffany medallions, and because all the other Lockwood silver of the period is from Tiffany's. (Mr. Lockwood's inkstand is shown in Figure 183, Chapter 6.)

The dining room of the Lockwood mansion in Figure 51 is from an 1868 photograph taken from the spacious alcove of the 32 x 35 foot room looking towards the double doors which open into the great center rotunda of the house. The rotunda towered forty-two feet through the middle of the four-story building. To the left in the photograph is one of two doors which open directly into the "fireproof and burglar proof" silver vault. The outer door is oak, paneled with brazilwood, to match the other doors in the room. The inner door is a massive three-inch thick steel safe door which is paneled and painted to simulate wood. The vault itself is triangular shaped, roughly 7 x 12 feet, and contains a marble sink for washing silver and high shelves for storage. It is a feature many modern householders might envy.

This vault was part of an overall security system which gave a fortresslike quality to this massive house. There was an extraordinary burglar alarm arrangement in the house connected to all exterior doors and windows on the first and second floors plus the door to the wine cellar. In addition, elaborate systems of wires were embedded in the floors under the carpeting in the main rooms of the house which led to burglar alarm indicators in the master bedroom and in the servants quarters.

Unfortunately, Le Grand Lockwood and his wife lived in the house only four years. The 1869 gold panic wiped out the firm of Lockwood & Co., and Lockwood was forced to take out a $400,000 mortgage on his Norwalk

50 Silver medallion portraits of Le Grand Lockwood and his wife Ann Louisa Benedict Lockwood made for their twenty-fifth wedding anniversary in 1867. Height: 3 in. (7.6 cm.). *(Lockwood-Mathews Mansion Museum, Norwalk, Connecticut).*

51 Dining room in Le Grand Lockwood house in Norwalk, Connecticut from a photograph taken in 1868, the year the house was finished. The door to the far left goes into the silver vault.

house. He died three years later in 1872 and, when his widow could not meet the last payment on the house, the mortgage holder foreclosed and took over the mansion.

P. T. Barnum's house in Seaside Park, Bridgeport, Connecticut was a comfortable medium-large Victorian house. The 1888 photograph in Figure 52 shows a fairly typical upper middle-class dining room of the period with its wainscoted walls and large built-in sideboard and mirror-backed shelves for the display of silver and china. The ceiling is floral decorated in an Oriental manner, and an Oriental rug is on the floor. The chandelier is a combination of gas and electric lighting. The chairs are typical Victorian dreams of past grandeur with embossed leather backs and seats. The basket on the table could be of silver or silver plate. Also on the table is a marble-topped plate with its Victorian silver frame and feet.

Above the built-in cupboard hangs a row of plates, among which are pieces of Chinese Rose Medallion and Dutch Delft. On the top shelf are three pieces of French Limoges, two tureens with covers, and a two-handled vase. There are nineteen pieces of silver displayed on the sideboard shelves and the shelf above it; a tea and coffee service, vegetable dishes, tureens, trays, a covered box, and a toast holder. The center of attention on the sideboard is the large hot water kettle resting on a footed tray. The silver flatware was probably kept in the drawers of the sideboard.

This rather casual collection of silver on display was quite typical both as to numbers of pieces and their arrangement. (We know nothing of the silver shown in the photograph. Some of it could well have come from Tiffany since Barnum had been a customer of the store since the 1850s.)

Silverware was often stored in the handsome locked chests that Tiffany made for their silver services. These

52 Dining room of P. T. Barnum's house in Bridgeport, Connecticut, from an 1888 photograph.

chests not only served as convenient storage places for the silver, they also protected the stored silver from dirt and the coal smoke which created such a problem of tarnishing in the nineteenth century. Servants could clean and polish the display silver once a week, but no one was anxious to polish the flatware any more often than necessary. Figure 53 shows a fine set of *Chrysanthemum* flatware and coffee and tea service in its original Tiffany chest. These chests were kept in the dining room or stored in closets off the dining room.

In this chapter we will illustrate a number of hollowware pieces showing the range of designs from the 1850s to the turn of the century. First we describe the Mackay service since it is *the* prototype of the really sumptuous dinner service of Victorian America. The Mackay service is so complete and so well documented that a study of it can give an excellent picture of the number and kind of pieces of silverware that were used or could have been used in the Victorian dining room.

The Mackay Service

Tiffany & Co. made one great silver service in the 1870s that epitomizes the sumptuous dining table of Victorian America. The largest, the grandest, the most elegantly ornate, and the most famous of its time, it was the "Dinner and Dessert Service for Twenty-Four Persons" which John W. Mackay had made for his wife, Marie Louise. The service consisted of some 1,250 pieces and was made from a half ton of silver sent by Mr. Mackay directly to Tiffany's from his fabled Comstock Lode mines of Virginia City, Nevada.

John Mackay, the "silver king," and his wife, with her separate career as a leader of European society, were among the best-known and most talked about Americans of their times. They both had humble beginnings. John Mackay arrived in New York in 1840 as a poor Irish immigrant boy of nine. In 1851 he followed the thousands and thousands who had already gone to California to seek his fortune in the gold fields. He had nothing to show for his first eight years of dawn to dusk labor but experience. However, this experience in mining and practical geology served him well when he left California for the silver and gold fields of Nevada in 1859. In Virginia City, Nevada, Mackay became a mining contractor and within a half-dozen years he became the chief owner of

53 Complete service for twelve of the *Chrysanthemum* pattern plus a matching seven-piece coffee and tea service and tray in its original red velvet-lined mahogany and walnut chest made about 1894. The top of the chest lifts up to give access to the tea and coffee service. The top drawer contains 34 serving pieces and the bottom drawer has 216 pieces of flatware. Many pieces of the service are gilt. Height: 24 1/2 in. (62.3 cm.). Width: 22 3/4 in. (57.8 cm.). Length: 33 in. (83.8 cm.). *(Mr. and Mrs. Frank R. Edwards).*

a profitable silver mine. When he met and married the twenty-three-year-old widow Marie Hungerford Bryant in 1867, he was already a man of means, a man on the way up. Mrs. Bryant, who was born in Brooklyn, had grown up in the mining towns of California and Nevada where she had married a bright young doctor, Dr. Edmund Cullen Bryant (a cousin of William Cullen Bryant) when she was sixteen years old. After two children were born in quick succession something happened to Dr. Bryant. He took to drugs and drink and abandoned his family and wandered off. In 1866, Mrs. Bryant received word that her husband was dying in LaPorte, California. She joined him and nursed him in his final days. When John Mackay met Marie Bryant she was supporting herself as a seamstress.

John Mackay built a Victorian bungalow for his new family at the corner of Howard and Virginia streets in Virginia City. "Virginia," as it was called, was a classic mining town, 6,000 feet high in the Sierras. It was a bare, dusty, noisy, brawling, jerry-built scar in the mountains. It was claimed there wasn't a blade of grass or shrub in the town and that strangers couldn't sleep at night because of the noise. It wasn't a woman's world and in the early 1870s when the Mackays became really rich, Mrs. Mackay left for good; first to San Francisco, then New York. She was snubbed by New York society so she soon left for Paris where her knowledge of the French language (her grandmother was French), her vast wealth, and her vaulting social ambitions soon propelled her to the top.

The riches came when John Mackay and his partners discovered the "Big Bonanza" of the Comstock in 1873. This discovery has been described in superlatives ever since. It is said to have been one of the greatest and richest mining discoveries in history. It made John Mackay and his partners among the richest men in America. In its comparatively short life (about twenty years) the Comstock yielded hundreds of millions of tax-free dollars to its owners at a time when the silver miners made $4 a day, a farm laborer about $1 a day and $500 bought a nice small house.

Before settling down permanently in Europe, Louise Mackay made one last visit to Virginia City in 1874, during which she made the fifteen-hundred-foot elevator descent down the mine shaft to see the famous Comstock Bonanza. It was here deep in the mine that she is said to have originated the idea for a silver service to be made from their own silver. Mrs. Mackay's granddaughter, Ellin Berlin, wrote about it this way in *Silver Platter*:

"How queer, John, that silver should look so plain. I knew it but I didn't expect it. The pyrites sparkle like diamonds, and those crystals! This pale blue one is like a giant jewel."

"Quartz crystals," John said, "We like to find them. They show there's life in the vein. But silver can be pretty too. I'll show you."

He led her to a chamber about ten feet square. Its walls were flecked with silver. The ceiling was covered with silver in the form of crystals.

"Silver sometimes shines in its natural state," John said. "Wait here a moment."

He left her and presently returned with what looked like a coil of polished silver wire. "I was lucky. One of the men just found a bright bit. Usually this crystalized silver is black. It's only once in a while that it shines like this. Keep it as a souvenir."

"I'll make some fine and memorable thing of it."

"There's not enough there to make much of anything."

"Can I have enough, John? Can I have enough silver from our own mine to make a memorable thing? A dinner service, I think, made by the finest silversmith in the country."

"You shall have it. I like the notion of eating off silver brought straight from the Comstock. Be damned if I won't bring it up for you myself."[2]

Tiffany submitted their design ideas for a silver service to the Mackays and Mr. Mackay sent the silver for its making directly from his Nevada mines to Tiffany's Prince Street works in New York. There was a story, possibly apocryphal, that Mackay wanted Tiffany to use pure "fine" silver in the making of his silver service. Tiffany was supposed to have pointed out to him that their sterling alloy containing 92.5 percent silver would be much stronger and wear far longer than the pure silver. Tiffany won the argument.

The service was made in 1877 and 1878, the patented pieces in the set being dated 1878. It is said to have taken two hundred men two years to complete the service which would mean that over a million man hours were devoted to it.

The Mackay service was delivered to Paris in 1878 where it was displayed publicly for the first time in the American Pavilion of the Paris Exposition, sharing honors in the Tiffany display with Tiffany's new silver in the Japanese style.

The critics were properly impressed with the Mackay service. One said:

Conspicuous in the American Department is the splendid exhibit of Messrs. Tiffany & Co. whose silverware is incontestably the finest, in point of design and workmanship, in the Exhibition. Prominent among the articles that they display is a magnificent service manufactured by them for the Bonanza King, Mr. J. W. Mackay. This gorgeous set, on which their workmen have been employed for over two years, comprises several hundred pieces, including nearly every article that ever is or has been made of silver—punch bowl, soup tureen, dishes, trays, tea things, spoons, forks, etc., in bewildering variety and number. All the work was done by hand, and the rich floriated designs are all in full relief, the tea caddies tall and three sided, are very elegant, and so is an exquisite tête-à-tête tea service, graceful and shapely and gorgeous in workmanship. This splendid service alone would form a very full exhibit.[3]

The correspondent for the New York *Daily Tribune* (May 30, 1878) thought the Mackay service was ostentatious although "Messrs. Tiffany's goods are worthy to be put in comparison with anything that can be seen elsewhere." He said this about the service:

For the convenience sake, permit me to call it the Mackay service, since everybody knows it as such. It consists of not less than 1,000 separate pieces; it fills nine huge boxes, which thirty-six porters carry with difficulty; 200 men have been a year in its manufacture; and the cost, reported in awestruck whispers to be $125,000,[4] exceeds that sum. Messrs. Tiffany display it with pride as a masterpiece of American silversmithery, and technically I have no doubt it is. You could not help liking it, said Mr. Marcus, if you had seen it making —if you knew how much labor had been spent on it. Very likely, but that is not quite the point. Mr. Marcus' appeal leads the way to the true criticism on this performance. The first impression it makes on you, and the last is the same. The millionaire who ordered it, the enterprising firm which undertook the commission, the artist who settled the composition and the design, the craftsmen who wrought their work into actual silver, were the victim of one and the same idea. The service is a monument of the wealth of the owner. To put as much silver into it as possible, to put as much work on the silver as possible to impress the beholder at the same time with the enormous costliness of the service and the skill of its makers—is apparently the object, and is beyond question the effect, of this large accumulation of coin and cunning.

The Mackay service adorned a series of spectacular banquets at the Mackay house at 9 Rue de Tilsitt, just off the Champs-Elysées, adjacent to the Arc de Triomphe, and later their house at No. 6 Carlton House Terrace in London. Mrs. Mackay's parties were landmarks even in this era of fantastic parties. She entertained and was entertained by the royalty of Europe. When she received President Ulysses S. Grant and his wife in Paris in 1877, a whole floor of the Mackay mansion was done over. The furniture was reupholstered in red, white, and blue satin, and the menu for the dinner was engraved on silver plaques.

For twenty-five years the Mackay balls, travels, and marriages were avidly reported in the American press. One of Mrs. Mackay's most publicized parties of the 1880s was for Buffalo Bill, an old friend.

The whole background of the Mackay silver gives it an almost legendary quality. But this does not mean that individual pieces of the service cannot stand on their own as works of art. They can. So let us examine the service itself.

The Mackay service consisted of about 1,250 pieces. There were 1,223 pieces listed in the Tiffany silver-clasped book of photographs that accompanied the service (Fig. 54) but there were at least a couple of dozen unlisted ones, making the estimated total of 1,250. The service was

54 Leather album, with silver fittings and the coat of arms and initials of Marie Louise Mackay, containing photographs of the Mackay service. Size: 11 x 14 in. (28 x 38.1 cm.). *(Private Collection)*.

delivered in nine sturdy beautifully made mahogany and walnut chests where each piece had its own plush-lined place. There was a silver plaque on each chest listing the contents. Chest No. 1, containing the 918 pieces of flatware and related pieces, is discussed in Chapter 5. A list of the hollow-ware pieces in chests 2 through 9 gives an idea of the variety and completeness of the service:

CHEST 2

6 Pepper boxes	24 Salt & peppers
2 Mustards	6 Claret jugs
6 Ash receivers	2 Liquor stands
24 Coffee cups & saucers	2 Oil & vinegars
24 Scallop dishes	

CHEST 3

1 Coffee urn	1 Chocolate pot & muddler
1 Tea kettle	1 Syrup jug
1 Water kettle	2 Sugars
2 Butter dishes	2 Creamers
1 Tête-à-tête set (3 pieces)	24 Ice cream plates
1 Waiter	8 Olive dishes
2 Tea caddies	6 Bottle coasters

CHEST 4

2 Salad bowls	2 Flacons
2 Water pitchers	2 Bottle wagons
4 Wine coolers	2 Segar stands

CHEST 5

1 Centerpiece*	2 Grape dishes
1 Plateau	2 Ice cream dishes
4 Side pieces	2 Cheese dishes
4 Compotiers high	2 Celery vases
4 Compotiers low	

CHEST 6

2 Soup tureens	6 Vegetable dishes, oval
2 Stands for tureens	4 Vegetable dishes, round
2 Sauce tureens	2 Entree dishes
2 Stands for tureens	2 Pudding dishes
4 Gravy tureens	2 Ice dishes

CHEST 7

1 24-in. Meat dish	1 20-in. Meat dish
1 24-in. Hot water stand	2 18-in. Meat dishes
1 22-in. Meat dish	2 16-in. Meat dishes
1 22-in. Hot water stand	2 14-in. Meat dishes

1 28-in. Fish dish	2 12-in. Meat dishes
1 24-in. Fish dish	24 Soup plates

CHEST 8

1 30-in. Waiter	2 Crumb trays
6 12½-in. Waiters	1 Punch bowl
2 12-in. Waiters for pitchers	24 Goblets
6 8-in. Waiters for cards	

CHEST 9

2 Candelabras	2 Salon lamps
2 Extinguishers	2 Trays for extinguishers

* The Tiffany plant records show that there was also a centerpiece made for the Mackays in 1879 which weighed 1,825 ounces (about 125 pounds avoirdupois). This enormous object had a making cost of $10,321.52. It is believed to have been since melted down.

We illustrate a number of pieces of the Mackay service in Figures 55 through 64 and Plate II. Although the designs vary somewhat from piece to piece, there is an overall unity, emphasized by having the monogram MLM and Mrs. Mackay's Hungerford family coat of arms on every piece of the service. The coat of arms, which was specially designed for the service, was topped by the Scottish thistle and bore the motto: ET DIEU MON APPUI (and God my support). All of the flatware pieces of the service and most of the hollow ware pieces incorporate the motif of the Irish shamrock and the thistle of Scotland for Mrs. Mackay's ancestors. The entire service is characterized by floral ornamentation ranging from the thistle and the shamrock to American garden and wild flowers to the flowers and plants of the Orient.

The covered vegetable dish in Figure 55 is in many ways an archetypical piece of the service. Its shape is conventional and is related to pieces Edward C. Moore designed in the 1850s such as the du Pont vegetable dish in Figure 21. However, the Mackay piece is far more complex than the relatively plain Classical Revival pieces of the 1850s; it is more sensuous and far more ornamented. The flower-encrusted design has its origin in Persia and Mogul India. In fact, Tiffany called the design of the whole service *Indian*. Unquestionably Edward C. Moore, who supervised the design of the service, was influenced by the dense overall designs of the Near-Eastern metal works in his own collection. But he did not copy the designs. His designs are not flat like their prototypes. They are more three dimensional, more sculptural,

and far more varied in their ornamentation.

From a silversmithing point of view the pieces are beautifully made. The repoussé work is quite different from that of Kirk and the so-called Baltimore silver. The Kirk repoussé work tends to cover almost all surfaces of a piece of silver rather uniformly. The Tiffany repoussé chasing is more architectural, more ordered. The formal elements of the piece come through with clarity—the repoussé ornamentation emphasizes the forms.

Each design area is carefully delineated. Note how the ornamental center band of the vegetable dish is kept in place by the strips of plain silver, and how the vertical thrust of the deep-grooved leaves outlining the lotus shapes is accentuated by the exaggerated loop of the lid handle. The coat of arms (and the initials on the opposite side) are carefully worked into the design and become an integral part of it.

The tête-à-tête service in Figure 56 was much admired when it was shown in the 1878 Paris Exposition. The ornamentation is in perfect scale with the small size of the pieces. The undulating forms have an easy grace, and the airy open handles add a whimsical touch to the sugar bowl.

The cloverleaf tray or waiter in Figure 57 accompanies the tête-à-tête set. The fanciful, flowered border grace-

55 Oval vegetable dish with cover of the Mackay service. The deep grooves on top, which are willowlike leaves, outline lotus shapes with repoussé roses. There are bands of flowers with columbine and cherry blossoms. The coat of arms in the photograph is balanced by the monogram on the backside. Height: 8 in. (20.3 cm.). Mark: NO. 19 (4851/5635). *(Private Collection).*

56 Tête-à-tête set from the Mackay service, repoussé chased with the shamrock and thistle motif. Height of pot: 5 7/8 in. (14.9 cm.). Mark: NO. 19 (4854/5635) on all three pieces. (*Private Collection*).

57 Tray which accompanies the Mackay tête-à-tête set in Fig. 56 in a shamrock-leaf form. The Japanese style background is made up of stylized thistle leaves, while the border is of more naturalistic thistles. Diameter: 13 5/8 in. (33.3 cm.). Mark: NO. 19 (4862/5635). (*Private Collection*).

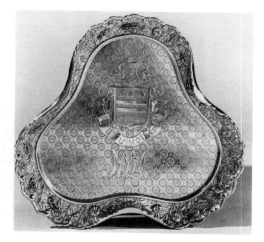

fully encircles the geometric field of stylized thistle leaves, whose design derives from Japanese ceramics and textiles. The coat of arms and monogram are proportionally enlarged, becoming the principal decorative elements of this masterful design.

All of the massive trays (originally designated as meat and fish *dishes*) which were listed for chest number 7 have similar repoussé flower borders surrounding plain serving surfaces. The meat dish in Figure 58 with its draining channels makes a strong and clear design statement. The border of the meat dish derives directly from Chinese lacquer and ceramic plates of the fifteenth to nineteenth centuries.

The round waiter in Figure 59 is delicate and graceful. A scalloped floral border surrounds geometric Japanese patterns with graceful swirling stylized thistle and leaf patterns in the middle. Even though every part of the surface is ornamented, the designs are clear and the overall effect is one of grace and lightness.

The handsome ice cream dish in Figure 60 is almost purely Indian from the rim of flowers around the top to the elephant trunk feet. Even the Chinese-type fretwork decoration between the feet is often found in Indian metal work. The rhythm of the panels around the bowl is gracefully and subtly controlled. The plain aras accentuate and show off the decorative elements. The gilt interior of the ice cream dish is delicately engraved with floral patterns.

The enameled silver pieces in Plate II are strikingly different from the other pieces of the Mackay service. About all the enameled pieces have in common with the other pieces of the service is the coat of arms and monogram. The enameled pieces are not repousséd. Their forms are simple and straightforward. The cups are porcelain-like in appearance and feel and we almost forget they are silver. The wings of the butterflies in Plate II fold back, opening a clamp on the underbody of the insect. These enameled butterflies (which are unmarked) were made by Tiffany in 1879, the year after the rest of the Mackay service was finished. Tiffany's plant records call them "Napkin Clips."

The opulent water pitcher in Figure 61 is almost pure Art Nouveau. If we did not know better, we might have guessed it was made in Paris in 1900 at the height of the Art Nouveau style. It is a remarkable object.

The huge punch bowl in Figure 62 is one of the most regal and flamboyant pieces of the Mackay service. It is certainly heavy, containing forty-eight pounds (avoirdupois) of silver. It is almost two feet in diameter and sixteen inches high. The inside is gold lined, and a Chinese dragon is engraved on the bottom. The bowl is divided into rhythmically arranged panels enclosing grape and vine decorations, with densely decorated undulating borders around the top. The overall effect is one of ripe, lush opulence, which is fitting for one of the largest and most festive pieces of this grand service.

The liquor stand in Figure 63 is a bit more prim than some other pieces of the service and eminently utilitarian. The lightly etched glass decanters are quite in keeping with the silver designs.

The bottle wagon in Figure 64 is a true Victorian whimsy. Small wheels are inset in the runners so the bottle can be sent rolling along the table. Although bottle wagons are seldom seen in American silver, we know that Tiffany made others since two were loaned to the Tiffany exhibit for the 1876 Centennial Exhibition in Philadelphia.

The Mackay service is a landmark of Victorian America, both for itself and for its fascinating history. It is a remarkable tour de force in silvermaking and a lasting tribute to those who made it—Edward Moore and his associates at Tiffany's.

58 Meat dish from Mackay service with floral border containing combinations of flowers including forget-me-nots, hibiscus or hollyhocks, magnolia blossoms, bleeding hearts, and false Solomon's seals. Length: 22 in. (55.9 cm.). Mark: NO. 19 (2111/5635). (*Private Collection*).

59 Waiter from the Mackay service with stylized thistles and thistle leaves in the center on a field of Japanese designs with floral border. Diameter: 12 1/2 in. (31.8 cm.). Mark: NO. 19 (5635). (*Private Collection*).

58

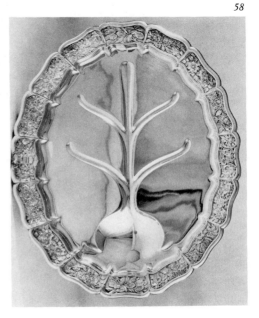

59

60

61

60 Ice cream dish from the Mackay service, gilt interior with engraved flowers and floral border; elephant trunk feet. Height: 5 1/2 in. (14 cm.). Diameter: 15 in. (38.1 cm.). Mark: NO. 19 (4878/5635). *(Private Collection)*.

61 Water pitcher from the Mackay service nelumbo water lilies, cattails, and flag lilies on stylized leaf background. The Persian decorative element coming down from the rim has stylized composite flowers. Fern encrusted handle. Height: 13 3/4 in. (35 cm.). Mark: NO. 19. *(Private Collection)*.

62 Mackay punch bowl with grapevine and grapes motif. The base with elephant-trunk feet is decorated with forget-me-nots. The gilt interior of the bowl is engraved with a Chinese dragon. This huge bowl weighs 48 pounds avoirdupois or about 700 troy ounces. Diameter: 23 1/4 in. (59.1 cm.). Height: 15 3/4 in. (40 cm.). Mark: NO. 19 (4885/5635). *(Courtesy of Mrs. Irving Berlin)*.

63 Liquor stand with four cut glass bottles from the Mackay service.
Height: 12 1/2 in. (31.8 cm.). Mark: NO. 19 (4891/5635). *(Private Collection)*.

62

63

64

64 Bottle wagon or sleigh from the Mackay service. It has small wheels concealed in the sled runners, and stylized lily-of-the-valley decorations on the runners. The bed of the sleigh is in the form of a leaf-and-flower-encrusted fig tree which appears to grow out of the runners. Height: 8 7/8 in. (22.5 cm.). Length: 13 1/8 in. (33.4 cm.). Mark: NO. 19 (4886/5635). (*Private Collection*).

65 Tea and coffee service made by Moore for
Tiffany, Young & Ellis about 1851. This service
combines the two dominant styles of the 1850s:
Classical Revival and rococo. The individual
pieces are rather small scale compared to others
of this period. The bird finial was a favorite
decorative motif. Height of coffeepot: 9 1/4 in.
(23.4 cm.). Mark: NO. 1. (*Anglo-American Art
Museum, Louisiana State University, Baton
Rouge, Louisiana. Gift of Major General Junius
Wallace Jones*).

Tea and Coffee Services

Tea and coffee services were the most typical silver
hollow ware forms of Victorian America. The great increase in the popularity of the afternoon tea party and
coffee hour made larger, more formal services, with up
to six or seven matched pieces, common. Tiffany's records
show there were many such services made in sterling
in every decade of the last half of the nineteenth century, particularly in the 1870s, and many have survived
intact.

In the first part of the nineteenth century the average
tea service was made up of three pieces: a teapot, creamer,
and sugar. Sometimes a coffeepot was included. In the
1830s and the 1840s the slop, or waste, bowl became
fashionable. Often a slop bowl was added later, usually
in a matching design. The slop bowl was meant to receive the cold dregs of a tea cup before a fresh cup of tea
was poured. Incidentally, the term slop bowl, which may
sound a bit inelegant, was regularly used in the nineteenth century.

By the 1850s larger services included the above mentioned five pieces plus a hot milk pot and/or a hot water kettle and stand with lamp. Occasionally a matching tray was part of the set.

After about 1860 teapots of a service tended to be short and squat and the coffeepots taller. The hot milk pot usually had the same shape as the coffeepot except it had a short pouring lip instead of a spout. Covers on coffee- and teapots were usually hinged. The handles of the tea- and coffeepots had ivory insulators in them to keep the handles from getting too hot. Silver is such a good conductor of heat that an uninsulated handle would become too hot to hold immediately after the pot was filled with boiling water. The largest services included a hot water kettle and stand as the ultimate addition. The kettle with stand was always an expensive item, being perhaps twice the price of the coffeepot, the next most expensive item in a tea service. This was due to the size and complexity of the kettle and stand, and consequently the time involved in making it. The kettle and stand actually involve four pieces of silver: the kettle, the stand, the alcohol lamp, and a snuffer. The kettle, stand, and lamp in Figure 73 are all marked in the same manner, but the accompanying snuffer is unmarked.

The earliest tea and coffee service which we illustrate is shown in Figure 65. This seven-piece service has an interesting blend of Federal and rococo styles, the shapes being classical while the ornamentation is rococo with cartouches prominently repoussé chased in the bodies of each piece and bird finials on the pieces with lids. It was made by John C. Moore for Tiffany, Young & Ellis about 1851. The service first belonged to Dr. and Mrs. William Jones Lyle of Smithfield Plantation in West Baton Rouge Parish, Louisiana. The silversmithing firm of Hyde and Goodrich of New Orleans later made hot water and hot milk pitchers (not illustrated) to match the Tiffany service.

The pieces of the service in Figure 66 have classical forms, bands of beading and cast lion handles (on the sugar bowl) which are characteristic of the silver of fifty years earlier, even though the rococo repoussé chased flowers and the overall effect is typical of the 1850s. The deep, three-dimensional chasing (see Fig. 314), the relatively large scale decorations balanced against the plain surfaces create strong virile compositions which are reinforced by the vigorously modeled bird finials.

66 Four-piece tea service made by Moore for Tiffany about 1855. Deep repoussé chased flowers; cast figure of a long-necked bird on the lids of the sugar bowl and the teapot. Height of teapot: 11 in. (27.9 cm.). Mark: NO. 11 (295/1271). *(Mr. and Mrs. Charles F. Murray).*

The creamer from a tea set in Figure 67 was originally part of a five-piece service, consisting of a teapot, creamer, sugar, coffeepot, and slop bowl. This exuberantly designed service is rather atypical of Tiffany silver of the period although we know of at least one other related set. The engraved strapwork is reminiscent of the 1850s while the Islamic handles are related to the Eastlake furniture of the period. Tiffany's records call the set Mooresque.

The Philadelphia service can be almost completely documented from Tiffany's records and Edward C. Moore's sketchbook. Figure 68 shows a drawing from Moore's Sketchbook II dated November, 1865 where he experimented with ideas for the service. The handle design on the left of the drawing was the basis for the handle of the creamer in Figure 67, with certain obvious changes.

On January 17, 1867 the cost for each piece of the newly finished service was entered in the plant journal. The plant costs of the pieces were:

Teapot	$119.25
Sugar	91.25
Creamer	78.50
Bowl	75.25
Coffeepot	136.75
Total plant cost	$501.00

The selling price in the store was about double the plant cost to cover sales costs, overhead, and, of course,

67 Creamer from "Mooresque" service made in
late 1866 or January 1867 by Moore for Tiffany.
Strapwork, chasing, parcel gilt, cast handle and
spout. Height: 7 in. (17.8 cm.). Mark: NO. 11
(1770/4189). (*Philadelphia Museum of Art*).

profit. This meant that the retail price of the five pieces
of the original service in 1867 was approximately $1,000.

Two tea services made in the late 1860s and the
early 1870s are shown in Figures 69 and 70. Both make
use of the same basic forms, the handles and spouts
are of the same design. The finials of the two differ
slightly but are about the same size. We know of
other tea and coffee services based on these same forms,
all of which are different in the treatment of their ornamentation. One service (not illustrated) is ornamented
with only center bands of a simple Greek geometric design, while another set (not illustrated) is completely
covered with shallow repoussé chasing, including even
the handles and spouts.

The coffee and tea service in Figure 69, dated 1874,
was made for Mary Pauline Foster at the time of her

68 Drawing from Edward Moore's Sketchbook
II dated November 1865 showing designs used in
the "Mooresque" creamer in Fig. 67.

marriage to Henry Algernon du Pont of Winterthur, Delaware. Her monogram, MPF, is engraved on each piece. The service is large being made up of eleven pieces including a matching water pitcher. The small bud vases are of different design and strictly speaking should not be considered as part of the set, although they are monogrammed in the same manner and were purchased at the same time from Tiffany's.

69 Tea and coffee service made about 1874 for Mary Pauline Foster at the time of her marriage to Henry Algernon du Pont with the initials MPF engraved on each piece. A pair of small bud vases and a matching water pitcher were added to the standard service of kettle and stand, teapot, coffeepot, cream pot, sugar bowl and cover, hot milk pot, and slop bowl. Height of coffeepot: 7 1/2 in. (19.1 cm.). Mark: NO. 16 on all pieces. Pattern and order numbers: teapot (1982/2852), kettle (1878/7203), coffeepot (1984/7203), hot milk pot (1982/2772), water pitcher (1653/2552 plus "1874"), sugar bowl (1942/3007), slop bowl (1982/2772), creamer (1982/3007), bud vases (3514/3307). (*The Henry Francis du Pont Winterthur Museum*).

The band of the du Pont set is Islamic in origin, giving the pieces a reticent, restrained look. The original Tiffany drawings for the service indicated that the customer had a choice of four different bands. The fact that these working drawings are quite worn indicates that a number of services were made based on these same designs.

It should be noted that these die-rolled bands have a practical as well as an esthetic purpose. They protect the vulnerable middle part of the pieces from bumps (like the chrome strip on an automobile), and they also hide the seam when two parts of a bulbous body are soldered together.

The other related tea and coffee service is shown in

Figures 70, 71, and 73. The seven-piece service (counting the hot water kettle and stand as one piece), which we have designated the Ivy Chased service, is decorated with rather deep repoussé chased undulating ivy vines with leaves. It is unusual in that six of the pieces (all except the hot milk pot) were designed and made at the same time. The hot milk pot was made a few weeks later and probably was delivered with the other pieces of the set.

It is instructive to study the differences and the similarities of the du Pont and the Ivy Chased services. The du Pont service has only a narrow applied foot ring while the Ivy Chased service has a substantially higher foot, which is the result of adding an extra "bezel" ring to the bottom of each piece. This not only adds height to the

70 Tea and coffee service with repoussé chased ivy decoration and pine cone finials. This service has a total weight of 161 ounces. Height of coffeepot: 9 in. (22.9 cm.). Mark: NO. 16 on all pieces. Pattern and order numbers: coffeepot (2243/5867), teapot (2243/2798), hot milk pot (2323/1934), sugar bowl (2243/5867), creamer (2243/2798), slop bowl (2243/2798), hot-water kettle (2243/2860). (*Private Collection*).

71 Slop bowl from "Ivy Chased" service in Fig. 70. Height: 3 1/2 in. (8.9 cm.). Mark: NO. 16 (2243/2798). *(Private Collection).*

72 Original Tiffany working drawing of slop bowl in Fig. 71 dated May 20, 1869. Note addition of bezel foot to drawing and the actual piece.

71

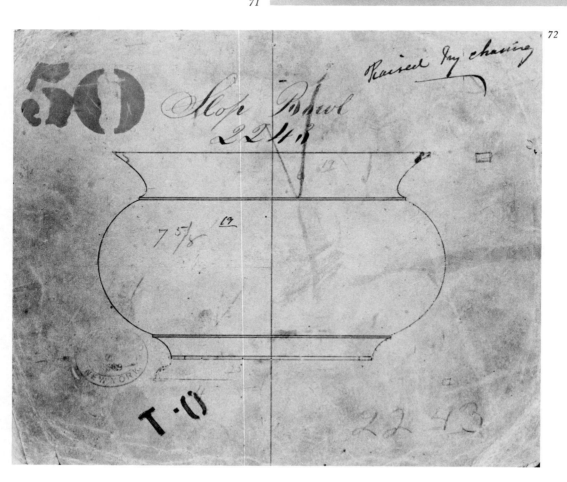

72

73 Hot water kettle and stand from Ivy Chased service in Fig. 70. Overall height: 12 1/4 in. (31.1 cm.). Mark: NO. 16 (2243/2860) on kettle, stand, and lamp. *(Private Collection)*.

Ivy Chased pieces, it also adds another plain undecorated strip to balance the decorated areas. The repoussé chasing of the Ivy Chased service is deeper, more vigorous, and more carefully organized than the shallow chasing on the du Pont service. The Islamic die-rolled band on the du Pont service is tighter and stronger in its composition than the chasing on the service, which gives an eclectic feel to the pieces. The necks of the du Pont coffee and hot milk pots are plain while the Ivy Chased service necks have a chased band on them. The stand for the kettle of the du Pont service has an applied ornamental band while the stand of the Ivy Chased service is plain.

The superb hot water kettle of the Ivy Chased service (Fig. 73) has the same cast parts—handle, spout, and stand—as the kettle of the du Pont service in Figure 69. The pinecone finials of the Ivy Chased service are slightly more slender and vertical, which, along with the bezel foot, adds to the illusion of height.

The repoussé chasing on the Ivy Chased service is tightly contained in the stippled background areas in such a way that it is most carefully balanced with the unadorned plain areas (see Fig. 71). The decorated areas reinforce and emphasize the basically simple spherical shapes of the service. The designer and the chaser obviously gave a lot of thought to orchestrating the design elements of this beautiful service. An analysis of one piece of it, the slop bowl, gives some indication of how the design process worked.

The original Tiffany shop working drawing of the slop bowl (Fig. 72), dated May 20, 1869, is the actual size of the piece of silver. The silversmith would use it to check (with calipers) the size and shape of the piece as it was being made. This drawing, like others for the service, does not say how the decoration should look, it only notes "Raised Ivy Chasing." The chaser was a highly skilled craftsman and it was his job to fit the ivy motif appropriately on each piece of the service. The pencil additions to the inside lip of the slop bowl in the drawing indicate how the metal was to be lapped over (compare the working drawing in Figure 72 with the actual bowl in Figure 71). The drawing also shows that the bezel foot was added to the piece *after* the original drawing was made, obviously because the designer thought it resulted in a more satisfying design.

The Ivy Chased service was made sometime between May 20th, 1869 (the date of the drawings) and June,

1870 when the finished work was entered in the Tiffany plant journal. The journal entry gives a complete breakdown of the cost of each piece of the service. Using the same formula as we mentioned earlier for the Philadelphia service (i.e., the plant costs are doubled to get the selling price), we estimate that the Ivy Chased service would have sold for about $2,500 in the Tiffany store.

Both of these services are superior examples of Tiffany silver. The number of pieces in both the du Pont and the Ivy Chased services is of course larger than today's sets. They were superbly designed for their original purpose and were widely used in their time when the afternoon serving of tea and coffee had not yet been replaced by the cocktail hour. In fact, the du Pont service is still regularly used at various Winterthur Museum functions. The individual pieces of these services are well balanced and usefully sized for today's living and make a handsome showing on a sideboard when not in use. The chased and engraved surfaces cut down on the reflectivity of the pieces, allowing plain surfaces and highlights to flicker in changing lights, particularly candlelight. This controlled glitter, surrounded by soft, opulently colored backgrounds, was a much sought after decorative effect in the nineteenth century.

The tea caddy in Figure 74 has two separate vermeil-lined compartments for two varieties of tea. Tea caddies were not common in American silver and were not usually a part of tea and coffee services. The engraved ivy designs on the two lids are similar to the engraved designs on Tiffany's *Antique Ivy* flatware.

The colonial revival of the 1870s, which was helped along by the Philadelphia Centennial Exposition, led to the introduction of simply designed tea and coffee services based on free interpretations of early American silver. The coffeepot in Figure 75 is based on earlier models. It is plainer in design than other Tiffany silver of the period. Occasional pieces of colonial revival silver were made throughout the nineteenth century, and the popularity of the "style" has continued in the twentieth century.

In 1880, the year Charles T. Grosjean's flatware pattern *Chrysanthemum* (Fig. 138) was introduced, a related design was used for pieces of a tea and coffee service which is now called *Chrysanthemum*. The individual pieces of the tea and coffee service (Fig. 53) are traditional baroque shapes with squat, apple-shaped bodies. Incised lines form

74 Tea caddy with cast handle and two separate gold-lined compartments with hinged lids. Persian die-rolled borders with interlocking circles. Top engraved with ivy leaf patterns. Made in the late 1860s. Height: 6 1/2 in. (16.5 cm.). Mark: NO. 14 (1687). *(Burt Collection).*

75 Coffee or chocolate pot in the colonial revival style made about 1878. Body and spout reeded, with engraved coat of arms of the Ridgely family of Baltimore. Ebony handle and finial. Height: 8 1/2 in. (21.5 cm.). Mark: NO. 19 (5232/8919). *(Private Collection).*

reeding at the corners of the pieces, leaving the rounded, swelling parts of the body unadorned. Shaggy chrysanthemum leaves and daisylike flowering heads are applied on feet, around rims, in between necks and bases, and on handles and lids. The original Tiffany plant working drawings for the *Chrysanthemum* pieces are worn almost to shreds indicating many services were made from the designs. The drawings, with the pattern number 5960, indicate that the individual pieces could be made either with or without scroll feet. The journal entries for the pattern call it Apple Shape and also B. Lorillard Style. There is no mention of the name Chrysanthemum either on the drawings or in the Tiffany plant journals. The sets were made from 1880 until well into the twentieth century. Figure 76 shows the *Chrysanthemum* coffeepot from the service illustrated in Figure 53 which was made in 1894.

A journal entry for a *Chrysanthemum* tea and coffee service, dated July 7, 1891, indicates the following weights and costs of the individual pieces:

76 Coffeepot of the *Chrysanthemum* pattern from the service in Fig. 53. Height: 9 5/8 in. (24.3 cm.). Mark: NO. 21 (5960/1928). (*Collection of Mr. and Mrs. Frank R. Edwards*).

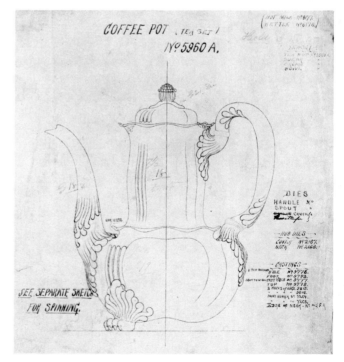

77 Working drawing of coffeepot in the *Wave* pattern.

	Weight-oz.	Plant cost
Teapot	44	$135
Sugar	31	100
Creamer	22	90
Bowl	21	85
Coffeepot	42	160
Hot milk	..	120
Kettle	..	205
TOTAL		$895

Using the standard formula of doubling the plant cost to find the retail price indicates that this seven-piece *Chrysanthemum* service would have sold for about $1800 in 1891.

There were many kinds of hollow-ware forms made in the *Chrysanthemum* pattern besides tea and coffee sets. Figure 190 shows a flower vase in the pattern. Other pieces include trays and waiters, candlesticks, compotes, vegetable dishes, tureens, fish platters, chafing dishes, gravy and sauce boats, individual and master salts, bowls and water pitchers.

In 1880, another hollow-ware pattern was introduced which is closely related to *Chrysanthemum*. The working drawing in Figure 77 with the pattern number 5960A indicates it is a variation of the *Chrysanthemum* pattern using the same forms with different decorations. The pattern is now called *Wave* although, like *Chrysanthemum*, there is no indication of the name on either the working drawings or in the Tiffany plant records. The *Wave* pattern is more innovative and looks forward to the Art Nouveau objects of the 1890s while the *Chrysanthemum* pattern looks back and is more traditional. A fine example of *Wave* pattern hollow ware is the chafing dish in Figure 41.

In the 1930s Tiffany introduced a simplified and modernized version of the *Chrysanthemum* and *Wave* pattern tea sets calling it the *George IV* pattern.

Compotes and Centerpieces

Most of the pieces we illustrate under this heading are classified as compotes, but all of them could be used as centerpieces on small tables, or in pairs on dining tables or sideboards. These were popular silver forms and many have survived. The large pieces were, of course, true cen-

78 Compote or centerpiece with gold-plated bowl, applied strawberry vine decorations, Greek key border on base, made by Moore for Tiffany about 1858. Diameter: 10 in. (25.4 cm.). Height: 6 in. (15.3 cm.). Mark: NO. 11. (*Burt Collection*).

79 Centerpiece with flaring pierced cast handles, four classical heads of women on the sides, on an oval pedestal resting on four animal claw feet. Made about 1873. Height: 9 1/4 in. (23.5 cm.). Length: 14 in. (35.9 cm.). Mark: NO. 16 (2575/728). (*New York State Museum, Albany*).

80 Gilt compote with pierced naturalistic fern decoration made about 1885. Height: 4 1/2 in. (11.4 cm.). Diameter: 9 1/4 in. (23.5 cm.). Mark: TIFFANY & CO./7533 MAKERS 6931/STERLING-SILVER. (*Museum of Art, Carnegie Institute*).

terpieces, such as "The Four Seasons" centerpiece in Figure 17 in Chapter 2. The compote in Figure 78 has applied cast strawberry vine decorations around the bowl and on the base, with a Greek fret border. The centerpiece in Figure 79, with its classical heads and Persian die-rolled decorative bands, is a typically chaste Tiffany version of mid-Victorian silver. The large unadorned

79

areas set off the decorated band and handles on top of the bowl from the decorated base. The gilt compote in Figure 80 with its cast naturalistic leaves, branches, and buds was made about 1885. The blackberry dish in Figure 81 with its rolled rococo edge is pierced and decorated with cast blackberries and blackberry leaves, and re-poussé and chased stylized leaves in the bowl. The cake plate in Figure 82, made about 1855 by Grosjean and Woodward for Tiffany, is related to the compote form—with the addition of a handle. Cake plates were often used as centerpieces.

Candlesticks and Candelabra

The use of one or more candelabra was de rigueur for large and fashionable Victorian dining tables. These ranged from simple two- and three-candle examples to large impressive objects such as the eight-candle *Chrysanthemum* pattern candelabrum in Figure 83. The largest Tiffany candelabrum that is known to us is the one in the Mackay service which is about 36 inches tall and 28 inches in diameter holding 29 candles. The relatively chaste pair of candlesticks in Figure 84 was made about 1900, although the design dates from 1882. The deceptively simple candlesticks in Figure 85 are related more

81

82

83

81 Blackberry dish made about 1903 based on a 1900 design. Engraved in the bowl are the dates 1877 and 1903. Diameter: 8 3/4 in. (22.2 cm.). Mark: NO. 22 (14619/6193). *(Private Collection).*

82 Cake plate made by Grosjean & Woodward for Tiffany about 1855, with floral and rococo repoussé decoration. Engraved with the initials MCM for Maria Catherine Manis who married William B. E. Lockwood in 1856. Length: 12 1/4 in. (31 cm.). Mark: NO. 7 (1354). *(Lockwood-Mathews Mansion Museum, Norwalk, Connecticut).*

83 This large candelabrum with eight branches in the *Chrysanthemum* pattern was part of a 165-piece dinner service given as a wedding present in 1890 to Daisy Beard Brown. [Note: In December 1890 Tiffany's records show a pair of these candelabra were sold for $2,200.] Height: 27 1/2 in. (69.9 cm.). Mark: NO. 19 (5727/3128). *(Museum of the City of New York).*

84 Pair of candlesticks with removable nozzles made about 1900. Four applied die-rolled bands decorated with cornucopia, shells, and scrolls. Height: 8 1/4 in. (20.6 cm.). Mark: NO. 21 (6780/6074). *(Private Collection).*

84

85

86

to twentieth-century design than they are to Victorian America. They have a contemporary look.

Plates

Silver and silver gilt plates ranged in size from small butter pat plates to full-sized dinner plates such as J. P. Morgan's gilt plate in Figure 86. Some plates such as the one in Figure 87 with its forty-three naked cherubs frolicking among the grapes were display plates and were not used on the dining table. They could of course be used as cake or serving plates. This plate is dated May 27, 1885.

87

85   Pair of candlesticks made in 1905, based on an 1895 design. Height: 9 1/4 in. (23.5 cm.). Mark: NO. 22 (12221/1329). *(Private Collection)*.

86   Gilt dinner plate, one of twelve, made about 1895 based on an 1883 design. Monogram JPM for John Pierpont Morgan. Engraved on the bottom is the inscription: "PRESENTED TO THE UNION LEAGUE CLUB / BY / MR. & MRS. HERBERT L. SATTERLEE / IN / MEMORY OF MRS. SATTERLEE'S FATHER / J. P. MORGAN—A V. P. OF THE / CLUB 1891–94 1906–1908." Diameter: 9 3/4 in. (24.8 cm.). Mark: NO. 21 (7616/2211). *(Union League Club, New York)*.

87   Plate with cherub border made about 1883. Engraved on the bottom is the inscription: "FROM / H.C.H. / MAY 27TH, 1885." Diameter: 8 11/16 in. (22.1 cm.). Mark: NO. 19 (7344/8824). *(Mr. and Mrs. Donald L. Fennimore)*.

Trays and Waiters

Trays were made in many sizes and shapes. The large trays used with tea services are usually oval in shape, with handles. The English call these tea trays as distinguished from waiters or salvers used for serving food and drink. Today we tend to use the word "tray" for all sizes and shapes of these useful and decorative objects.

The original inventory of the Mackay silver listed fish and meat *dishes,* even for the largest sizes. The Mackay "dishes" were made in matching, graduated sizes so that the smaller sizes fit into the next larger ones. There were seven sizes of the meat dishes or trays: 12 in., 14 in., 16 in., 18 in., 20 in., 22 in., and 24 in. The 24 in. and 28 in. fish "dishes" were similar to the meat dishes, but narrower in width. (See pp. 61–62.)

The rectangular tray with feet in Figure 88 was made

about 1870. It has a typical die-rolled border and a neatly engraved center. The oval tray in Figure 89 with four cast shell feet, delicately pierced border, open handles and engraved center was made in 1886.

88

89

The large two-handled tea tray in Figure 90 was designed by Paulding Farnham in what he called the Renaissance style. The border is decorated with raised clusters of fruit enclosed by strap work which spreads to the center of the tray. Note the winged cherubs at each end below the foliate scroll handles.

Paulding Farnham was trained as a silversmith under Edward C. Moore and he afterward became secretary and a trustee of Tiffany & Co. In addition to his career at Tiffany & Co., Farnham had an independent career as a sculptor. During the 1890s he shared a studio with his wife Sallie Farnham who was also a sculptor. Farnham designed many well-known Tiffany pieces of his time such as a presentation sword for Admiral Dewey and the Adams Gold Vase.

88   Tray, die-rolled border, engraved center, four rococo cast feet. Engraved inscription: M. de C. C. for Mary de Camp Corning, widow of Edwin Weld Corning, and second wife of General Robert Lenox Banks. Length: 10 15/16 in. (27.8 cm.). Mark: NO. 16 (1670/4711). *(Albany Institute of History and Art)*.

89   Oval tray with pierced border and engraved center, made in 1886. Length: 11 in. (27.9 cm.). Mark: NO. 20 (8863/5829). *(Private Collection)*.

90

91

92

90 Tea tray designed by Paulding Farnham about 1900. Border decorated with raised clusters of fruit with strapwork spreading to the center of the tray. There are winged cherubs at each end below the foliate scroll handles. Length: 34 1/2 in. (82.6 cm.). (*Sotheby Parke Bernet*).

91 Water pitcher made about 1855, the baluster body repoussé chased with floral sprays and centered by a vacant scrollwork cartouche. The cast spout and the double scroll handle decorated with shell work and acanthus, the circular foot with gadroon border. Height: 11 1/2 in. (29.2 cm.). (*Sotheby Parke Bernet*).

92 Water pitcher of vase shape made about 1869. Die-rolled band of stylized speartips and interlaced circles. Engraved with reserves of strapwork on matted grounds and with armorials and monogram. The handle is decorated with stylized foliage, on pedestal foot. Engraved on bottom. "FROM R. & M. I. DEC. 9TH, 1869." Height: 13 3/4 in. (34.9 cm.). Mark: NO. 14 (1959/5814). (*Collection of the Authors*).

Water pitchers were a popular form in American silver of the nineteenth century. They were used on the dining table for ice water and on the veranda to serve lemonade or iced tea during steamy tropical summers long before the days of air conditioning. Silver water pitchers were a favorite gift item and many of those found today bear dated inscriptions.

The earliest Tiffany silver pitchers of the 1850s were often made in the then popular rococo style. Figure 91 shows a typical pitcher of the era with its body repoussé chased with floral sprays and centered by a vacant scroll-work cartouche, the cast spout and the double C-scroll handle decorated with shell work. The quality of the chasing is first-rate, being clear and sure, giving the design an abstract quality.

The stately vase-shaped water pitcher in Figure 92 shows the type of flat decoration that was popular in the post–Civil War era. The shallow engraved and chased decorations on a mat (chased) background give this piece a quite different feeling from the previous pitcher. It is more restrained and at the same time more monumental. It was obviously designed as a work of art rather than just a water pitcher, even though it functions perfectly well.

We noted earlier that often the chaser did not work from drawings. However, most of the more complicated pieces of Tiffany hollow ware did have drawings as a guide for the chaser or engraver. Figure 93 is an example showing the engraving pattern for the pitcher in Figure 92. These engraving-pattern drawings were in addition to the regular working drawing for the actual fabrication of the piece itself.

In the 1870s Tiffany's introduced a form of water pitcher that was so simple, straightforward, and logical in its design that it became a favorite Tiffany form during the last three decades of the nineteenth century. Figures 94 and 95 show two of the more elaborate versions of this form. We also use this form in Chapter 12, "The Making of Tiffany Silver," as a demonstration of the making of a hollow-ware piece (Fig. 309). The pitcher form is in three principal pieces: the spherical bottom part which is essentially the center slice of a ball; the straight-walled neck with a lip inserted in it; and the handle which is joined to the mid-section of the bottom

93 Original Tiffany full-scale pencil drawing of the engraving pattern for the pitcher in Fig. 92. The die-rolled band around the middle is designated as "Bor[der] 90."

94

95

96

part and to the top of the neck. We have already pointed out the similarity these pitcher shapes have to the fifteenth-century jug in Edward C. Moore's collection (Fig. 29).

The repoussé pitcher in Figure 94 is unusual for Tiffany silver in that the entire body and handle of the pitcher is chased, with no relieving plain areas. However the wide areas of stylized band leaves between the neck and the body and around the base do isolate the repoussé work into two areas. But the first effect is one of overall decoration; a sea of leaves and flowers.

The water pitcher in Figure 95 is a fine example of what one could call the Tiffany style. It is similar in shape to the repoussé pitcher, but both more typical and classical in style. The undulating bands emphasize and dramatize the full ripe shape. The reeded base firmly anchors the wide band to the center of the bowl. The intricate monogram is carefully sized and spaced in order not to clutter up the plain area of the bowl.

The monogram on the pitcher is CdeBM for Corinne de Bebian Moore and was a wedding present "From Many Friends with Tiffany & Co." in 1889 when she married Edward C. Moore's grandson, John C. Moore, who afterward was president of Tiffany's from 1907 to 1938 (Fig. 96).

The robust wine cooler in Figure 97 is dated April 19, 1888. The rim and the foot are appropriately decorated with grape clusters and leaves. The bombé body is reeded and deeply repoussé with chased stylized acanthus leaves. A silver tube to receive the wine bottle has been inserted as a sleeve inside the cooler leaving space around it for ice. This allows the bottle to be removed from the cooler dry, thus doing away with the towel drying routine.

The important punch bowl, repoussé chased with grape leaves and grapes, in Figure 98 is one of the finest objects Tiffany ever made. If one had to put this bowl in a style category it would be Art Nouveau, because of its treatment of nature, particularly the swirling tendrils around the top. Its decoration could also be compared with the naturalistic treatment of twigs and leaves in the silver of the 1850s. But we think this great punch bowl transcends any stylistic considerations. Its treatment of nature is different from either mainstream Art Nouveau or the silver of the 1850s. The leaves are precisely and formally orchestrated around the bowl and the base.

97

94 Water pitcher, globular shape with cylindrical neck. Acanthus band between neck and bowl, and around base. Flowers repoussé chased over entire surface: roses, peonies, violets, etc. Engraved on base: "JEANETTE A. DWIGHT FEBY. 12TH 1879." Height: 8 1/2 in. (21.6 cm.). Mark: NO. 19 (5066/225). (Brooklyn Museum).

95 Water pitcher with die-rolled bands of garland flowers, bottom of bowl reeded. Initials engraved on bowl CdeBM for Corinne deBebian Moore. Height: 8 1/4 in. (21 cm.). Mark: NO. 19 (5066/8528). (Private Collection).

96 Bottom of water pitcher in Fig. 95 showing mark and inscription.

97 Wine cooler with the date APRIL 19, 1888 engraved on the bottom. Height: 8 7/8 in. (22.6 cm.). Mark: NO. 19 (8973/2819). (Private Collection).

98 Punch bowl, repoussé chased, bowl vermeil inside. Made in March 1906. Height: 10 1/4 in. (26 cm.). Width: 16 3/4 in. (42.6 cm.). Weight: 180 oz. Mark: NO. 22 (16613/3439). (S. J. Shrubsole).

98

99

100

There is just enough asymmetry in the placement of the grapes on the base and the vines and tendrils around the top to keep the design from becoming too stiff. The plain rim of the bowl plays off well against the twig rim outlining the base. The decorations all have a feeling of inevitability. They seem exactly right for the object. It is a triumph of silversmithing made at the very time when there was a letdown in the design quality of some of Tiffany's silver.

The punch bowl was made in March, 1906. We have not been able to locate any drawings or any records of the piece beyond a simple plant journal entry. Because of its beautiful ordered treatment of nature we inevitably think of Louis Comfort Tiffany who was artistic director of Tiffany's at the time the bowl was made. It is a wonderful object, whether or not he had anything to do with it.

Mugs and Cups

Mugs and cups with handles have always been a popular gift item in silver, particularly for children. The earliest of those we illustrate (Fig. 99) was made by Wood & Hughes for Tiffany, Young & Ellis about 1850. The repoussé work is typical of the period, with the moth or butterfly lending a nice touch.

At the end of the nineteenth century children's cups became more pictorial in their decoration with a definite tendency towards whimsy. The mug in Figure 100 with its delightful decorative band of playing children is quite realistic in its approach. We can tell exactly what kind of clothes the children are wearing and the individual faces are almost portraits. The bucolic scene etched in the cup in Figure 101 features the classic cock perched kinglike on the barnyard fence. The cup has a curious C-shaped rococo handle.

Pepper Shakers

We end this chapter on Tiffany hollow ware with the delightful pair of pepper shakers in Figure 102 with bands of discrete engraving and ruffled necks.

99 Mug with double C-scroll handle. Repoussé chased moth or butterfly and chrysanthemum. Cartouche enclosing engraved "CARRIE." Made by Wood & Hughes for Tiffany, Young & Ellis about 1850. Height: 4 1/4 in. (10.8 cm.). Mark: NO. 2. (*The Smithsonian Institution*).

100 Child's cup with cast handle. Applied die-rolled border of children playing. Engraved (above border) "ARTHUR WALLACE DUNN, JR." and below JBM. Height: 3 3/8 in. (8.6 cm.). Mark: NO. 20 (5470/1902). (*The Smithsonian Institution*).

101 Child's cup with etched barnyard scene with chickens and chicks lorded over by the cock on the fence. Inside of cup is gilt. Engraved: "VIRGINIA FROM UNCLE MORGAN / JUNE 20, 1900." Height: 3 7/16 in. (9.1 cm.). Mark: NO. 21 (7995/9684). (*The Smithsonian Institution*).

102 Pair of pepper shakers made about 1874. Height: 5 in. (12.7 cm.). Mark: TIFFANY & CO / 3146 M 3964 / STERLING SILVER. (*The Preservation Society of Newport County, Rhode Island*).

5. The Sumptuous Table—2: Flatware

Tiffany Sells Other Makers' Flatware 1848–1868

Dᴜʀɪɴɢ the twenty-year period 1848–1868, before they had their own silverware manufacturing facilities, Tiffany sold other makers' flatwares. As we have already mentioned, much of their hollow ware of this period was made by Edward C. Moore. The flatware sold by Tiffany during this period was supplied by several New York makers.

The first flatware design sold by Tiffany, Young & Ellis (c. 1850) was the traditional *Thread* pattern. Figure 103 shows an elaborately engraved crumber knife with a beautifully simple curved and pointed oval *Thread* handle. The piece has an unidentified pseudo-hallmark which was common for New York silversmiths of the period. It could have been made by Henry Hebbard or John Polhemus (also spelled Polhamus), both well-known New York makers of quality sterling flatware. Both Polhemus and Hebbard made flatware for Tiffany later in the 1860s as did Polhemus and Strong, successors to Henry Hebbard.

The *Thread* pattern, particularly the *Fiddle and Thread* version, had been a popular pattern in England

103 Crumber with oval thread handle. The crumber pan is engraved with baroque cartouches enclosing rabbits and a rose, made around 1850. Length: 12 3/8 in. (31.4 cm.). Mark: ᴛɪꜰꜰᴀɴʏ, ʏᴏᴜɴɢ & ᴇʟʟɪꜱ plus pseudo marks (see mark ɴᴏ. 33). *(The Smithsonian Institution).*

since the late eighteenth century and in America since the early nineteenth century. Therefore the Tiffany, Young & Ellis *Thread* patterns could have been made by either American or English silversmiths, although we know of no early Tiffany flatware with English hallmarks.

During the 1860s, and particularly during the latter part of the decade, Tiffany's flatware sales expanded rapidly. They sold the sterling flatware of the above mentioned makers plus that of Gorham. The usual practice on Tiffany flatware before 1868 was to include both the maker's mark and TIFFANY & CO. STERLING.

John Polhemus's work is shown in the handsome fish serving knife and fork in Figure 104. Polhemus had been a silversmith in New York since about 1833. At various times he was connected with other makers. In 1833–40 he worked with Albert H. Van Cott.

Tiffany seemed to have particularly favored the sterling flatware of Gorham during the 1860s. Many pieces of Gorham *Medallion* pattern with Tiffany marks have survived (Fig. 105).

104

105

104 Fish serving knife and fork made by John Polhemus for Tiffany, in the *Ionic* pattern, patented in 1860. Length of knife: 12 3/16 in. (31 cm.). Mark: PATENT 1860 TIFFANY & CO. STERLING. *(Burt Collection)*.

105 Serving spoon and table knife of the *Medallion* pattern made by Gorham for Tiffany. The Medallion pattern was designed by George Wilkinson and was patented June 7, 1864. Length of spoon: 8 3/8 in. (21.3 cm.). Mark: TIFFANY & CO. / STERLING plus Gorham mark (Lion passant, anchor, G). *(Burt Collection)*.

In the first part of the nineteenth century there were relatively few silver flatware forms made in the United States compared to the large number of forms that proliferated late in the century. From surviving examples we know that many of these early pieces were spoons—teaspoons, tablespoons, serving spoons, and salts—plus an occasional dipper and ladle. In the 1820s dessert spoons came into general use. Early American silver forks and silver-handled knives are seldom seen. Silver forks in two sizes—the large dinner fork and the smaller breakfast or dessert fork—only came into general usage in America in the third quarter of the nineteenth century.

After the Civil War, American makers rapidly added to their repertory of silver forms. A variety of new serving pieces were made. Specialized pieces were developed for serving different kinds of food. Fish knives and forks, asparagus tongs, salad forks, ice cream spoons (and forks), as well as many others were made. It reached the point where almost every conceivable bit of food had a tool designed to transport it from one place to another.

The number of pieces of table silver faced by the dinner guest and the servants of the 1880s and 1890s was indeed formidable. Imagine coping with just the spoons listed in Tiffany's 1880 catalog: berry spoons, egg spoons, grapefruit spoons, ice spoons, bonbon spoons, dessert spoons, ice cream spoons, jelly spoons, mustache spoons (the bowl had a partial cover to keep the gentleman's moustache out of the soup), mustard spoons, nut spoons, olive spoons, orange spoons, preserve spoons, sherbet spoons, teaspoons, and toddy spoons. Tiffany also listed in the 1880 catalog other spoons—pap spoons, medicine spoons, salad spoons, salt spoons, serving spoons of various sizes, sugar spoons, and vegetable spoons.

Many of these forms were promoted as gift items. Of course there were more kinds of spoons and other flatware than any one house would have used. However, some of these specialized tools are extraordinarily well designed for their usage. For example, the snub-nosed, rather narrow grapefruit spoon is definitely a more satisfactory tool for eating grapefruit than a tea or coffee spoon. Such spoons as egg spoons and mustard spoons serve their purposes well.

The Scarcity of Knives

With all this variety of flatware sold by Tiffany & Co. one is struck by the present-day scarcity of knives, particularly in the early patterns. One factor in this was the common practice of using ivory, bone, or mother-of-pearl handled knives with a silver flatware service. And when steel bladed knives with silver handles were made for a service, they had the problem of rusting blades. It has been customary to replace such blades with stainless steel, but relatively few seem to have survived.

Many collectors today use modern knives or old ivory or pearl handled knives with their antique silver.

The Dinner Party

The etiquette books of the nineteenth century give a vivid picture of the formal dinner parties of society. It was an opulent, extravagant age—and they knew it. Most Victorian Americans were quite conscious of what Thorstein Veblen called conspicuous consumption. Cartoons in such magazines as *Life* poked gentle fun at these events. Florence Howe Hall in her book *Social Customs* (Boston, 1887) noted: "The extravagance of our modern dinner table has grown to be so great that it rivals those ancient Roman feasts where dowries were expended on a single meal, and almost surpasses Cleopatra's famed and costly beverage."

We quote below parts of Mrs. Hall's detailed description of a dinner party. There was a stately succession of food courses. No wonder some of the participants in those fabulous dinner parties were outrageously fat. It also indicates clearly why such huge quantities of silver and chinaware were required for these parties.

In Chapter 8, "Dinner-Parties; Service and Arrangements of the Table," Mrs. Hall first describes the tablecloth ("always white"), the correct lighting, flowers and ornaments on the table, and the centerpiece. Then:

A "cover" signifies the place laid at table for each person; and should consist of two large knives, a small silver knife and fork for fish, three large forks, a table-spoon for soup, a small "oyster-fork" for eating oysters on the half-shell, a goblet for water, and claret, hock, champagne, and sherry glasses, which are placed around it. The knives and forks should always be placed on the right and left of the plate, and never across the table.

In England, where raw oysters are not usually given at dinner, the dinner-napkin, with the bread folded in it, is placed between the knives and forks. But with us, the napkin and bread are placed on the left, as raw oysters, served on a majolica oyster-plate, with a piece of lemon in the center, are set at each place before the guests enter. The oyster-fork is usually placed at the right side of the plate, but the other forks should be on the left.

Seven and even nine wine-glasses are sometimes put beside each plate, but most of us would not approve of such a profusion of wine as this would imply. At other tables, two extra glasses, one for sherry or Madeira, and the other for claret or Burgundy, are put on with the dessert. These late-coming glasses are usually very delicate, as they accompany choice wines. No table-spoons (save those for soup) or other extra silver are placed on table for diner à la Russe, and no cruets or casters.

After the raw oysters, soup is served. At very stylish dinners it is customary to serve two soups,—white and brown, or white and clear. A thick soup is purée, and a clear soup is consommé. The soup, like the rest of the dinner, is served from the sideboard.

Fish is the next course, and is followed by the entrées, or "those dishes which are served in the first course after the fish." It is well to serve two entrées at once at a very elaborate dinner, and thus save time. To these succeed the roast, followed by Roman punch, and this in turn is followed by game and salad. Roman punch should only be given with a dinner, where there is only one course of meat. It is properly an "entremet," or "dish coming after the roast, in the second course."

Salad is sometimes served with the game, or again, it is served as a separate course, accompanied with cheese and with bread and butter. The bread should be cut very thin and nicely buttered, although sometimes the butter and bread are served separately.

Cheese is often made a course by itself; indeed, the general tendency of the modern dinner is to have each dish "all alone by itself," like the one fishball of classic memory. This style, however, may be carried too far. Only one or at most two vegetables are served with one course, and many vegetables make a course by themselves, as asparagus, sweet corn, macaroni, etc.

Some people think it is very barbarous to eat corn from the cob, but many others consider it entirely allowable to do so. A lady who gives many elegant dinners at Newport causes to be laid beside the plate of each guest two little silver-gilt spike-like arrangements. Each person then places these in either end of the corn-cob, and eats his corn holding it by two silver handles as it were.

After the salad and cheese come the ices and sweet dishes, then the fruit, then the bonbons. Coffee is usually served in the drawing-room, although it may be handed around in the dining-room if the guests have not already sat too long at the table.

Gentlemen stay at table a short time after the ladies have left it, discussing wine, cigars and liqueurs (or cordials), and no doubt indulging in the most improving conversation. After dinner coffee should always be cafe noir, or strong black coffee. It should be poured out in the kitchen or butler's pantry and handed round on a salver in tiny cups, with tiny gold or silver spoons and lump sugar, but no cream or milk.

For a dinner of many courses the knives and forks laid besides the plates will not be sufficient. Therefore at a later stage of the entertainment a fresh fork, or fork and knife, as the course may require, is set before each person on a fresh plate.

For the dessert, a silver dessert knife and fork and a gold or silver dessert spoon are put at each place. To these is often added an ice-spoon,—a compromise between a fork and a spoon. The finger-bowl comes with the fruit; it is set on the plate (usually a glass one or a handsomely decorated china one), a fruit napkin or one of the embroidered doilies now so fashionable being placed between.

Finally, Mrs. Hall gives a note on washing up:

The washing of plates, silver, etc. at a dinner-party should if possible be performed at such a distance from the dining-room that the clatter will be inaudible to those seated at table. In order to give an elaborate dinner it is almost indispensable that one should have a large quantity of china and plate, otherwise the delay from washing the dishes will be endless. Those that have been used should be at once removed from the dining-room, a page or maid-servant carrying them away; and one or two servants should be employed in washing them.[1]

Even in smaller middle-class houses of the nineteenth century the intimate servantless dinner party for four would have had a table set with many more pieces of silver than is usual for a similar party today. Mrs. Dewing's *Beauty in the Household* in 1882 suggested the table setting shown in Figure 106. There are thirty-six pieces of flatware and cutlery indicated for the four place settings all of which would have been silver or silver

DIAGRAM OF DINING-TABLE WHERE NO SERVANT WAITS.

A. Candles. B. Dishes of one course. C. Flowers. D. Dinnerplates with napkins and bread. E. Knives and forks. F. Carving forks and knives and gravy spoons. G. Glasses. H. Small corner dishes of olives, pickles, nuts, and bonbons. I. Strawcovered flask of oil, bottle of vinegar, and mustard-pot, for salad dressing. K. Salad bowl, with fork and spoon. L. Decanter of wine. M. Pitcher of water. N. Dish of fruit. O. Two small dishes of cakes. P. Small silver trays of pepper and salt. Q. Large napkins spread before host and hostess.

106 Drawing and caption from Mrs. Dewing's [Maria Richards Dewing] *Beauty in the Household* (New York: Harper & Brothers, 1882), p. 73.

handled in the proper household. And this did not include the flatware which appeared with the dessert or the coffee or demitasse spoons used after the meal.

Today we use far less silver on our dining tables. Many of the more informal tables in *Tiffany Table Settings*[2] showed only three pieces of silver flatware at each place setting: a fork, knife, and teaspoon. The standard five-piece Tiffany place setting of today includes: a teaspoon, luncheon fork, luncheon knife, dessert spoon, and a flat butter spreader.

Tiffany Makes Their Own Flatware—1869 Onward

When the Edward C. Moore Company was integrated into Tiffany & Co. in 1868 a decision was made by Tiffany to add a complete line of flatware patterns to their line of hollow ware. Even though the Moore Company had not made flatware prior to the merger, Tiffany had already established the market by selling other makers' flatware. The move to self-manufacture was an obvious next step when the Moore organization became part of Tiffany's.

The proliferation of flatware forms after the Civil War was accompanied by a flood of new flatware patterns. Gorham led the way by introducing a dozen new patterns in the immediate postwar years. Most of the new patterns were protected by design patents, a practice which Tiffany adopted for their own patterns. But design copying and plagiarism were widespread. Makers wanted to have copies of their competitors best-selling designs in their own lines.

Complete matched services of sterling flatware became the vogue. By the end of the first decade after the Civil War most families of social pretension owned a flatware service, usually sterling but sometimes silver plated.

There was a great flurry of design activity at Tiffany's from 1868 to 1872. During that period Tiffany introduced thirteen (including variations) new sterling silver flatware patterns. During this period they also started a campaign to promote custom-designed flatware. These new special custom designs were not for everyone. The design and cost of dies alone could run into thousands of dollars. The designs could remain exclusive since their customers usually purchased the dies and the patterns for the pieces.

With all this Tiffany still wanted the public to know

that their prices were not out of line. They made a big point in their newspaper advertisements that they were strictly competitive in their prices. An early 1870s advertisement noted:

Their Forks, Spoons and Table-ware are the richest in designs and finest in finish in this country, and are sold at the same price per ounce as the ordinary trade patterns.

Complete outfits, put in strong plate chests, always in stock.

For the convenience of persons out of New York, photographs of articles or careful selections from stock will be sent on approval.

Designers of Tiffany Flatware Patterns

It is clear, from a study of U.S. Patent Office records, that Edward C. Moore single-handedly propelled Tiffany & Co. into the flatware business. All of the patentable designs of early Tiffany flatware were obtained by Moore. (By law only the actual inventor is able to obtain a patent. This law has always been strict in the United States and there is no doubt that Edward C. Moore—and not his associates—was solely responsible for these designs.)

The following list shows that Moore obtained six flatware design patents (assigned to Tiffany & Co.) in the 1869–1872 period and two more in 1878 and 1879. The list of known Moore flatware patents ends with the two in 1889, just two years before his death in 1891. The undecorated, plain patterns *Antique* and *Queen Ann,* both introduced in 1870, were variations of traditional silver flatware patterns and would of course have been unpatentable.

FLATWARE PATTERNS PATENTED BY EDWARD C. MOORE

Pattern	Patent No.	Date Issued
Tiffany	3588	July 27, 1869
Italian	3917	March 22, 1870
Cook (Saratoga)	4476	November 15, 1870
Japanese	4831	April 18, 1871
Palm	5077	July 4, 1871
Persian	6205	October 15, 1872
Mackay (private pattern)	10524	March 12, 1878
Olympian	11333	August 12, 1879
Old French (electroplate pattern)	19210	July 16, 1889
J. P. Morgan (private pattern)	19211	July 16, 1889

We have already seen that Edward C. Moore had been sketching flatware ideas since the 1850s. In Figure 8 we pointed out the similarity between the sketch of an 1855 design and the 1869 *Tiffany* pattern. In addition to the above mentioned designs we attribute to Moore the *Vine* pattern and the *Grape Vine* and *Tomato Vine* serving pieces.

Most of the important flatware designs of the 1880s were by Charles T. Grosjean. He started off brilliantly in 1880 with *Lap Over Edge,* the most innovative of Tiffany's regular flatware patterns. In 1880 he also designed the popular *Chrysanthemum* pattern which was noteworthy for its rich flowing design and the decoration extending to the back of spoon bowls. Grosjean used this device of decorating spoon-bowl backs with particular effectiveness in the Searles pattern presented in 1886 (Fig. 110).

FLATWARE PATTERNS PATENTED BY CHARLES T. GROSJEAN

Pattern	Patent No.	Date Issued
Lap Over Edge	11728	April 13, 1880
Chrysanthemum	11968	September 21, 1880
Wave Edge	15144	July 15, 1884
Cornelius Vanderbilt (private pattern)	15675	December 30, 1884
W. K. Vanderbilt (private pattern)	15715	January 13, 1885
Mt. Vernon (electroplate pattern)	15716	January 13, 1885
Regent (electroplate pattern)	15717	January 13, 1885
Floral (electroplate pattern)	15784	February 10, 1885
*Indian Spoons**	15785	February 10, 1885
*Indian Spoons**	15831	February 17, 1885
King (electroplate pattern)	16216	September 1, 1885
Searles (private pattern)	16560	March 9, 1886
J. Carter Brown (private pattern)	16561	March 9, 1886

*Indian spoons are discussed in Chapter 10.

Charles Grosjean died on February 23, 1888 and his passing was noted in the *Jewelers' Circular* (April 1888):

Chares T. Grosjean, of Tiffany & Co., died on February 23d, at Hamilton, Bermuda, whither he had gone in quest of rest and a change from the busy life in the silverware factory of his firm. He was forty-seven years of age, and learned the silversmith's trade with his father, of the late firm of Grosjean & Woodward. He soon made his mark and became very adept in his art. He was admitted into his father's firm, and about twenty years ago was offered a position with Tiffany & Co., as superintendent of the silverware branch of their business. He was very devoted to his art, in which he achieved distinction, being spoken of as one of the best living decorators of silver. He overworked himself, however, and when his physician got him to consent to go to Bermuda it was already too late and he died two days after landing there.

In 1890 a patent on the *Broom Corn* pattern was issued to John T. Curran (Patent No. 20173, September 30, 1890) and in 1893 his design for the Christopher Columbus souvenir spoon was patented (No. 22698, August 15, 1893). In 1899 Burnett Y. Tiffany patented the *Atlantus* pattern, also known as *Ailantus* and *B. Tiffany* (Patent No. 31345, August 8, 1899). Burnett Tiffany was the youngest son of the company's founder, Charles L. Tiffany.

Private Custom-Designed Flatware Patterns

Tiffany made six known custom-designed "private pattern" flatware sets in the last quarter of the nineteenth century, and another six early in the twentieth century. These private patterns were made from dies specially designed and made for the particular set. All six of the known nineteenth-century private patterns were protected by U.S. design patents. The fact that only six true private pattern flatware sets of the nineteenth century could be identified from Tiffany's records was surprising. We had expected more. The private patterns should not be confused with the hand-worked flatware patterns on page 105 which are hand-decorated versions of Tiffany's *Antique* and *Lap Over Edge* patterns, some of which were custom made. The latter hand-decorated patterns are scarce, but pieces regularly appear on the market.

The custom-designed private pattern sets were quite expensive, even for those extravagant times. The time-consuming and laborious process of designing and hand making new dies ran the cost of these sets into the thousands of dollars. The New York *Herald* for December 29, 1889 had a story on J. P. Morgan's service. (See right)

J. PIERPONT MORGAN'S CHRISTMAS PRESENT.

A $50,000 Silver Dessert Service from the Directors of the New York Central Railroad.

GRATEFUL WORDS WITH IT.

The Gift Intended as a Recognition of His Labors in the Reorganization of the West Shore

Of all the Christmas gifts which were made in this city last week it is probable that the most magnificent was the present which J. Pierpont Morgan received from the directors of the New York Central and Hudson River Railroad Company. It consisted of a dessert service of gold and silver of three hundred pieces, manufactured by Tiffany. The intrinsic value could not be ascertained in exact figures, but some of those who have seen it estimated that it cost as much as $50,000. Superintendent Cook, of Tiffany's, said that it cost "many thousands of dollars," but he was not permitted to state the exact figures.

But whatever its intrinsic value may be that is a secondary consideration with Mr. Morgan, who is a very rich man himself. He prizes it most as a recognition of his services as chairman of the Reorganization Committee of the New York, West Shore and Buffalo Railway Company, the control of which, as every man familiar with railroads knows, has greatly enhanced the value of the Vanderbilt system of roads. For his services on that committee Mr Morgan refused to take any compensation. It was resolved, therefore, to give him a present.

The Morgan service of course included pieces other than flatware such as a centerpiece, candelabra, compotes, and side dishes. The flatware for the service was designed by Edward C. Moore and his design was patented on July 16, 1889 (Fig. 111).

The largest and one of the most ornate of Tiffany's early custom-designed flatware services was the one made for John W. Mackay which was part of the great dinner and dessert service for twenty-four discussed in Chapter 4. Chest No. 1 of the Mackay service contained the flatware—a formidable array of 918 pieces.

CONTENTS OF CHEST 1—THE MACKAY SERVICE

48	Table spoons	
48	Dessert spoons	
24	Coffee spoons	
24	Coffee spoons Euld	
48	Tea spoons	
24	Egg spoons	
24	Ice cream spoons	
24	Fruit spoons	
48	Salt spoons, individual	
72	Table forks	
48	Dessert forks	
2	Soup ladles	
2	Oyster ladles	
4	Gravy ladles	
2	Punch ladles	
2	Cream ladles	
2	Macaroni servers	
2	Ice cream servers	
2	Push ice cream servers	
2	Pudding servers	
2	Pie knives	
2	Crumb knives	
2	Fish knives	
2	Fish forks	
2	Salad forks	
2	Salad spoons	
2	Ice spoons	
4	Berry spoons	
2	Mustard spoons	
6	Vegetable spoons	
4	Gravy spoons	
2	Sugar spoons, large	
2	Sugar spoons, small	
2	Sugar tongs, large	

2	Sugar tongs, small
2	Asparagus tongs
2	Sugar sifters
2	Cheese scoops
4	Cheese knives
4	Butter knives
2	Cake knives
2	Melon knives
6	Olive forks
6	Olive spoons
2	Caddy spoons
72	Dinner knives
48	Breakfast knives
36	Fish knives, individual
36	Fish forks, individual
36	Oyster forks
36	Fruit knives
36	Nut picks
36	Melon knives, individual
2	Pair meat carvers
2	Pair game carvers
2	Steels
4	Champagne bottle holders
2	Ham holders
12	Skewers
2	Pair grape scissors
4	Knife rests
6	Nut crackers
2	Tea strainers
2	Corkscrews
1	Bell
1	Syphon pump
6	Marrow spoons
12	Wine labels

107 The Mackay flatware pattern which incorporates the motifs of the shamrock of Ireland and the thistle of Scotland for Mrs. Mackay's ancestors. The front has the family crest and the monogram MLM on the back is for Marie Louise Mackay.

Figure 107 shows in detail the heavy ornamentation of the Mackay flatware with the family coat of arms and monogram on the pieces. The Mackay flatware is far

more ornamented than most of Tiffany's contemporary flatware patterns. Figure 108 shows a few of the serving pieces listed above in chest No. 1 of the Mackay service. Note the intricate ornamentation on the blade of the cake knife and the fancy pierced bowl of the olive spoon.

The flatware services designed for the Cornelius and William K. Vanderbilt families were also highly ornamented. Figure 109 shows the backside of the W. K. Vanderbilt pattern with the monogram WKV and emblems of the chase—a stag's head, horn, and quiver of arrows. The front side of the Cornelius Vanderbilt pattern in Figure 109 has a basket filled with fruit and flowers above a vase of flowers. The reverse side of the pattern has the Vanderbilt coat of arms.

In some ways the most remarkable and interesting of Tiffany's private custom-designed flatware sets is the silver and gilt dessert service for eighteen made for Mary Frances Hopkins (Searles) in 1886 (Fig. 110). Charles T. Grosjean's patented design for the service is different from any other Tiffany silver. The handles are hand-

108 A sampling of parcel gilt serving pieces from the 918 pieces in Chest No. 1 of the Mackay service. From left to right: olive spoon, tea caddy spoon, cake knife, berry spoon, olive fork, and melon knife. Mark on all flatware pieces: TIFFANY & CO. PAT. 1878. (*Private Collection*).

109

pierced (there are twenty-seven openings pierced through the spoon handles in Figure 110). The grape and vine design is extraordinarily complex, as are the marvelously baroque initials MFS on the backs of the pieces. Yet the individual pieces of the Searles service have a buoyant lightness which is partly because of the piercing in the handles and partly because of the sharp clarity of the design.

The Searles service is not only fascinating from a design point of view, it also has an interesting history. It was involved in a life story more flamboyant and certainly more lurid than the Mackay story. Mary Frances Searles was Mrs. Mark Hopkins when as a woman in her fifties she married Edward T. Searles, a young decorator, in 1887. Her first husband was Mark Hopkins, one of the founders of the Central Pacific Railroad, who is probably best remembered today for the hotel named for him in San Francisco with its spectacular barroom the "Top of the Mark." He died in 1878 leaving his widow, Mary Frances, a vast fortune. The newspapers called her "America's Richest Widow." Mrs. Hopkins first met Edward Searles when she was furnishing her

110

109 Flatware designed for the Vanderbilt families in 1884 by Charles T. Grosjean. On the left is the pattern of W. K. Vanderbilt and center and right is the pattern of Cornelius Vanderbilt.

110 Dessert spoon (back), serving spoon, dinner fork (back), and luncheon fork from a dessert service for eighteen designed by Charles T. Grosjean for Mary Frances Hopkins [Searles] in 1885. The initials MFS are on the back of each piece. The service consisted of eighteen of each: silver serving spoons, dessert spoons, teaspoons, dinner forks, and luncheon forks; gilt dessert spoons, gilt luncheon forks, gilt ice cream spoons, and gilt after-dinner coffee spoons. Length of dessert spoon 7 in. (17.9 cm.). Mark: TIFFANY & CO STERLING PAT. 1886 M. *(Private Collection).*

mansion on Nob Hill in San Francisco. Searles, described as being swarthy and muscular "with exquisite manners and of a romantic and poetic temperament," was a decorator with the well-known New York firm of Herter & Company. He was twenty-eight at the time. Mrs. Hopkins and Edward Searles's mutual interest in houses and furnishings made them fast friends. When she married Searles in 1887, it was over the strong objections of her adopted son, Timothy. Searles and Mrs. Hopkins were married in a private ceremony in Trinity Chapel in New York. During their six-month honeymoon in Europe they were presented to Queen Victoria of England and King Humbert of Italy.

During the 1880s Mrs. Hopkins moved East and went on a monumental house-building and buying spree. She built a two million dollar chateau, modeled after Chambord, in the Berkshire town of Great Barrington, Massachusetts, acquired a house at 60 Fifth Avenue in New York, and places on Block Island and at Methuen, Massachusetts.

Mrs. Searles died in 1891 at the age of sixty. Her will created a sensation. She cut out everyone—her adopted son Timothy, relatives, and disgruntled servants—and left her estimated sixty million dollars to Edward Searles. Timothy and the others sued. The widely publicized trial at Salem, Massachusetts made marvelous newspaper material. Searles testified that Mrs. Hopkins pursued *him* for three years before they were actually married and that it was not a love match. He stated that his current income was more than $500,000 per year (this was still before income taxes) but was not allowed by his attorneys to state his income before his marriage to Mrs. Hopkins. The trial came to an abrupt halt because of an out-of-court settlement of about ten million dollars. The San Francisco *Call* noted: "Evidentally Mr. Searles didn't want another day on the witness stand."[3]

There is a curious discrepancy between the date of the dessert service in Figure 110 and the date of the marriage of Mrs. Hopkins to Edward Searles. The dessert service, which is identified in Tiffany's records only with the name Mark Hopkins, must have been ordered in 1885 since Charles T. Grosjean's application for a design patent for the service was filed on December 26th of that year. It was almost two years later when Searles and Mrs. Hopkins were married—November 8th, 1887—and she became Mary Frances Searles, the MFS of the dessert service.

111 Coppers of private custom-designed flatware patterns. *Left to right:* (1) A. D. Russell—early 1900s. Mark: TIFFANY & CO STERLING. (2) Archibald Rogers—after 1907. Mark: m TIFFANY & CO STERLING. (3) Unknown—after 1907. Mark: TIFFANY & CO STERLING m. (4) J. Carter Brown—1886. Mark: TIFFANY & CO STERLING PAT. 1886 M. (5) "Cuban"—after 1907. Mark: TIFFANY & CO STERLING m. (6) J. P. Morgan—1889. Mark: TIFFANY & CO STERLING PAT. 1889 M. (7) Unknown—Solid Gold [no date]. (8) A. J. Fuller. Mark: TIFFANY & CO STERLING m PAT. [no date].

The only other private custom-designed flatware patterns of the nineteenth century that could be identified from the Tiffany files are the J. Carter Brown pattern patented in 1885[4] and the J. P. Morgan pattern patented in 1889. Figure 111 shows the "coppers"[5] of these two patterns plus the six known private patterns made by Tiffany in the early part of the twentieth century. The J. Carter Brown pattern has a paddle-shaped handle with a raised molding. At the head is a shell-like ornament over the family coat of arms. The J. P. Morgan pattern has undulating stemwork leaf forms and scroll ornaments.

We feel that the six nineteenth-century private pattern designs are far more interesting than the twentieth-century designs. The latter tend to be dull and, in one or two

104

cases, downright derivative. The best of the private pattern designs of Edward Moore and Charles Grosjean of the 1878–1889 period are among the most interesting and important of all of Tiffany's flatware.

Special Designs for Serving Pieces

Tiffany's designed a number of serving pieces with handle designs different from their regular flatware patterns. Such serving pieces as ladles, serving spoons and forks, berry spoons and jelly spoons were popular gift items that were not expected to be part of a patterned flatware set.

Two patterns introduced in the early 1870s, which we call *Grape Vine* and *Tomato Vine,* are shown in Figure 112. The *Grape Vine* berry spoon shown at the left in Figure 112 is similar to the regular *Vine* pattern introduced in 1872. Raised vines and leaves and grapes are displayed on a stippled background. The designs wrap around the edges of the handle to the back. The handle edges are hand filed to accentuate the forms. The gold vermeil bowl of the berry spoon was not only a decorative effect, it prevented tarnishing and corrosion from acidic fruits.

The *Tomato Vine* ladle on the right of Figure 112 has a very high relief design of tomatoes, vines, and leaves which also goes around the edge of the handle to the back, as shown in Figure 114. These large ladles, with their dramatic large-scale leaf and tomato designs and swelling, sharply curved handles, are among the most spectacular of Tiffany's flatware pieces.

The *Holly* pattern is a charming and whimsical design which has an Art Nouveau feel. There were a number of serving pieces made with this handle design, one of the most successful being the jelly server in Figure 113.

113

112 Berry spoon *(left)* with gilt bowl in the *Grape Vine* pattern and punch ladle *(right)* in the *Tomato Vine* pattern, first made around 1872. Length of ladle: 11 1/4 in. (28.6 cm.). Length of berry spoon: 9 1/2 in. (24.1 cm.). Mark: TIFFANY & CO STERLING M (see Fig. 114). *(Private Collection).*

113 Jelly server in the *Holly* pattern. Length: 7 in. (17.8 cm.). Mark: TIFFANY & CO STERLING M. *(Private Collection).*

114 Reverse side of handle of a *Tomato Vine* ladle showing engraved initials LGS and the Tiffany mark.

115 Cake server, pierced and engraved blade. Length: 8 3/4 in. (22.2 cm.). Mark: PAT. 1885 TIFFANY & CO. (*The New-York Historical Society, New York City*).

116 Berry spoon with cast grape motif handle, engraved monogram EAR, for Ethel Agnes Robinson. About 1905. Length: 9 3/8 in. (23.8 cm.). Mark: TIFFANY & CO MAKERS STERLING C. (*Mr. and Mrs. Donald L. Fennimore*).

The rococo bowl of the jelly server with its lovely upswept tip compliments beautifully the design of the handle. Note how carefully the monogram is placed so that it integrates smoothly into the overall design.

Creatively suitable monograms are a hallmark of Tiffany silver. Often the engravers were true artists. The stunning monogram (Fig. 114) on a *Tomato Vine* ladle shows the undulating line of the engraver filling the space with all the grace and precision of a first-rate abstract painter. See also the complex and handsome monogram on the Moore pitcher in Figure 95.

114

The cake server in Figure 115 with its engraved and pierced flat scoop was patented in 1885. It is similar to John Polhemus's Oriental pattern and the decorative elements on the handle are of Islamic origin. The berry spoon with the grape-encrusted handle in Figure 116 dates from about 1905.

115

116

At the end of the nineteenth century Tiffany made some delightful sterling for children. Figure 117 shows a nursery rhyme set of knife, fork, and spoon. The knife handle is Little Red Riding Hood with a rather benign wolf. The fork handle depicts a stylish turn-of-the-century Little Bo-peep, and the spoon shows Jill observing Jack's fall and the spilling water bucket.

Before showing Tiffany's regular flatware patterns, the first of which was offered for sale in 1869, we will discuss a small, remarkable group of handworked and, in some cases, handmade, flatware types and patterns designed by Tiffany in the 1870s.

The Handworked Flatware Patterns

In the 1872–1880 period Tiffany introduced a small group of expensive handworked flatware patterns that involved one or more hand operations: engraving, chasing, etching and/or applied ornamentation. The fact that each piece was hand ornamented meant that such flatware was more costly to make than even the most expensive of the regular Tiffany patterns made from dies, such as the *Olympian* or *Chrysanthemum* patterns. For this reason the handworked patterns described below are scarcer today than most of Tiffany's regular flatware patterns.

The first group of these patterns makes use of the plain *Antique* pattern (Fig. 128), which was ornamented either by hand engraving or chasing:

Antique Engraved No. 4 (Fig. 118) has a simple geometrically engraved triangle below an engraved loop on the handle end for initials if desired.

Antique Ivy (also called *Antique Engraved No. 20*) (Fig. 119) has an engraved ivy vine on a hand-stippled background. The latter was the most expensive of the engraved versions of *Antique* because of the labor involved. For example, three hours were involved in engraving the two sides of a knife. Spoons and forks, which are engraved on one side only, took about an hour and three quarters to engrave. The time (and cost) of engraving an initial or initials on a piece is not included in these figures.

Figure 120 shows a piece of a custom-made set in the *Antique* pattern of the 1890s that has been beautifully engraved and chased.

The *Lap Over Edge* pattern was introduced in 1880,

117   Child's knife, fork, and spoon, late nineteenth century. Each piece depicts a nursery rhyme: Little Red Riding Hood, Little Bo-Peep, Jack and Jill. Length of knife: 7 1/2 in. (19 cm.). Mark: TIFFANY & CO STERLING. (*The New-York Historical Society, New York City*).

107

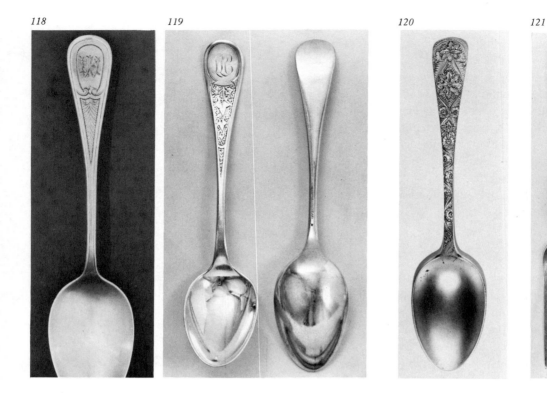

118 *Antique Engraved #4.*

119 *Antique Ivy* (also called *Antique Engraved #20*).

118–119 Hand-decorated styles based on plain *Antique* pattern, first made in 1870. These hand-decorated versions of *Antique* were first made after 1870, but probably no later than 1875.

120 A variation of the engraved *Antique* pattern. This custom design of the 1890s has very deep engraving on an exceedingly heavy spoon. Length: 8 1/2 in. (21.6 cm.). Mark: TIFFANY & CO STERLING. *(Collection of Mr. and Mrs. Cruger D. G. Fowler).*

121 *Lap Over Edge* pattern blanks. The lap was usually on the back *(right)*, but occasionally it was on the front *(left)*. The blanks were usually decorated by etching, engraving, and/or chasing.

122 Pieces from a 62-piece *Lap Over Edge* service made about 1890. Each piece of this hand-hammered set is different, with applied mounts in copper, gold, and silver. Mark: TIFFANY & CO. / STERLING SILVER / AND OTHER METALS PAT. 1880 / M 915. (Different numbers for each piece.) *(Courtesy of George L. K. Frelinghuysen).*

122

and the patent date of 1880 is included in the mark on these pieces. The *Lap Over Edge* handle blanks have rolled edges, with the roll usually to the back but sometimes to the front (Fig. 121). This makes the edges of the handles thicker than the middle.

Figure 122 shows five pieces from an unusual 62-piece *Lap Over Edge* service which was completely handmade. The spoons were entirely hand hammered as were the handles of the forks and knives. The handles of the knives are solid—not lapped. The applied ornaments are brass, copper, gold, and silver. The background decorations are engraved and chased. Each piece of this most interesting service is different.

Etched versions of *Lap Over Edge* are shown in Figure 123. In these etched pieces the high places are protected (stopped out) with asphaltum paint and the unprotected part of the design is etched down with acid. This is followed by handworking—chasing and engraving.

Occasionally *Lap Over Edge* pieces were hand engraved. The handsome crumber in Figure 124, with its crisply engraved "bright cut" bamboo branches and spider and web, is in the Japanese taste. The *Lap Over Edge* designs were developed at about the same time as

123 *Lap Over Edge* fish forks etched with marine designs. From a set of twelve, each of which is different. The design is identified with a scratched mark on back of handle. *Left to right:* ENCAMPMENT CONE, FLYING FISH, KINGFISH, WINKLE. The fork on the right shows the reverse side scratch marked CORAL. Length: 6 15/16 in. (17.6 cm.). Mark: C TIFFANY & CO. STERLING PAT. 1880. *(Private Collection).*

124 *Lap Over Edge* crumber with bamboo branches and spider web engraved on handle. Length: 12 3/4 in. (32.4 cm.). Mark: TIFFANY & CO STERLING PAT. 1880. *(Private Collection).*

123

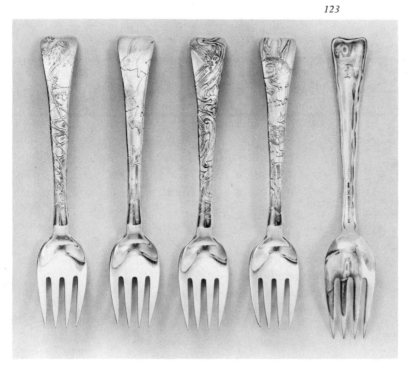

124

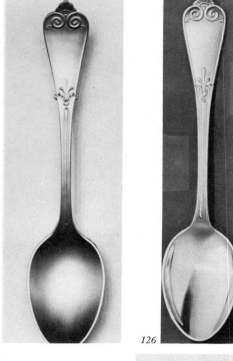

125 *Tiffany*, first made in 1869.

126 *Beekman*, formerly *Tiffany*, with two side knobs removed, introduced in 1956.

127 *Italian*, first made in 1870.

the hollow ware in the Japanese style discussed in Chapter 10. Both wre important precursors to Art Nouveau.

Standard Tiffany Sterling Flatware Patterns

The first standard Tiffany flatware pattern, which appeared in 1869, was appropriately named *Tiffany* (Fig. 125). A similar pattern, *Beekman* (Fig. 126), without the knobs on the sides of the handles, was introduced in 1956. The *Italian* pattern (Fig. 127) which came out in 1870 was more ornamented and typically Victorian. The simple undecorated *Antique* (Fig. 128) and *Queen Anne* (Fig. 129) patterns were remarkable for their time. They were related to traditional early patterns and were most severe when compared to other mid-Victorian sterling flatware.

The *Japanese* pattern introduced in 1871 (Fig. 131), now called *Audubon* (Fig. 132), and the *Persian* pattern (Fig. 134) introduced in 1872 are direct results of the interest in exotic cultures which became so widespread later in the nineteenth century and which led into the Art Nouveau movement (see Chapter 10).

The *Vine* pattern (Fig. 135) first appeared in 1872. The stamped undulating vine and gourd decoration is on a mat background which shows off the raised decorations. The top and the thickened edges of the *Vine* handles are similar to *Lap Over Edge,* although the edges of *Vine* are not actually lapped. The *Vine* pattern includes a number of stamped flatware handle designs such as daisies (breakfast forks), wheat (dinner forks), iris (oyster forks, nut picks, demitasse spoons), and tomatoes (knives). There are numerous related serving pieces such as *Grape Vine* and *Tomato Vine* (Fig. 112).

The *Olympian* pattern, which was first made in 1878, was obviously the result of a major design effort. It was the most elaborate and complex of all of Tiffany's regular flatware patterns. In ornateness it rivaled the Mackay and Vanderbilt silver, but it was more pictorial and the designs, which completely cover the front of the handles, are more tightly enclosed in the strong, raised border-edges of the handles.

Figure 136 shows a typical front and back side of the *Olympian* pattern. Figure 137 is a cheese scoop with vermeil blade and a different mythological scene.

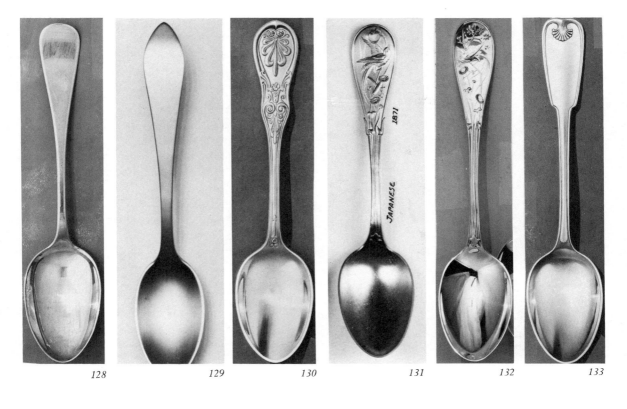

128   129   130   131   132   133

134   135

128 *Antique*, first made in 1870. Renamed *King William* in 1956.

129 *Queen Anne*, circa 1870.

130 *Cook*, renamed *Saratoga* in 1956.

131 *Japanese*, first made in 1871; each piece is different.

132 *Audubon*, formerly *Japanese*, with two side knobs removed, introduced in 1956. Briefly named *Plantation*.

133 *Palm*, first made in 1871.

134 *Persian*, first made in 1872.

135 *Vine*, first made in 1872 (front and back).

111

The subjects vary with the size of the handles of the different pieces and are as follows:

Teaspoon	Diana and her nymphs, while hunting, are surprised by Pan, from whom they run in fright (Fig. 136).
Tablespoon	Venus born of the sea is drawn in her shell by dolphins driven by Cupid, who bears the laurel branch.
Dessert spoon Salad fork Soup spoon	Orpheus in search of his wife, Eurydice. He is playing upon the lyre presented to him by Apollo, from which he produced such sweet music that he charmed all that came within its sound.
Dessert fork	The sybil unrolling the scroll of fate, which is being eagerly read by one of her votaries.
Dinner fork	Hercules and Omphale. Hercules became so enamored of Omphale, Queen of Lydia, that he would sit by her side among her women and hold her distaff while she spun.
Coffee spoon	Bacchantes amusing the infant Bacchus and teaching him to dance.
Salt spoon	The satyrs receiving instruction from Sylvanus, a rural deity.
Dessert knife	Bacchus and bacchante.
Dinner knife	Bacchus, feeding with the juice of grapes the panther which was sacred to him. Two bacchantes are lying nearby.
Breakfast knife	Orpheus charming wild animals with the sweetness of his music.
Serving pieces	Paris, the son of Priam the king of Troy, presenting to Venus the golden apple, having been called upon by Juno, Minerva, and Venus to adjudge the prize of beauty to the fairest of those goddesses (Fig. 137).
Meat carver	The fourth labor of Hercules, which was to bring alive to Eurystheus the wild boar that had ravaged the country around Erymanthus.
Game carver	Actaeon devoured by his own dogs, after having been changed by Diana into a stag.
Mustard spoon Iced teaspoon Sauce ladle Oyster ladle	The sleeping Diana. While the goddess of hunting and her dogs sleep, the animals of the wood rest.
Oyster ladle	Hebe, the cupbearer of the gods, watched over by the eagle of Jove. The wine jars and vine indicate her vocation.

136 Child's fork and spoon in the *Olympian* pattern, first made in 1878. The spoon handle shows Diana and her nymphs being surprised by Pan. Engraved on back "HARRIET / 1884." Mark: M TIFFANY & CO STERLING PAT. 1879 (*The New-York Historical Society, New York City*).

| Soup ladle | Jupiter with the eagle and sceptre surrounded by the gods and goddesses on Mount Olympus. |
| Nut picks | The second labor of Hercules. He kills the Lernean hydra which has seven heads. |

The *Chrysanthemum* pattern (Fig. 138), first made in 1880, has been from the beginning one of the most popular of all of Tiffany's patterns. The *Chrysanthemum* pattern was also adapted for use in hollow-ware patterns (see page 78).

On the following pages in Figures 139 through 176 we list chronologically up to the present (1978) all of Tiffany's regular flatware patterns, noting with each illustration the date of introduction.

The 1972–73 Tiffany *Blue Book* illustrated a flatware pattern, "Ward Bennett," which was never actually made. It was a squarish handle design based on the spikelike form of a surgeon's bone chisel.

Sterling Spoons and Forks Were Sold by Weight

During the latter part of the nineteenth and early twentieth centuries Tiffany sold sterling spoons and forks by weight. There were three different weights: light, medium, and heavy. The 1904 Tiffany *Blue Book* explained how this worked:

Weight:
The spoons and forks are made to conform as nearly as practicable to the weights given below; small variations are unavoidable.

Price:
The price is figured according to the actual weight of the silver, and NEVER AVERAGED, thus always assuring a full equivalent for the price paid.

The table on page 118 shows the variations in average weights per dozen of the various pieces and the price per ounce.

137   138

137 Cheese scoop in the *Olympian* pattern. Length: 9 in. (22.9 cm.). Mark: M TIFFANY & CO STERLING PAT. 1879 (*Collection of Mrs. Raymond L. Thomsen*)

138 *Chrysanthemum*, also known as *Indian Chrysanthemum*, first made in 1880.

113

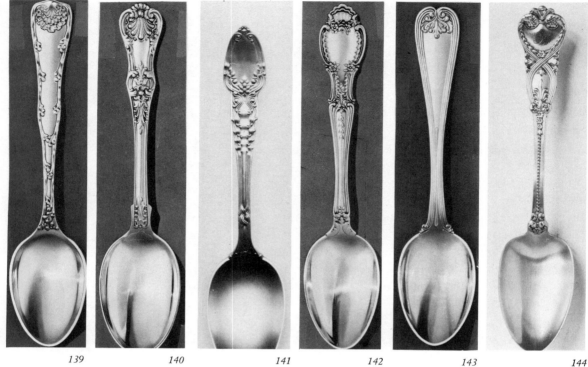

139   140   141   142   143   144

145   146   147

139   *Wave Edge*, first made in 1884.

140   *English King*, first made in 1885 (also *King* plated).

141   *Broom Corn*, first made in 1890.

142   *Richelieu*, first made in 1892.

143   *Colonial*, first made in 1895.

144   *St. James*, first made in 1898.

145   *Atlantas*, also called *Ailanthus, Ailantus,* and *B. Tiffany.* First made in 1899.

146   *Florentine*, first made in 1900.

147   *Marquise*, first made in 1902.

148 *Marquise Engraved* #226.

149 *Shell and Thread*, first made in 1905.

150 *Renaissance*, first made in 1905.

151 *St. Dunstan*, first made in 1909.

152 *Winthrop*, first made in 1909.

153 *Faneuil*, made in 1910; modification of *Queen Anne* pattern.

154 *Faneuil Engraved*. Date unknown.

155 *Reeded Edge*, formerly called *Faneuil* #225.

156 *Feather Edge*, formerly called *Faneuil* #95.

148   *149*   *150*

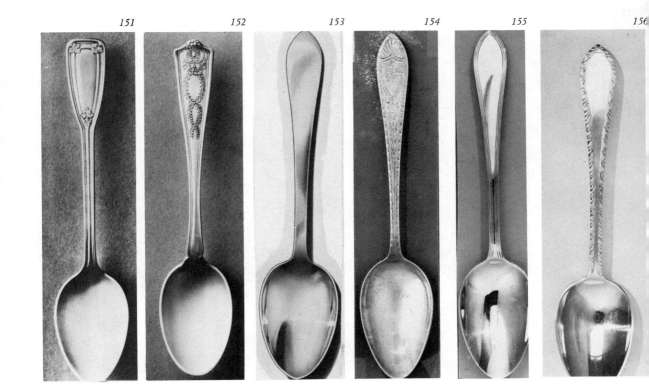

151   *152*   *153*   *154*   *155*   *156*

157 *Flemish*, first made in 1911.

158 *Clinton*, first made in 1912.

159 *Clinton Engraved*, date of introduction unknown.

160 *San Lorenzo*, first made in 1916.

161 *Gramercy*, first made in 1921. Replaced by Hamilton.*

162 *Windham*, first made in 1923.

163 *Castilian*, first made in 1929.

164 *Hampton*, first made in 1934.

165 *Century*, first made in 1937. This Art Deco pattern celebrated the hundredth anniversary of Tiffany & Co.

* The spoon illustrated is part of a set which belonged to Eleanor and Franklin Delano Roosevelt before they were in the White House. *(Courtesy of Mr. and Mrs. William D. Roosevelt.)*

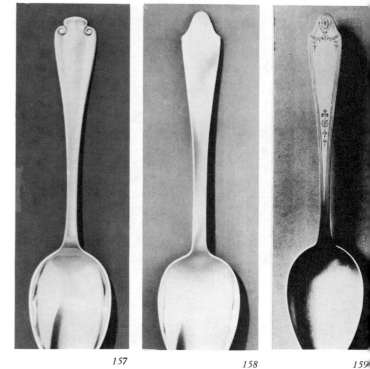

157   158   159

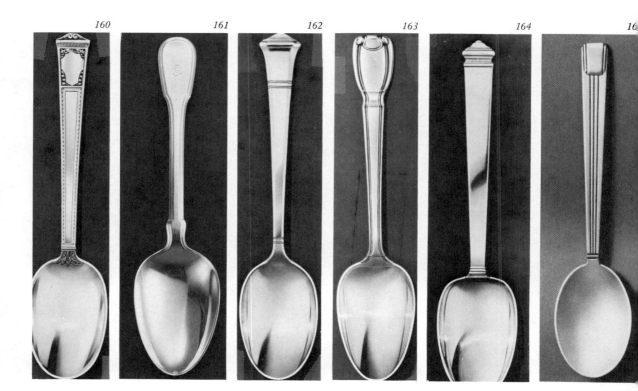

160   161   162   163   164   16

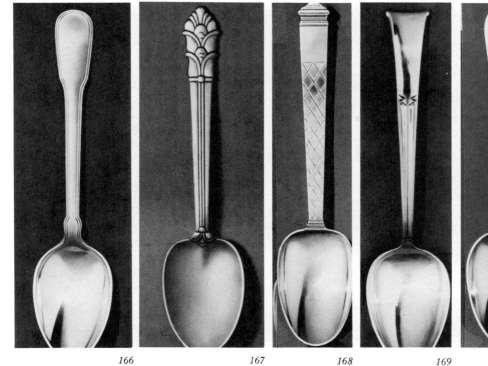

166   167   168   169   170

171   172   173

166 *Hamilton*, first made in 1938. Replaced *Gramercy*.

167 *Palmette*, first made in 1947.

168 *Harlequin*, derived from *Hampton*, first made in 1956.

169 *Linenfold*, first made in 1956.

170 *Salem*, first made in 1956.

171 *Governor*, derived from *Clinton*, first made in 1956.

172 *Fox Head*. Trifid end on *Antique* pattern, first made in 1956.

173 *Cordis*, first made in 1957.

117

| | | Tea Spoons | | | Dessert Spoons | | | Table Spoons | | |
| | Price | Light | Med. | Heavy | Light | Med. | Heavy | Light | Med. | Heavy |
Pattern	Per Oz.	Oz.	Oz.	Oz.	Oz.	Oz.	Oz.	Oz.	Oz.	Oz.
Ailantus	$1.00	12	13	15	21	23	25	33	35	38
Colonial	1.00	11	13	15	20	23	25	28	32	35
English King	1.00	15	17	19	25	27	30	39	43	46
Marquise	1.00	12	14	16	21	24	28	29	32	36
Palm	1.00	11	13	15	18	21	23	26	28	32
Richelieu	1.00	12	14	16	20	23	26	28	32	34
Tiffany	1.00	11	13	15	18	21	23	25	28	32
Wave Edge	1.00	11	13	15	19	21	24	26	30	34
Florentine	1.15	15	16	18	22	24	27	35	37	39
St. James	1.15	12	14	16	21	24	26	32	35	38
Chrysanthemum	1.35	14	15	17	22	24	26	33	35	38
Olympian	1.35	15	17	19	23	25	28	36	38	40

Average Weights per Dozen Given in Ounces Troy

		Soup Spoons			Dessert Forks			Table Forks		
Ailantus	$1.00	31	34	37	20	22	24	28	31	34
Colonial	1.00	26	30	34	19	22	24	25	29	33
English King	1.00	39	43	46	23	26	28	31	35	38
Marquise	1.00	20	32	36	20	23	27	27	30	34
Palm	1.00	26	28	32	17	20	22	23	26	30
Richelieu	1.00	28	32	34	19	22	24	26	30	33
Tiffany	1.00	25	28	32	17	20	22	23	26	30
Wave Edge	1.00	26	30	34	18	21	23	25	29	32
Florentine	1.15	33	35	38	21	23	26	29	32	35
St. James	1.15	31	33	36	20	22	25	27	32	34
Chrysanthemum	1.35	31	34	38	20	22	24	29	32	35
Olympian	1.35	34	36	39	22	24	26	32	34	36

The price varied according to the production costs of various patterns. The prices of *Ailantus, Colonial, English King, Marquise, Palm, Richelieu, Tiffany,* and *Wave Edge* were all $1.00 per troy ounce. *Florentine* and *St. James* were $1.15 per ounce and *Chrysanthemum* and *Olympian* were the most expensive at $1.35 per ounce.

It is interesting to compare the price of the Tiffany flatware per ounce with the actual value of the silver contained. In 1904 the price of fine or pure silver on the New York market was about fifty-seven cents per troy ounce. This meant that in one ounce of a Tiffany spoon there was silver worth about fifty-two cents (remembering that sterling is 92.5 percent fine silver). Thus for such patterns as *Ailantus*, Tiffany's price was approximately

118

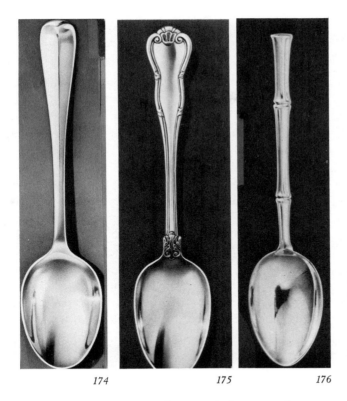

174   175   176

174 *Rat Tail*, made in England to Tiffany specifications. First made in 1957.

175 *Provence*, first made in 1960.

176 *Bamboo*, first made in 1961 as coffee spoons. Other pieces have been added.

double the silver value. The remainder was of course production and sales costs and profit. The $1.35 per ounce price for the more expensive *Chrysanthemum* and *Olympian* pieces was about two and a half times the cost of silver contained, reflecting the higher labor costs of these patterns.

Tiffany Souvenir Spoons

Souvenir spoons first appeared in America in about 1888 and by the early 1890s the production of these spoons reached flood proportions. Souvenir spoons by the hundreds were made. It was a true craze. Organizations, religious groups, towns, states, presidents, world fairs, holidays, historic sites, flowers, Indians—almost anything was an excuse for a souvenir spoon. They were made in sterling and silver plate. Some were handsome and interesting in design and some were awful.

It didn't take Tiffany long to get involved. The *Jewelers Circular* of May 20, 1891 noted:

Tiffany & Co., New York, have produced several elegant spoons to represent the metropolis and the city of churches. These are the High Bridge, the Trinity Church (two designs),

119

the Washington Statue on Union Square and in front of the Sub-Treasury Building, the Brooklyn Bridge, the Obelisk and Liberty Enlightening the World (two designs).

At an even earlier date Tiffany was exhibiting its Indian spoons, which have sometimes been classified as souvenir spoons. The Indian spoons, which were shown in the 1889 Exhibition, will be discussed in more detail in Chapter 10.

The Tiffany *Blue Book* of 1893 gave a complete listing with prices of their souvenir spoons. The floral spoons were smaller and more inexpensive than the New York souvenir spoons. The Forget-me-not spoon in Figure 177 has "souvenir forget-me-not" in Art Nouveau script on the handle. The spoon is about 5 inches (12.7 cm.) long compared to the approximately 6-inch (15.2 cm.) length of the Statue of Liberty spoon in Figure 178. All of the Tiffany souvenir spoons were available in both plain silver and gilt (vermeil) bowls.

SOUVENIR SPOONS IN TIFFANY'S 1893 BLUE BOOK

COFFEE SPOONS

Foreign Spoons:
German, French, Italian, and Norwegian
each $2.50 to $5.00

Floral Spoons:

Clover	Marigold
Daisy	Morning Glory
Forget-me-not	Pansy
Fringed Gentian	Ragged Sailor
Golden Rod (New York State)	Thistle
Iris	Wild Rose
	Violet

each $1.50 to $2.00

New York Spoons:
Academy of Design
Brooklyn Bridge
Castle Garden
Castle William, Governor's Island
Christmas, Holly and Mistletoe
City Hall
Cooper Institute
Harlem Bridge
Metropolitan Museum of Art
Obelisk, Central Park
Statue of Liberty
Statue of Farragut, Madison Square
Statue of Washington, U.S. Sub-Treasury
St. Patrick's Cathedral

St. Paul's Church
Trinity Church
Washington Bridge
Worth Monument, Madison Square

each $2.25 to $4.00

Orange Spoons:
Brooklyn Bridge
St. Paul's Church

each $3.50 to $5.00

Tea Spoons:
Brooklyn Bridge
Christmas, Holly and Mistletoe
Christopher Columbus
Continental Soldier
Father Knickerbocker
Statue of Liberty
Spinster
St. Paul's Church
Trinity Church
Union League Club

each $2.25 to $5.00

Additional souvenir spoons were designed and sold by Tiffany's well into the twentieth century:

1894 Second Presbyterian Church of Richmond, Va.
1898 Admiral Dewey
1901 Statue of Liberty (second version)
1909 Seal of New York
1909 Flatiron Building
1911 Atlas Holding up Tiffany Building
1923 Woolworth Building
1929 Statue of Liberty (third version)
1939 New York World's Fair

We show photographs of three of the Tiffany souvenir spoons listed in the 1893 *Blue Book:* The Forget-me-not floral spoon (Fig. 177), the Columbus spoon, and the first version of the Statue of Liberty spoon (Fig. 178). We also illustrate Tiffany's original working drawings of three of their later souvenir spoons (Fig. 179): the Admiral Dewey (1898), the Hudson-Fulton (1909), and the Flatiron Building (1909).

Figure 180 shows Atlas holding up a coinlike disc on which is depicted the Tiffany Building. This is the famous nine-foot wooden Atlas holding a clock that has adorned the front of all Tiffany stores since 1854. The drawing of the Tiffany Atlas spoon with its note of Louis Comfort Tiffany's change in its design indicates a part he played in Tiffany & Co. at a time when his major

177 *Forget-me-not,* souvenir spoon.

121

178

energies were devoted to the Tiffany Studios. It is most interesting that he would have become involved in a minor design detail of a souvenir spoon, even if it was one which pictured the store itself.[6]

178   Souvenir spoons. *(Left)* Chicago Columbian Exposition, 1893. *(Right)* New York, Statue of Liberty. Length of both spoons: 5 13/16 in. (14.8 cm.). Mark on Chicago Spoon: NO. 38. Mark on New York Spoon: TIFFANY & CO STERLING. *(Albany Institute of History and Art).*

179   Original Tiffany drawings for souvenir spoons.

179a

179a   *Admiral Dewey* 1898

179b   *Hudson-Fulton* 1909

179c   *Flatiron Building* 1909

179b   *179c*

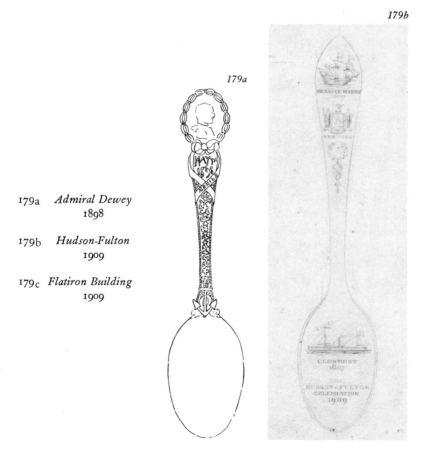
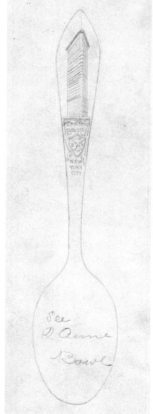

180   Original drawing of Tiffany Building spoon
with change *ordered* (written over twice and
underlined for emphasis) by Louis Comfort
Tiffany on May 17, 1907. The spoon was originally designed by Paulding Farnham in 1905 but
was not actually offered for sale until 1911.

6. Silver Out of the Dining Room

SILVER ARTICLES were used throughout the Victorian house and many personal articles were made of silver. The number and variety of such pieces are so great we can only illustrate a sampling. In order to show some idea of the range of household and personal silver made by Tiffany & Co. in the latter part of the nineteenth century we will list items and prices from two typical *Blue Books:* the 1880 and the 1893 editions. Unfortunately none of the nineteenth-century editions of the *Blue Book* was illustrated.

The first silver article usually encountered in a Victorian house was the card tray or card receiver in the front hall. In rare cases one might have entered the house through a front door with a silver knob, a silver door knocker, and a silver name plate. We know of no examples in New York but such door furnishings still exist on the whaling mansions on Main Street on Nantucket Island.

The card tray was a necessity in the Victorian house. Everyone carried cards. The ritual of calling cards was so complicated that the etiquette books of the time had long and detailed chapters on how and when to use or not to use them. For example, here are two short paragraphs from the twenty-one page chapter, "Visiting Cards and Their Uses," from Florence Howe Hall's *Social Customs* published in 1887:

In making a first call, a card should be left for each lady of the family; where there are several young ladies who are sisters, and their mother is living, it suffices to leave two cards,—one for the mother and one for the daughters. A lady also leaves the cards of her own immediate family, in making the first call of the season, including those of her husband.

One married lady in calling upon another leaves two of

181 Card salver with die-rolled border on four Chinese scrolled feet. Engraved monogram ER for Ella Rivers (Mrs. Edward King). About 1873. Width: 9 in. (22.8 cm.). Height: 3/4 in. (1.9 cm.). Mark: NO. 16 (1888/2354/9). *(The Preservation Society of Newport County, Rhode Island).*

her husband's cards,—one for the lady of the house and the other for the husband. Even if admitted, the caller leaves these cards on the hall table. [P. 44]

The Victorians *needed* their Florence Howe Halls!

Card trays were usually silver, often in the form of a small dish. Sometimes salvers—round or square—with feet were used. Figure 181 is an example of the latter. In the 1893 *Blue Book* sterling card trays were listed at $25 to $50.

Silver card cases, often beautifully engraved, were made for carrying calling cards. The small case in Figure 182 was probably for calling cards in spite of the playing card symbols. It is too thin to hold a deck of playing cards.

The use of silver inkwells or inkstands was widespread in the post–Civil War era. They seemed to have been real status symbols and many famous and powerful men had them on their desks. There was a Tiffany inkwell on Lincoln's desk in the White House at the time of his assassination.

The inkstand of LeGrand Lockwood (see p. 53) is shown in Figure 183. This rather strange piece is based on classical motifs. It is an amusing conceit to have the chubby cherubs holding the inkwell.

The handsome inkstand in Figure 184 was involved in an odd and unusual story coming out of the 1976 U.S. bicentennial celebration. A television newscast in the summer of 1976 showed President Gerald Ford examin-

182 Card case etched with spades, hearts, diamonds, and clubs, slightly curved or bowed. Engraved FJB. Made about 1905. Length: 3 3/16 in. (9.7 cm.). Mark (in line): TIFFANY & CO. 16046 MAKERS 603 STERLING 925/1000 C. (*The Smithsonian Institution*).

183 Inkwell and stand with gilt silver inset. Cast cherubs and handles, engraved lid. Made about 1867. Length: 11 1/8 in. (28.2 cm.). Height: 5 1/2 in. (13.9 cm.). Mark: NO. 14 (1940/3050). (*Lockwood-Mathews Mansion Museum, Norwalk, Connecticut*).

182

183

184 Inkstand with two inkwells, cast handle and cast animal feet. The engraved inscription on the tray reads CENTENNIAL WELCOME between a sword and a sheathed sword. Engraved on the left-hand lid is "1776" and a pine tree in a shield. On the right-hand lid is "1876" and a shield with stars and stripes. Length: 8 1/4 in. (21 cm.). Height: 6 1/4 in. (15.9 cm.). Mark: NO. 16 (2889/1752). *(Architect of the Capitol of the United States)*.

ing this same Tiffany inkstand which had recently been removed from a safe that had been in the United States Capitol since 1877.

The idea of a depository, filled with historical material linking the 1876 centennial with the expected bicentennial celebration in 1976, was conceived by Mrs. Charles F. Deihm of New York City, a publisher, a Civil War widow, and a very determined woman.

The 64-inch high safe was exhibited at the Centennial Exposition in Philadelphia in 1876. At the exposition it attracted much attention, providing publicity for Mrs. Deihm's ambitious program to collect autographs and photographs of presidents and their cabinets, the Supreme Court, members of Congress, top Army and Navy officers, governors, business leaders, and "men and women of mark." Her goal was 100,000 signatures. Visitors to the exposition were invited to autograph pages of the large albums for inclusion in the safe. In addition to the autographs and photographs, books, collections of poems, and miscellaneous literature were deposited in the safe. Of tangible value was the Tiffany inkstand holding two pens of gold and mother-of-pearl used to autograph the books.

At the close of the exposition, Mrs. Deihm, armed with a letter of introduction from President Rutherford B. Hayes, toured the country to gather additional photographs and signatures for her albums.

In December 1877, the safe was moved to the United States Capitol where it was displayed in the old House Chamber—known as Statuary Hall. In 1879 Congress passed a law prohibiting such exhibits in Statuary Hall, and the safe was placed under the east central portico of the Capitol. There it remained semi-protected, yet exposed to the elements, for nearly eighty years. In 1958 the heavy safe was moved to a closeted area off the crypt to allow work on the extension of the east front of the Capitol.

In 1976 the centennial safe was opened in a ceremony under the direction of the Joint Committee on Arrangements for the Bicentennial, chaired by Congresswoman Lindy Boggs. The books were there, including one on temperance by Mrs. Elizabeth Thompson, as was the Tiffany inkwell. But not the three large books of autographs; they had disappeared without a trace.

Boxes of all kinds have had a continuing fascination. Tiffany's silver boxes were made in a variety of sizes and shapes and decorations. Even today some of the most attractive and well-designed silver items in Tiffany's are their boxes. We illustrate a box with lid and drawings for three match boxes, all displaying an unexpected sense of humor. Conscious whimsy and humor were not the most prominent characteristics of Tiffany silver, or Victorian silver in general, so we welcome these pieces. The charming little box with the engraving of a pair of spectacles with a broken glass and the date 1888 engraved on the front (Fig. 185) and a check for ten dollars engraved on the rear (Fig. 186) is most interesting. Nothing is known of the history of the box, but the conjecture is that F. B. Cushing broke Fred E. Gilbert's spectacles in 1888 and this was his way of repaying him. It is a delightful and amusing piece.

The three working drawings for match boxes in Figure 187 are downright cute. The giraffe with his extraordinary neck, the injured cat being taunted by his bird friend, and momma mouse with her key (to the cheese box) are, unfortunately, rare excursions (for Tiffany)

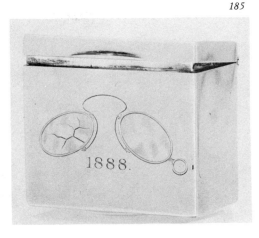

185

186

185 Box with hinged lid. Engraved with spectacles and the date "1888." Height: 2 in. (5 cm.). Mark: TIFFANY & CO STERLING. (*Private Collection*).

186 Back side of box in Fig. 185 showing engraved lid and pseudo bank check: "No. New York 1888 / GARFIELD NATIONAL BANK / Pay to the order of / Fred E. Gilbert / Ten Dollars / $10 F. B. Cushing."

127

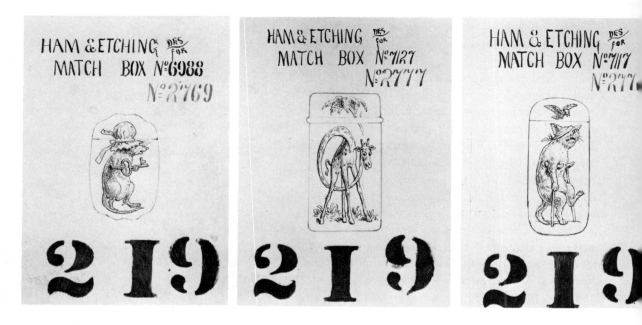

187 Original Tiffany hammering and etching designs for match boxes, dated 1882.

188 Candy dish in the form of a shell with rustic pine branch to form feet and cast head of an Egyptian lady with oak leaves and pine cones. Length: 7 3/4 in. (19.7 cm.). Mark: NO. 15 (2442/5587). (*Burt Collection*).

into light humor. It would have been fun to have had more.

Silver dishes for bonbons and other edibles were available in a variety of forms and sizes. The shell with classical head (Fig. 188), made in the late 1860s, has realistic tree branch feet much like the silver of the 1850s.

Vases have always been a popular item in Tiffany silver. They could be used for flowers or as an item of display by themselves. The small vase in Figure 189 with its classically simple shape is decorated only with the two rams' heads and monogram. This restraint is no longer felt in the two vases in Figures 190 and 191. The vase in Figure 190 is decorated in the *Chrysanthemum* pattern with regularly spaced, swaying stems. The three-handled cup in Figure 191 with repousséd cherubs, roses, and acanthus leaves is a presentation piece dated June 15, 1892. It was made about 1890.

We show two pieces of so-called personal silver, that is, silver worn or carried on a person: a small silver pocket flask owned by the Vanderbilt Mansion, Hyde Park, New York and a sterling Spanish-type handmade back comb. The flask in Figure 192 is oval in shape with a flat and slightly curving profile. Both the flask and the circular cap are of elaborately chased silver. The front of the flask is dominated by a large bird with outstretched wings and arched neck. The flowering plant upon which it is perched branches to encircle it; two doves perch on

189

191

190

189   Vase with cast rams' heads. Made by
Moore for Tiffany about 1860. Height: 7 3/4 in.
(19.7 cm.). Mark: TIFFANY & CO / M / STERLING.
1076/9215. (*Private Collection*).

190   Vase with chrysanthemum decorations.
Made about 1905. Height: 11 3/4 in. (29.7 cm.).
Mark: NO. 22 (13206/4945). (*Museum of Art,
Carnegie Institute, Pittsburgh, Pennsylvania*).

191   Three-handled cup, repoussé chased with
angelic cherubs emerging from stylized acanthus
leaves. Dated June 15th, 1892. Height: 8 7/8 in.
(22.6 cm.). Mark: NO. 19 (521/1961 "6 1/2
pints." (*Burt Collection*).

192

193

each side in the shelter of its wings. The back of the flask is chased with a chrysanthemum plant with blossoms symmetrically arranged around a large central flower. It is framed by a border of laurel leaves. The sides of the flask are decorated with a stylized floral design, and the rim of the cap by a border of flowers.

The sterling Spanish-type back comb in Figure 193 has an astonishing amount of handwork on it for a piece of silver of this kind. There are more than seventy handmade cutouts piercing the decorative fan, with a considerable amount of line and bright cut engraving on both the front and back. There is approximately two days of handwork on this piece according to present-day Tiffany engravers.

A wide assortment of silver items were used on ladies' dressing tables. Combs, brushes, jars, pill boxes, glove stretchers, nail files, and fingernail polishers came in patterns ranging from plain or simply engraved pieces to the elaborate repoussé pieces shown in Figure 194 and Plate III. Repoussé dressing table silver was very popular in the latter part of the nineteenth century and many companies made it. Unless it is marked, it is often difficult to know the maker since so many firms made similar designs. These pieces were not repoussé chased with hand tools in the way a hollow-ware bowl would have been made, but were stamped out from thin sheet metal and then applied to the appropriate wood, plastic, or base metal shapes. The designs are not usually very well integrated—the whole surface is simply covered with flowers and leaves and occasional rococo flourishes.

Figure 195 shows twelve pieces from a very elegant gilt dresser set of the 1890s decorated with cast symbols

192 Oval flask chased with a large bird and two doves on each of the two flowering branches. On the back of the flask is a large chrysanthemum plant with blossoms arranged around a large central flower. Made about 1880. Height: 5 1/8 in. (13 cm.). Mark: TIFFANY & CO. 3529 M 6408 STERLING SILVER. (*Vanderbilt National Historical Site, Hyde Park, N. Y.*).

193 Handmade and hand-decorated back comb of the 1870s. Length: 5 7/8 in. (14.9 cm.). Mark: STERLING TIFFANY & CO 69. (*Private Collection*).

130

of amour: buds, flowers, cupids, musical instruments, bows and arrows, and quivers. The pieces are from a matched set, and all have the same order number (7884). The Tiffany records call the pattern *Cupids and Flowers* and *Princess Hatzfeldt*.

In addition to silver sets, Tiffany also made some sumptuous solid gold dressing sets.

Silver Out of the Dining Room in the 1880 Blue Book

The following items from the 1880 *Blue Book* are pieces that would normally be used in rooms of a house other than the dining room. This is not meant to be a rigid classification. Obviously many items of silver such as candlesticks, small trays, and tea and coffee services were not confined to any one room in the house. The 1880 *Blue Book* was divided into a number of sections and we excerpt the household and personal silver from the sections "Presents for Ladies," "Presents for Gentlemen," and "Presents for Infants." It is difficult to translate the 1880 prices listed below into 1978 prices but a rough rule of thumb is to multiply the 1880 prices by a factor of ten to find an approximate equivalent of present-day prices.

194 Dresser set with repoussé floral designs of composite flowers, wild roses, ferns, and violets. All pieces made by Tiffany & Co. in the 1880s except the whisk broom on the right by Howard & Co. and the hairbrush third from right by Gorham. The Tiffany brush (second from right) is engraved "JANUARY 16, 1888 L.D.B." Length of Tiffany hair brush: 8 1/4 in. (21 cm.). Mark: TIFFANY & CO STERLING. (*Brooklyn Museum*).

131

Belt and Cloak Clasps

All silver, $7 to $75. Some of the new hammered silver, with enrichments of other metals and colored alloys.

Belts

Leather, velvet, and silver, $7 to $100.

Bon-bon Boxes

Silver, Limoges enamel, to carry in the pocket, $12 to $50. Some larger ones of hammered silver, decorated with raised fruits and flowers in colored alloys and laminated metals.

Bouquet Holders

Silver, for the hand, $10.50 to $16.

Call Bells

Silver, $10 to $100.

195 A gilt silver dresser set with pincushion, two toilet bottles, a shoehorn, powder box, puff box, hairpin tray, clothes brush, hairbrush, mirror, comb, nail file and buff, and scissors. Monogram MEP. Height of toilet bottle: 7 3/4 in. (19.7 cm.). Mark: TIFFANY & CO. T. (Collection of Annette K. Diehl).

Card Cases
  With silver edges or corners, $4.50 to $15. Some with
  gold mountings as high as $175.
Chatelaines
  Silver, with one or more pendants for fan, smelling bot-
  tles, and other articles. Plain and variously enriched, $6
  to $100.
Combs
  Richly chased or engraved silver, $4.75 to $30.
Dog Collars
  Leather and velvet, silver mounted, and all silver, $6
  upwards.
Fan Holders
  Worn as chatelaine. Plain bright, "hammered," pierced
  or enameled gold, and with ornamentation of birds,
  foliage, etc., in relief, $24 and upwards. Some of plain
  or "hammered" silver oxidized or with enrichments of
  colored alloys of other metals are very novel and elegant,
  and cost from $10 upwards. Plain silver ones are as low
  as $4.
Garters
  With silver clasps, $6.50 to $30; gold, $20 to $85, and
  upwards, and some richly enameled and jeweled ones at
  higher prices.
Glass Toilet Bottles and Boxes
  For tooth-brush, powder, lip salve, soap, etc., with plain
  and engraved silver tops, or tops decorated with colored
  alloys in the new Japanese-American style. They range
  in price from $5 for the smallest and plainest, to $38 for
  the largest and most elaborate. Bags, cases, or trays for
  bureau drawers, are fitted with these to order, or they
  are sold singly as required.
Glove Boxes
  Gilt, $28 to $60.
Hair Brushes
  Ivory; oval and oblong, with plain and twist handles,
  $5 to $15.50. Tortoise-shell, $10 to $20; some with rich
  silver handles, and others with handles of plain wood.
Hair Ornaments of Silver
  Arrows, daggers, pins with pendants, and other novel
  articles, $5 to $20.
Odor Bottles
  Silver, $40 to $250, pair. Richly cut glass, $3 to $28.
Paper Cutters
  Buffalo horn, silver-mounted, $13; tortoise-shell, $4 to
  $20; Silver, $8 to $75 and others of bronze, gilt, and
  polished brass.
  The Stanley paper cutters, natural tusks, $30 to $60.

Photograph Frames

Gilt, from $10 to $40. Some very rich ones with doors that open for two pictures, $65; polished brass, $8 to $12; wood, with nickel mountings, $4; velvet, $5; with two doors opening in center, $15; folding for two pictures, $15; for small card, $3.50; with two doors, $13, Russia leather, plain, $5; for small card, $3. These frames are made in MESSRS. TIFFANY & CO.'s own shops, and are quite unlike any others.

Puff Powder Boxes

Ivory, $7 to $25; Silver, $15 for a small plain one, up to $100, or even higher. Some are very richly ornamented with designs of fruits and flowers in other metals and colored alloys.

Sets of Brushes

Ivory or silver handles, in cases, $35 to $350.

Shopping-Bags

Of leather and velvet, with elaborate silver clasps, monograms and other ornaments, $9 to $100.

Silver Jewelry

Lace pins and brooches, $2 to $10; scarf pins, $1 to $8; sleeve buttons, $3 to $10; ear-rings, $1.25 to $7.50; hair pins with ornamental heads, $5 to $20; combs, $4.50 to $30; belt clasps, $7 to $45; chatelaines from $6; necklaces, $10 to $35; lockets, $6 to $25; bracelets and bangles, $1.50 to $30; shopping bracelets with pencil attached, $20.

Silver Link Purses

These novel and pretty purses are made of joined rings of silver like chain armor. Some have one and some two pockets and silver clasps. The prices are $4.50 to $9.

Silver-Mounted Umbrellas

With crutch and other handles, ornamented with colored alloys on a hammered surface, $24 to $30.

Silver Portrait Frames

With secret for opening, from $30.

Tape Measures

Thimbles

Plain, Etruscan, engraved, faceted, or enameled gold, $5 to $12. Some richly jeweled at higher prices. Silver, plain, 30 to 50 cents; ornamented borders, $1.25, all sizes.

Traveling Inkstands

Leather and silver, plain and richly ornamented, $1.50, $1.75, $2.50, $5, $10 to $36.

Umbrellas

Tiffany & Co.'s umbrellas are made of superior English silk, woven for the purpose, and more pliable and closer than the ordinary weighted or prepared silks, which are liable to cut. A great variety of beautiful and curious natural sticks are tastefully mounted with or without silver or gilt tip cups, $11 to $15. Mourning umbrellas, with black sticks, and long black onyx handles, $12 to $35. Silver and other fancy handles, $12 to $35.

PRESENTS FOR GENTLEMEN

Ash Receivers
Silver, $8 to $40.

Beer Mugs
Silver, with glass bottom, $30, $55, to $100.

Bell Trays
Silver, $14 to $18.50

Bells
Silver, for library or dinner-table, $10 to $100.

Bottle Handle
For holding bottle of champagne or other wine when pouring, silver, $24.

Canes
Malacca and other woods, with ivory, tortoise-shell, silver, and gold handles, $2 to $75. Some of the new crutch-handles of hammered silver with enrichments of colored alloys and other metals, $15 to $45. These are exclusively made by TIFFANY & CO.

Card Cases
$2 to $24. Some with costly gold mountings. Some with letter case combined and with secret locks, $5 to $11.

Casters with three bottles
Silver of individual use, $25 to $40.

Cigarette Cases
For the pocket, silver, leather with silver mountings, ivory, and tortoise-shell, $4 to $32.

Claret Pitchers
With silver lids, $25 to $100. Glass with silver mountings.

Compasses
Set in various nautical devices of gold, $7 to $10. Silver in gimbal balls and other forms, $2 to $6.50.

Decanters
With silver mountings, for claret and other wines, $25 to $75 each.

Dressing Cases
With silver or silver-plated fittings, $18 and upwards.

Drinking Cups
That telescope and close compactly. Silver, $14 to $30.

Funnels
Silver, $14 to $30.

Glass Toilet Bottles and Boxes
With silver tops, $2.50 to $38.

Horses' Bits

Silver, made to order.

Inkstands

Bronze, silver, polished brass, marble, and glass, for the library, and leather, silver, and other metals, for traveling, $4 to $200.

Match Boxes

For the pocket. Silver, $5 to $42. Gold, $35 to $135. The $5 solid sterling silver match boxes are made both bright and satin finished, and make useful, handsome, and inexpensive presents.

Match Stands

Silver, bronze, and leather; for house use, $5 upwards.

Nutmeg Graters

Silver, $5.50 to $15.

Paper Cutters

Silver, ivory, tortoise-shell, lacquered and gilt and enameled, $2.50 to $45.

Penholders

Ivory, mother-of-pearl, and silver, handsomely mounted for the library, $2.75 and upwards.

Punch Ladles

Silver, $18 to $110.

Punch Bowls

Silver, $200 to $1,000.

Scissors

Some to fold up, for the pocket, 75 cts. to $8 for silver-mounted ones.

Segar Cases

$5 to $50. Richer gold-mounted ones made to order.

Segar Lighters

Flint, steel, and combustible wick, with silver or gold mountings, for the pocket, $4.50 to $85.

Segar Lighters

Silver. With alcohol lamps for the dinner-table, from $30.

Shaving Cups

Silver; some with strainer for soap, and others with attachment in which to burn alcohol to heat the water.

Silver-mounted Corks

Plain and with ornamental silver tops, $2 to $25 each.

Silver Jewelry

Silver Rules

6 or 12 inches, $12 and $20.

Silver Trowels

For use at ceremonious laying of corner-stones, $50 to $75.

Silver Wax-taper Case and Match Box Combined

Carried in the pocket, furnish a ready light at all times, $12.

Siphons
Silver, for decanting liquors, $22 to $70. Plated, $6.50.
Snuff Boxes
Silver, from $12.
Suspender Mountings
Gold and Silver, $12 to $125.
Tankards and Loving Cups
$90 to $500.
Thermometers [see Fig. 196]
$4.50 to $80.
Tobacco Boxes
Silver, for the pocket, from $12.
Toddy Kettles
Silver, $110 to $220. T. & Co.s hard-metal silver-soldered plated ware, $37.50 to $60.
Traveling Candlestick Lantern
Silver, for use in stateroom of vessel, or to hang from lapel of coat, or from back of car seat in traveling. Closes compactly. $50.
Water Pitchers
Silver, $75 to $750.
Whistles
Gold, of many styles, to hang from watch-chain, $8.50 to $28. Silver, some with match-box and compass combined, $4.50 to $9.
Wine Coolers
Silver, $225 to $700.
Wine Labels
Silver, $1.50 to $15.
Wine Stands
Silver, with two or three bottles, $160 to $250.

PRESENTS FOR INFANTS

Silver Pap Boats
$15 to $28 and upwards.
Silver Plates
$18 to $70.
Silver Knife and Fork, in case
$8 to $18.
Silver Knife, Fork, and Spoon, in case
$8 to $50.
Silver Fork, Spoon, and Napkin Ring, in case
$12.
Silver Sets
Including all or any part of the above, put up in handsome cases, $30 to $400.
Silver Rattles
$4.50 to $20.

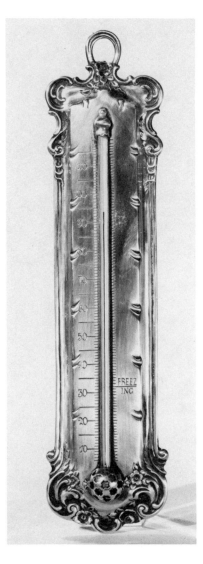

196 Thermometer on silver frame, made around 1895. Height: 9 1/4 in. (23.5 cm.). Mark on back: TIFFANY & CO / STERLING. (Brooklyn Museum).

137

Coral and Silver Bells
$4.50 to $25.
Biting Pieces
Mother-of-pearl, silver-mounted, $4 to $10.
Silver Mugs
$8 to $75.
Silver Cups and Saucers
$25 to $80.
Silver Bowls and Saucers
$27 to $150.
Silver Porringers
$20 to $85.
Napkin Rings
$1.50 to $25.
Feeding Spoons
$1.50 to $10.
Feeding Trays
Sterling silver, $60 to $150.
Finger Rings
$1 to $15.
Safety Pins
Of gold and silver, from $1.50.
Toilet Sets
Ivory-handled brushes, with puff-box, comb, and rattle, in case, from $20.

A pleasing style of decoration for children's cups, bowls, spoons, and other articles, is the adaptation of characters from *Mother Goose,* sometimes with an explanatory line from the verse illustrated. Cups adorned in this way, range in price from $30 upwards.

The 1893 Blue Book

The types of silver made and sold by Tiffany & Co. changed constantly over the whole last half of the nineteenth century. There were a number of items in the 1893 *Blue Book* which were not mentioned in the 1880 edition. For example, in 1893 ecclesiastical silver was being advertised: alms basins, baptismal bowls, chalices, christening bowls, communion sets, processional crosses, croziers, and flagons, patens, and pyx for communion purposes.

Cocktail mixers and cocktail strainers were new items in the 1893 *Blue Book* along with traveling clocks in silver cases. The latter cost from $125 to $800. The 1893 *Blue Book* featured antique Dutch silver and modern Russian silver. There were eight pages listing Russian silver, ranging from enameled bonbon spoons for $10 to enameled and silver-gilt jewel caskets from $100 to $250. The *Blue Book* noted:

Tiffany & Co., recognizing the continued favor of Russian silver with their patrons, have made preparations to meet an increased demand for this ware, and in their stock this season will be found a large selection of the choicest examples of the most artistic of Russian productions. Noted alike for their fine niello and gilt work, and for the rich color of their beautiful transparent smooth and raised enamelling.

An interesting example of the kind of Russian enameled silver sold by Tiffany's is shown in Figure 197. The architectural salt and pepper with onion domes have decorative touches of blue, white, and red enamels; they were made by A. Kuzmichev.

197 Russian salt and pepper, gilt with touches of white, blue, and red enamels. Heights: *(left)* 3 7/8 in. (9.8 cm.), *(right)* 4 13/16 in. (12.2 cm.). Mark: "A.A/ 1896/ 84/ DOUBLE EAGLE/ AK" plus "MADE FOR TIFFANY & CO." (*Collection of Harry Hilbert*).

7. Presentation Silver

198 Massive water pitcher made by Moore for Tiffany in 1859. Within the cartouche is the engraved inscription "To Col. I. A. Duryea this TESTIMONIAL IS PRESENTED on his retireing [*sic*] from the Colonelcy of the SEVENTH REGIMENT NATIONAL GUARD as a mark of high appreciation. From his Fellow Citizens for his soldierlike qualities and for the valuable services rendered by the Regiment during the eleven Years that he commanded it. New York, 1859." Height: 14 3/4 in. (37.5 cm.). Mark: NO. 10 (1004/6248). (*Museum of the City of New York, Bequest of Emily Frances Whitney Briggs*).

IN HER ADMIRABLE PAPER on "Presentation Pieces" Margaret Klapthor of the Smithsonian Institution had this to say about presentation silver:

The custom of giving a piece of silver to an individual in recognition of services or in appreciation of accomplishment probably began as soon as man developed the fashioning of that metal into objects. Such a presentation piece was a tangible and durable form of recognition which could be appreciated, used, displayed, and enjoyed by the recipient. Many of these silver pieces became for succeeding generations the cherished evidence of recognition accorded to an ancestor, and they were preserved long after the more customary family silver had worn out or been lost.[1]

Presentation silver not only has a long history in classical Western cultures, it is also part of the past of the Far East. Marco Polo, in telling how the Great Khan rewarded his leaders, said:

Upon their respective merits he advances them in his service, raising those who commanded a hundred men to the command of a thousand, and presenting many with vessels of silver, as well as the customary tablets or warrants of authority.

The tablets given to those commanding a hundred men are of silver; to those commanding a thousand, of gold or silver gilt; and those who command ten thousand receive tablets of gold, bearing the head of a lion.[2]

Tiffany & Co. from the beginning sold silver presentation pieces and they represented an important part of their silverware business, not only from an income point of view but also for their advertising and public relations value. Presentation pieces often received wide publicity in the nineteenth century and no doubt introduced many customers to Tiffany's household silverware. We have already illustrated some of the most famous and noteworthy Tiffany presentation pieces in Chapters 2 and 3. Such pieces as the gold box given to Cyrus Field in 1858 (Fig. 10), Tom Thumb's horse and coach (Fig. 28), the Bryant Vase (Fig. 33), and the Gladstone Testimonial (Fig. 35) were newsmaking pieces, famous in their time, which have a continuing interest.

Tiffany's presentation silver falls into three distinct categories. For convenience we treat each in a separate chapter:

7. Presentation Silver (hollow ware)
8. Presentation Swords and Guns
9. Yachting and Other Sporting Trophies

Tiffany's hollow-ware presentation pieces were of two kinds: those that were custom designed for the occasion, and stock pieces which were used "as is" after being suitably engraved. We have already illustrated in Chapter 2 two such "stock" presentation pieces: the Four Seasons Centerpiece in Figure 17 and the service presented to Admiral du Pont for his services at the 1853 New York Exposition (Fig. 21).

Many of Tiffany's presentation pieces are more interesting for their historical associations and the men they honored than they are as works of art. The designers sometimes overloaded these objects with ornament. Such ornamentation may have obvious symbolic meanings but often it was poorly integrated into the overall design. An example is the large 1859 water pitcher in Figure 198. It has a strong martial air and the armor, the leopard on the handle, the flags, and the cannonballs almost make one forget about its stylistic derivations. Its rococo and Renaissance decorations are characteristic of the 1850s but the literal storytelling quality of its warlike applied and repoussé ornamentation has a stronger meaning to us today than do the style notes. It seems to clearly forecast the Civil War to come.

The silver gilt ewer or pitcher with hinged lid (Fig. 199) which was given to Abraham Lincoln in honor of his inauguration in 1861 is, stylistically, a transition piece. The angular handle with cast head and the Greek key borders with beading show remnants of Greek revivalism, but the flat stylized, *néo-grec* engraved surfaces are characteristic of the middle and late 1860s. Note also the contrast between the martial helmet on the lid and the sweet

199   Classical pitcher with hinged lid presented to Abraham Lincoln at the time of his first inaugural. Made by Moore for Tiffany, ca. 1861. Height: 13 1/2 in. (34.3 cm.). Mark: NO. 10 (809-2/5790). *(The Smithsonian Institution).*

200 The great seal of the United States engraved on the Lincoln pitcher in Fig. 199. Around the seal is inscribed "FOR THE PRESIDENT OF THE UNITED STATES — ABRAHAM LINCOLN — FROM HIS WASHINGTON FRIENDS — MARCH 4, 1861." (*The Smithsonian Institution*).

classical face on the handle.

The engraved Great Seal of the United States on the Lincoln ewer (Fig. 200) includes thirty-three stars for the states in the Union. This was one short of the actual number of states on March 4, 1861 since Kansas had been admitted to the Union on January 29, 1861 as the thirty-fourth state. In addition, the number of stars in the seal completely ignored the fact that seven states—South Carolina, Mississippi, Florida, Alabama, Georgia, Louisiana, and Texas—had already seceded from the Union to form the Confederate States of America by the time of Lincoln's inauguration on March 4, 1861. The War Between the States had not really started yet (Fort Sumter was not attacked until April 12) but the die was cast. In the weeks following Lincoln's inauguration four more states initiated secession—Virginia, Arkansas, Tennessee, and North Carolina.

Both the Lincoln ewer and the Duryea pitcher in Figure 198 have obvious deficiencies as works of art, but both are well made from a silversmithing point of view and both are important historically. They are characteristic and poignant mementos of their times.

142

The covered sugar bowl in Figure 201 is one of the most interesting pieces of Tiffany's presentation silver, both as an object and for its historical associations. The sugar bowl was part of a five-piece set presented to Alban C. Stimers of the *Monitor* by Captain John Ericsson. The inscription reads:

Presented to / Alban C. Stimers C H Eng. USN / To Commemorate Important Services / Rendered to His Country / on Board / THE MONITOR / Before and During Her Memorable Conflict / THE MERRI-MACK / In Hampton Roads / March 9th 1862.

The finial on the lid is made up of a Watts type centrifugal governor (used for regulating the speed of engines), a cannon, and a bayonet. There are applied rope borders encircling the inscription on top and a border of anchors around the middle. The classical handles display heads of Neptune.

The silverware memorializes one of the pivotal events of the Civil War, the famous battle between the *Monitor* and the *Merrimack* at Hampton Roads. John Ericsson,

201 Sugar bowl, part of a five-piece tea set presented to Alban C. Stimers of the *Monitor* by Capt. Ericsson. Dated March 9th, 1862. Height: 6 in. (15.2 cm.). Mark: NO. 10 (1000/8392). (*The New-York Historical Society*).

202 Five-piece tea and coffee service made ca.
1868. On each piece is engraved a paddle-wheel
steamboat. On opposite side of pot is the inscription "PRESENTED TO/ PETER B. ANDERSON/ BY
THE/ OLD DOMINION STEAMSHIP CO./ 1868."
Height of coffeepot: 9 in. (22.8 cm.). Mark: NO.
14 (1516/2740). *(Brooklyn Museum)*.

one of the great inventors and engineers of the nineteenth
century (he had already developed the "caloric" engine
and "invented" a screw or rotary propeller for ships),
designed and helped build the ironclad *Monitor* for the
United States Navy. The Ericsson design of the *Monitor*
with its low profile deck and armored revolving turret
was to revolutionize naval design in the future. Although the actual battle between the *Monitor* and the
Merrimack on April 9, 1862 was inconclusive, the ideas
of iron- (or steel-) clad warships and the revolving gun
turret were proven once and for all.

Alban C. Stimers was a volunteer on board the *Monitor*
as an observer for the Navy with the title of Chief Engineer. Stimers was a well-known Navy engineer who had
once served as chief engineer on the old *Merrimack*.
Although he was mainly aboard as an observer, he
volunteered to operate the turret machinery and served
heroically in the actual battle. Later, in fact, Ericsson

made it clear that any success of the *Monitor* at Hampton Roads was directly attributable to Stimers being at Captain John Worder's side during the battle.

The battle of the *Monitor* and the *Merrimack* propelled John Ericsson to world fame and the Tiffany tea set was his expression of gratitude to Alban Stimers.

The coffee and the tea service in Figure 202 was presented to Peter B. Anderson in 1868. Each piece of the Anderson service is engraved with a Currier and Ives type paddle-wheel steamship with flags flying (Fig. 203). This is the type of presentation silver that must have been most welcome to the recipient. It was a useful, well-designed set, attractively engraved.

203 Detail of coffeepot in Fig. 202.

204 The Thomas Nast vase. Inscription: "THIRTY SIX MEMBERS/ OF THE/ UNION LEAGUE CLUB/ UNITE IN PRESENTING THIS VASE/ TO/ THOMAS NAST/ AS A TOKEN OF THEIR ADMIRATION/ OF HIS GENIUS AND OF HIS ARDENT DEVOTION/ OF THAT GENIUS TO THE PRESERVATION OF HIS/ COUNTRY FROM THE SCHEMES OF REBELLION/ APRIL 1869." Height: 15 in. (38.1 cm.). Mark: NO. 14 (2179/3824). *(The Metropolitan Museum of Art, Gift of Mrs. Thomas Nast, 1907).*

203

204

The parcel gilt Thomas Nast vase in Figure 204 is oval in shape, with gadrooning on the foot, base of the body, and shoulder. It has applied putti fighting dragons with spears in the form of charcoal holders. (Putti are representations of children in swaddling bands, much used in Italian art.) The charcoal holders were symbolic of the drawing instruments used by Thomas Nast in making his brilliant, highly influential cartoons of the Civil War and the post–Civil War era. His caricatures in *Harpers Weekly* and other publications helped mold public opinion of the time. His fierce cartoon attacks on Boss Tweed in the 1869–1872 period were a major force in overthrowing the corrupt Tweed ring in New York. Nast also invented the symbols for the two American political parties—the Democratic donkey and the Republican elephant.

The Nast Vase (which was incidentally once a candidate for de-accession by the Metropolitan Museum of

145

205 Presentation fireman's speaking trumpet made ca. 1880. *(A nineteenth-century photograph from the Tiffany files).*

Art) has a classical symbolism that looks very Victorian to us. Nevertheless, once the symbols are understood, we can see that the vase does have a kind of baroque power, and it does fittingly honor a man who truly deserves the word "fearless."

Figure 205 shows a Tiffany presentation speaking trumpet for a fireman. This photograph from the Tiffany files has no identification but we believe it was from the 1870s or early 1880s. These most interesting objects were a favorite gift for firemen in the nineteenth century. They are found both in sterling and silver electroplate. This trumpet, which is the only Tiffany example we know of, is most elaborately decorated with repoussé work and chasing.

The delightful three-handled cup in Figure 206, with its ivy-clad base and handles, and body etched with a view of the Yale campus, was a presentation piece for the first child born to a member of the class of '88, Allen Trafford Klots, given on June 23, 1891.

The large complex presentation vase in Figure 207 has as its decorative theme the transportation exhibit at the 1893 Columbian Exposition in Chicago. The pace-setting portal to the building designed by the architect, Louis Sullivan, is depicted in a three-dimensional model on the front of the cup. Various methods of transportation are shown pictorially and symbolically on the cup, while center back carries the inscription:

From / American Exhibitors, / Department of Transportation Exhibits. / World's Columbian Exposition / Chicago, U.S.A., 1893, / TO / Willard A. Smith, Chief. / In commemoration of the Conception, Perfection and / Administration of the First Distinctive Transportation / Department in the History of International Expositions. / Committee [followed by names].

The Adams Gold Cup in Figure 208 is the most extravagant of Tiffany's presentation pieces. It was made in 1893 to 1895 under the supervision of Paulding Farnham for presentation to Edward Dean Adams. Adams, Chairman of the American Cotton Oil Company, "had saved the company from ruin" and a grateful board commissioned this gold vase for him since he would take no compensation.

The gold vase is studded with pearls and semiprecious stones. The base has pieces of gold quartz in it and the lid is carved rock crystal. The classical figures and the

206

207

208

206 Three-handled cup with etched view of Yale campus. On the back sides are etched a cap and gown over a tree branch and the inscription "PRESENTED TO/ OUR CLASS BOY/ ALLEN TRAFFORD KLOTS/ BY THE CLASS OF '88/ YALE COLLEGE/ JUNE 23-1891." Height: 9 7/8 in. (25.1 cm.). Mark: "TIFFANY & CO/ 10797 MAKERS 4889/ STERLING SILVER" plus "9 PINTS." *(Courtesy of Allen Klots)*.

207 Presentation vase made by Tiffany in 1893 for Willard A. Smith who organized and supervised the building of the Transportation Building (Louis Sullivan, architect) at the 1893 World's Columbian Exposition at Chicago. Height: 24 in. (61 cm.). Mark: NO. 21 (11839/5600). *(The Smithsonian Institution)*.

208 The Adams Gold Cup designed by Paulding Farnham, made in 1893–5. This solid gold vase has gold quartz in the base and a carved rock crystal lid. The piece is set with 4 large pieces of quartz, 18 pieces of rock crystal, 38 pearls, 38 garnets, 116 tourmalines, and 10 "unusually large" amethysts. Height: 19 1/2 in. (49.5 cm.). Weight: 274 ounces. Marks on underside: TIFFANY & CO./ MAKERS/ SOLID GOLD, and on a tube inside, TIFFANY & CO./ STERLING SILVER/ T. *(The Metropolitan Museum of Art, Gift of Edward D. Adams)*.

lush, jewellike Renaissance richness of the piece would have seemed to have been more appropriate for the Czar of Russia than for an American businessman, but the Tiffany designers made a big point of the American qualities of the vase. A Tiffany booklet on the vase said: "Every piece of material used, and the artist and his principal assistants, are American, which shows an independence that many countries in the old world might be proud of."

The three-handled cup with eagles on its base in Figure 209 was presented to the French ambassador, Jules Cambon, for his services in helping to end the Spanish-American War. Spain had known from the beginning

209 Three-handled cup made in 1899. Under the rim is the inscription "PRESENTED BY THE PRESIDENT OF THE UNITED STATES TO HIS EXCELLENCY M. JULES CAMBON, AMBASSADOR OF FRANCE IN TOKEN OF HIS FRIENDLY SERVICES IN THE NEGOTIATION OF THE PROTOCOL OF PEACE BETWEEN THE UNITED STATES AND SPAIN, AUGUST 12, 1898." The cartouches under the handles of the cup include the seals of the three countries involved in the negotiations in 1898: the United States, Spain, and France. Height: 13 3/4 in. (34.9 cm.). Mark: NO. 21 (14078/6606). (White House Collection).

209

211 Massive sterling tray engraved with a map of the New York City subway which was completed in 1904. Given to August Belmont, president of the Rapid Transit Subway Construction Company. Length: 37 7/8 in. (96.3 cm.). Mark: NO. 22 (16015/6070). (Museum of the City of New York, Gift of August Belmont).

that their 1898 war with the United States was hopeless, so after three months' fighting their government initiated peace negotiations through M. Cambon, the French ambassador in Washington. Hostilities ended on August 12, 1898 and the peace treaty was signed in Paris on Dec. 10, 1898. Through the war Spain lost Cuba, Puerto Rico, Guam, and the Philippines.

The trophy, which was presented to Ambassador Cambon by President McKinley in 1899, is now (1978) in the

Treaty Room of the White House. In the same White House room is a painting of the signing of the 1898 peace treaty in Paris by the French artist Theobald Chartran.

The handles of the trophy are hollow and pierced with holly leaf decorations. The three vigorously modeled eagles on the base hold in their beaks a garland symbolizing peace.

The nautical three-handled presentation cup in Figure 210 was made in 1901. It has etchings of three New York ferries with their great side-wheel paddles. The inscription is in Art Nouveau script.

The massive tray in Figure 211 is more than a yard in length and has a brusque, no-nonsense engineer's quality. It was presented to August Belmont by the Rapid Transit Railroad Commissioners for the City of New York at the completion of the New York City subway line in 1904. A map of Manhattan and the subway is engraved on the tray. Around the tray are the ties and rails of the subway and, in the vignettes, views of the subway construction with a stern portrait of Mr. Belmont in the middle. The pickaxes in the handle describe sweeping arcs, and the handles themselves are hollow openwork.

The Spanish-American War greatly increased the

210 Three-handled cup with etchings of the ferryboats *Fort Lee* (shown), *City of Englewood,* and *George Washington.* Low relief inscription: "TO/ EDWARD/ WATKINS/ LAWSON/ UPON THE COMPLETION OF/ TWELVE YEARS OF VALUED/ SERVICE AS SUPERINTENDENT,/ FROM THE OFFICERS AND DIRECTORS/ OF THE RIVERSIDE & FORT LEE/ FERRY COMPANY/ APRIL 15TH 1901." Height: 6 in. (15.3 cm.). Mark: NO. 21 (18076/3329). (*The New-York Historical Society*).

211

American consciousness of naval vessels, and battleships were very much in the public eye. The fact that these vessels were named after states was a source of great pride to the states involved. An expression of this pride was the presentation of silver services to the ships. Tiffany made two such services, one for the battleship *New York* and the other for the battleship *New Jersey*.

The *New Jersey* service is considered to be the largest and most ornate of the battleship silver services with a total of 119 pieces. Almost half the silver service, 55 pieces, was presented to the original old battleship *New Jersey* on August 14, 1907, by Governor Edward C. Stokes at ceremonies in the North River. (The tea tray was etched with a picture of the battleship.) The service was purchased from an appropriation of $10,000. The original pieces were designed by Albert A. Southwick.

Somewhere along the line (no one seems to know when) 15 more pieces were added to the set. Then in 1952 an additional 49 pieces were added, these later pieces being designed under the direction of A. L. Barney. The additions, which were purchased by Rear Admiral Francis D. McCorkle, included 18 service plates costing $5,400, 18 goblets at $2,175, 3 pepper shakers at $750, 5 salt shakers at $750, and 9 salt spoons at $91.67.

When the original 14,948-ton battleship *New Jersey* was doomed under terms of a post–World War I disarmament program and was sunk in 1923 by airplane bombing off Cape Hatteras, the original silver was turned over to the light cruiser *Trenton*. The *Trenton* went out of business in 1943, and the silver was slated to have been sent back to the vault in Philadelphia.

However, when it came time to turn the service over to the second battleship *New Jersey*, it could not be found. The Navy conducted an intensive search and it was eventually found in the Brooklyn Navy Yard. There was never any explanation of how it got there.

The only time the silver traveled with the ship in combat was when it was on the old *New Jersey*. It was during World War I with the old "J" that the huge punch bowl (Fig. 212) was struck a glancing blow by a bullet or a piece of shrapnel, which canted the bowl a bit to the side; officers who have commanded the ship since have refused to have the battle marks removed.

When the second battleship *New Jersey* was fighting in the Pacific during World War II, the silver was still in Brooklyn. It was presented to the ship when it came

out of mothballs at Bayonne, New Jersey for the Korean War and was left at Pearl Harbor while the ship was in action. At present the service is at Governor's Mansion in Princeton, New Jersey.

The service for the battleship *New York,* now in the U. S. Naval Academy in Annapolis, includes a range of objects from the decorative flower bowl in Figure 213 to the copper and silver smoking set in Figure 214. The flower bowl is topped by a sculpture of explorer Henry Hudson's *Half Moon* which entered New York harbor on September 3, 1609. The bowl has a perforated cover for the arrangement of flowers.

In the first decade of the twentieth century Tiffany made a variety of objects combining silver and copper. They made both silver objects inlaid with copper and copper objects inlaid with silver. Examples of the latter are pieces of the smoking set for the *New York* in Figure 214.

From the time of the Civil War to the present, Tiffany has made hundreds of medals. Many are distinguished examples of the art and some were designed by the lead-

212 Punch bowl and stand given to the U.S.S. Battleship *New Jersey* by the state of New Jersey in 1906. This is the largest piece of the U. S. S. *New Jersey* silver service which was used in the officers' mess. Height: 21 in. (53.3 cm.). Length of base 32 in. (81.3 cm.). *(Collection of the State of New Jersey).*

151

213 Flower bowl from the U. S. S. *New York* silver service. Height: 24 in. (61 cm.). Mark: NO. 23 (0975). *(United States Naval Academy Museum)*.

213

214 Copper and silver smoking set from the U.S.S. *New York*. Humidor height: 12 in. (30.5 cm.). Mark on all pieces: TIFFANY & CO. MAKERS 0975 STERLING SILVER & COPPER m. *(United States Naval Academy Museum)*.

214

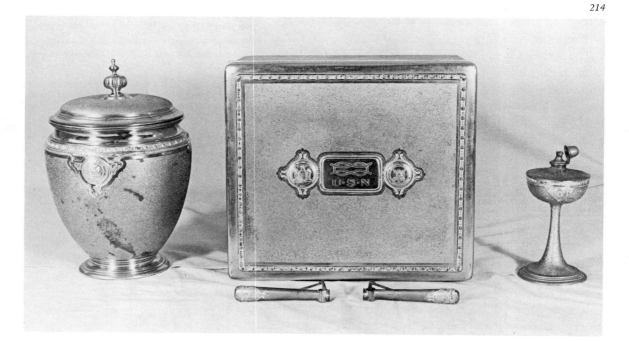

ing artists of the day. Although Tiffany's medals are outside the scope of this book we show two examples since they are, of course, presentation pieces.

The first is the Dewey medal (Fig. 215) for participants in the Spanish-American War. The Dewey medal was designed by Daniel Chester French, whose best-known sculpture is the great brooding figure of Abraham Lincoln in the Lincoln Memorial in Washington, D.C. The Dewey medal is dated 1898. The second is America's highest military honor, the Congressional Medal of Honor. The medal in Figure 216 was for Navy personnel.

215 Front and back views of the Dewey Medal designed by Daniel Chester French in 1898. Diameter: 1 7/8 in. (4.7 cm.).

216 U.S. Congressional Medal of Honor used by the Navy from 1917 to 1942. Designed by Tiffany & Co. (*United States Naval Academy Museum*).

8. Presentation Swords and Guns

ALTHOUGH THE CIVIL WAR obviously slowed down the making of household silverware by Tiffany & Co., it opened up an entirely new field for them: the selling and making of swords. Charles Tiffany and Edward Moore soon pushed the company ahead of their rivals. Of the twenty or twenty-five swordmakers in the United States during the Civil War, Tiffany & Co. was acknowledged the leader almost from the beginning. First they sold other people's weapons ("swords warranted to cut wrought iron from Sollingers Passants") and then they made their own with blades bought from German, English, and American manufacturers.

In 1861 Tiffany started making presentation swords which were the real basis for their reputation.[1]

The Tiffany presentation swords of the Civil War era were among the most ornate ever made and they were magnificently crafted. By their very nature they are among the great rarities in collecting and have long fetched high prices. Jay P. Altmayer estimated "that possibly one hundred [Tiffany] presentation swords of medium ornateness were sold, and probably thirty swords of extreme ornateness."[2] Most of the famous swords given to the leading military figures of the Civil War period are in museums and of course are not available to collectors.

American presentation swords date from the time of the Revolutionary War when the Continental Congress voted to present swords to ten officers in recognition of their services. Although these swords bear the United States shield and eagle on the hilt, they were actually made in France. Soon after the War of 1812 Thomas Fletcher of Fletcher and Gardiner of Philadelphia made some beautiful gold- and silver-hilted swords. Presenta-

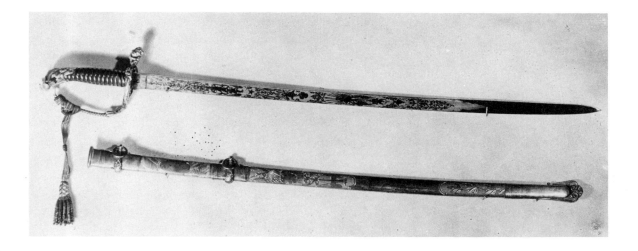

tion swords were also made in America during and after the period of the Mexican War.

These early presentation swords were conventional in style, being based entirely on European models. Their comparative simplicity reflected the plain, classically oriented styles of their time. The Tiffany swords of the Civil War period, particularly the later ones, were more ornate. Altmayer has pointed out that stylistically the Tiffany Civil War presentation swords derive from French models, particularly the designs of Nicholas Noel Boutet who was a well-known gunsmith at Versailles during Napoleonic times.[3] This is quite natural because of Edward C. Moore's close contacts with Paris.

In this chapter we show examples of some of the best known of the Tiffany Civil War swords in public collections plus two fine swords from Mr. Altmayer's collection. In most cases we have only shown details of the hilts of the swords and in some cases details of scabbards and blades. Photographs of full-length swords lose detail and have a look of sameness to the uninitiated. The detail photographs show the intricate craftsmanship of the swords. They were meant to be looked at this way since they were created and received as works of art in homage to a great man or an auspicious event. They were never meant to be instruments of war.

An early example of Tiffany presentation swords is shown in Figure 217. This relatively plain sword was presented to Captain John B. Coster for saving a man from drowning. The blade is beautifully etched on both sides with floral and military symbols. It has a silver

217 Sword and scabbard presented to Captain John B. Coster, 1st Regt. N.Y.S. Volunteers, in 1861. Length overall: 40 1/8 in. (102 cm.). Mark: TIFFANY & CO./ NEW YORK. (The New-York Historical Society, New York City).

covered grip wound with silver wire, a brass quillon terminating in a lion's head, brass knuckle guard of twisted metal, and a brass pommel with helmeted shape. The brass scabbard has heavy floral motif mounts. It is engraved with the recipient's name "Captn. John H. Coster" flanked by American flags, swords, and bayonets. Below the middle of the scabbard flanked by a winged trumpet is the inscription:

Presented to Captn. John B. Coster 1st. Regt. N.Y.S. Volunteers / by Compy. K. Engineers Corps 7th Reg. National Guard N.Y.S. Militia as a slight expression of their esteem and appreciation of his noble conduct in / saving from drowning A. M. Stetson, Quarter Master 11th Regt. N.Y.S. Volunteers at New Port News, Va. Oct. 12th 1861.

A sword presented by the Congress of the United States to General William Tecumseh Sherman in 1862 is shown in Figure 218. The hilt of this magnificent sword is very sculptural. The vigorous clear modeling is full of Victorian symbolism, just as the historical associations of the sword are full of this most bloody of American wars. The sword was presented to General Sherman in recognition of his services during the Battle of Shiloh. The blade is long and straight with two edges and a flat surface. The obverse is inscribed as follows:

Headquarters Department of the Mississippi, Pittsburg, Tenn., April 13, 1862. Hon. E. M. Stanton, Secretary of War; Sir, It is the unanimous opinion here that Brigadier General W. T. Sherman saved the fortune of the day on the 6th and contributed largely to the glorious victory of the 7th. He was in the thickest of the fight on both days, having three horses killed under him and being wounded twice. I respectively request that he be made a Major General of volunteers to date from the 6th instant. Very respectfully; your obedient servant H. W. Halleck, Major General Commanding.

The figure of Columbia on the hilt supports the American flag. The pommel consists of the figure of an eagle standing on a globe decorated with stars. The knuckle guard is a silver gilt strip covered with laurel leaves, and the end near the pommel is decorated with a scroll inscribed: "Pittsburg Landing, April 6 & 7, 1862." The quillon terminates above the blade in the head of Mars, and a blue enamel shield on the obverse bears in gold letters, set with diamonds, the initials WTS. The scabbard (not shown) is gilt with three mounts, the one nearest the hilt bearing the head of Mars on a trophy of United

218 Hilt of sword presented in 1862 to General William Tecumseh Sherman of the United States Army, in recognition of his services during the Battle of Shiloh. Length of sword: 38 3/4 in. (98.5 cm.). Mark: TIFFANY & CO., N.Y. (*The Smithsonian Institution*).

States flags, and the other two consisting of oak and laurel sprays.[4]

The sword of Admiral David Glasgow Farragut (Fig. 219) was presented to him in 1864 by the Union League Club of New York when he had become a national hero in the North. Farragut, a Southerner, had had a fifty-year career in the U. S. Navy when the Civil War broke out. He immediately moved from his home in Norfolk, Virginia to Hastings-on-Hudson, New York and became a strong Union supporter. He played an important role in the war, in 1862 capturing New Orleans and in 1863 cutting the Confederate communications at Vicksburg on the Mississippi River. It was in the Battle of Mobile Bay in 1864 that he shouted his famous battle cry "Damn the torpedoes," ordering his flagship ahead, that made him part of American folklore.

Admiral Farragut's sword is considered the most notable Civil War naval sword in the Smithsonian Institution in Washington. The blade is of medium size with a wide shallow groove on each side. The obverse is decorated in silver etching on a gold background with the letters "U.S.," the United States coat of arms, a figure of Fame, a naval trophy, and various floral and scroll designs. The reverse is decorated in a similar manner with a naval trophy inscribed "E Pluribus Unum," a naval monster, and various floral and scroll designs. The grip is covered with silver plate decorated with thirteen grooves wound with silver gilt wire. The pommel is designed in the form of a Phrygian helmet, the front of which bears a large anchor with a gold wreath. The rim is encircled by a row of thirteen diamonds set in blue enamel stars, and upon the top stands an eagle with outstretched wings. The guard consists of a circular strip encircled by oak sprays, which expand into an oval plate at the blade, the obverse of which bears the monogram DGF outlined in diamond chips on a background of blue enamel, the whole being flanked by sprays of laurel. The scabbard bears three heavy mounts of silver gilt, two of which bear anchors flanked by oak sprays in high relief. Between the two appears the inscription, "Presented to / Rear Admiral David G. Farragut / by the members of the Union League Club as a token of / their appreciation of his gallant services rendered / in defense of his country, New York, / April 23, 1864."

A sword of exceptional historical interest is the one presented to Major General Winfield Scott Hancock,

219 Hilt of sword presented to Admiral David G. Farragut by the Union League Club of New York in 1864 in recognition of his services during the Civil War. Length of sword: 38 1/2 in. (97.8 cm.). Mark: COLLINS & CO., HARTFORD, CONN. 1862 and TIFFANY & CO., N. Y. (*The Smithsonian Institution*).

United States Army, at the Mississippi Valley Sanitary Fair, St. Louis, in 1864 (Fig. 220). General Hancock, a career Army man, was a brilliant leader known as "Hancock the Superb." He commanded the Second Corps at Gettysburg which bore the brunt of Pickett's famous charge, in the course of which the Second Corps lost 4,000 killed and wounded out of less than 10,000 men, and Hancock was shot from his horse. In 1864 he was in command of Northern troops in the battles of the Wilderness and Spotsylvania Court House. In 1880 Gen. Hancock was the Democratic candidate for the presidency, but was defeated by James A. Garfield by less than ten thousand votes out of a total of four and a half million.

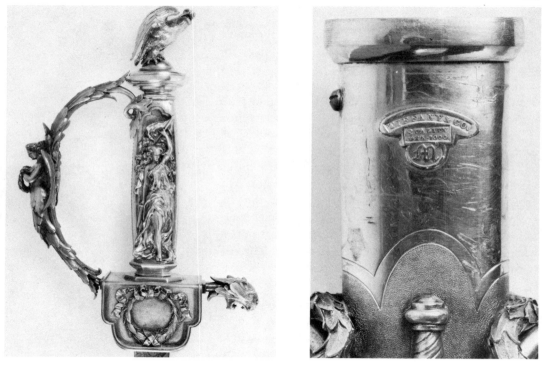

220 Hilt of sword presented to Major General Winfield Scott Hancock, United States Army, at the Mississippi Valley Sanitary Fair, in 1864. Length of sword: 39 in. (98 cm.). Mark on sword: TIFFANY & CO., NEW YORK. (*The Smithsonian Institution*).

221 Close-up of the upper part of the scabbard of the Winfield Scott Hancock sword in Fig. 220 showing the Tiffany mark.

The blade of the Hancock sword is straight with two edges. The obverse is decorated in silver on a gold background with the letters "U.S." in script, the figure of a United States Infantry officer in full uniform standing with a sword in the right hand and a standard in the left; the whole is flanked with floral and scroll designs. The reverse is similarly decorated with a medieval trophy, a man-at-arms, and floral and scroll designs. The grip is four sided and is silver gilt; on both the obverse and reverse sides is represented a standing female figure personifying War, a sword in her right hand and a standard raised above her head. The oval-shaped pommel is surmounted by an eagle poised for flight. The knuckle guard consists of two sprays of laurel leaves arranged in the form of a bow with a female figure of Victory superimposed upon the lower part. The quillon terminates above the blade in a monster's head; a large shield attached to the obverse bears a laurel wreath; and a small one on the reverse bears the inscription "Voted to Maj. Gen. W. S. Hancock at the Mississippi Valley Sanitary Fair, St. Louis, June 4, 1864." The scabbard, which is gold mounted, bears on the obverse, near the top, an eagle, in gold surrounded by a circle of thirty-six diamond chips set in gold stars; the whole rests on a blue enamel background flanked by two standards and surmounted by palm sprays and a square standard; in the center is an oval shield inscribed "U.S." with a Greek helmet and a sword above and a spray of laurel below. The tip is decorated on each side with a battle-ax between laurel wreaths and a lion's head. The reverse is decorated near the top with a Roman sword about which laurel sprays are entwined.

Figure 221 shows the upper part of the Hancock sword and the Tiffany mark. The cast mark has been soldered on to the scabbard.

Probably the most famous of Tiffany's presentation swords is the one given to General U. S. Grant in 1864 at the Metropolitan Sanitary Fair in New York. Tiffany had contributed the sword, "valued at one thousand dollars," to the fair to be presented to the general who received the largest number of votes from subscribers who made a contribution of one dollar per vote. There was a comparable sword for the Navy. General Grant won the Army sword and Admiral Farragut won the Navy sword. *Frank Leslie's Weekly* showed a drawing of the event (right).

The sword presented to General Grant was somewhat reminiscent in design of the presentation swords of the period of the War of 1812. The grip (Fig. 223), which is silver mounted, is decorated on the obverse side with the heads of Mars in an oval surrounded by military trophies; and the reverse (not shown) is decorated with a female figure of Victory. The pommel is in the form of a female head surmounted by a helmet, the lower por-

222 The Metropolitan Sanitary Fair.

223 Hilt of sword presented to General Ulysses
S. Grant at the Metropolitan Fair in New York
of the United States Sanitary Commission in
1864. Length of sword: 39 in. (97 cm.). Mark:
TIFFANY & CO. / NEW YORK / COLLINS & CO. /
HARTFORD CONN. (*The Smithsonian Institution*).

tion of which is set with rubies and diamonds. The
knuckle guard consists of a heavy gilt strip, the center of
which is decorated with a medallion bearing the head of
Medusa and terminating above the blade in a quillon
bearing on the end a ram's head. The counterguard is
formed of a large oval shield bearing the figure of Ulysses
strangling the lion.

The blade of the Grant sword, which was made by
Collins & Co. of Hartford, is wide and heavy and bears
on the obverse in etched silver the figure of a youthful

United States Infantry officer, with a sword in his right hand and the American flag raised above his head in his left hand (Fig. 224). Floral and scroll designs are above and below the soldier.

The engraving on Tiffany's Civil War sword blades is attributed to one man, John W. Orr, one of the leading engravers of his time. An 1860s Tiffany brochure on their swords had this note:

The illustrations, cut upon wood and admirably printed in gold and silver, are the work of John W. Orr, of this city. In their desire to present the details of ornament and design in as effective a manner as possible, the publishers [Tiffany and Co.] believe that they are doing but simple justice in thus awarding the credit of their success.

In addition to the custom-designed swords of the Civil War period, made for the great and the famous, Tiffany also carried in stock "(1) straight swords for general officers, and (2) straight swords for generals." An example of the latter is the handsome sword given to Major General John McAllister Schofield in 1864 (Fig. 225). A contemporary Tiffany catalog described the sword:

Washington Pattern Octagon Grip of silver, surmounted by head of Washington in gilt. Knuckleguard heavy gilt, with medallion relief of Hercules in silver. Wrist-guard, a crosspiece, with ram's head finials, and draped with flags. Scabbard chased and etched. Blade etched and gilt.

The scabbard bears the inscription "To Major General Schofield. From the Citizens of St. Louis, Mo. Jany. 30th 1864."

Schofield had a long and distinguished career in the U.S. Army. After the Civil War he became secretary of war (1868–1869), and commanded various army departments until 1888 when he was assigned to the command of the Army of the United States as senior major general.

The sword in Figure 226 was presented to Major General John Cleveland Robinson in 1865. The vigorously modeled eagle on the ball pommel holds the ribbon from the knuckleguard in its beak; a snake encircles the grip. The inscription on the gilt silver scabbard reads: "Presented To / Maj. Gen. John C. Robinson / By his friends / New York 4th July, 1865." Robinson's military career included action in the Mexican and Seminole Wars, the successful defense of Fort Henry in the Civil War followed by the battles of Fredericksburg, Chancellorsville,

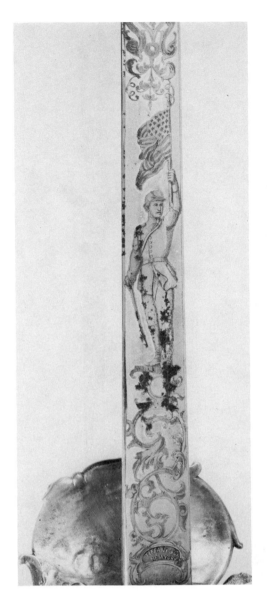

224 Close-up of blade of General Grant's sword in Fig. 223 showing engraving of Union soldier and Tiffany mark.

161

225 Sword of "Washington Pattern" presented to Major General John McAllister Schofield in 1864. Length: 31 1/2 in. (80 cm.). Mark: TIFFANY & CO / M. *(West Point Museum)*.

Gettysburg, Wilderness, and Spotsylvania. In the last he lost a leg which forced his retirement from active service. He was voted the Medal of Honor by Congress.

The Robinson sword is cased with yellow silk sash, knot, gold belt buckle and is accompanied by a sheepskin scroll of presentation signed by a group of prominent New Yorkers including Charles L. Tiffany, and finally, a Mathew Brady photograph of General Robinson. The blade of the Robinson sword was made by Collins and Co. of Hartford, Connecticut and is engraved with flags, military trophies, and the motto "Stand By the Union."

The straight sword in Figure 227, a silver-hilted sword with a scabbard of gilt brass, was presented to Brigadier General William A. Pile by Negro noncommissioned troops after the capture of Fort Blakely, Alabama in April 1865. The blade is engraved with Union officer, garlands, and military trophies. An eagle is on the pommel, the quillon terminating in acorns and a silver chain attaches from the pommel to the quillon. The counterguard bears the inscription "Presented to / Brig. Genˡ. Wm. A Pile / By the Non. Com. / Officers / and Privates / of the 68th / U.S. Infty. Colᵈ. / Ten Thousand Freedmen Speak His Praise."

The Civil War period was the real heyday of the American presentation sword. There were only a few made in the 1870s and 1880s; a small flurry of them were made for the heroes of the Spanish-American War at the turn of the century. But never again would they reach the heights of spectacular craftsmanship and be presented with such patriotic fervor as during and immediately after the Civil War. The greatest of these swords were ornate and sometimes fussy in their details, and the symbolism of the sword decorations often seems excessive to our late twentieth-century eyes. However, they were very much in tune with the era. The emotions of the Civil War ran deep and strong and, even though the decorative symbolism of the swords is now sometimes obscure, and the events which they celebrated are dim and only half-remembered, they spoke loudly and clearly to that passionate and partisan time. Men *did* die by the sword and the sword itself had a profound emotional meaning that few of us can understand today. A great presentation sword was the ultimate tribute to the great military leaders of the time.

Paulding Farnham designed a few presentation swords at the time of the Spanish-American War which are

226 Hilt and scabbard of sword presented to
Major General John C. Robinson of the United
States Army in 1865. *(Collection of Jay P.
Altmayer)*.

227 Sword and scabbard with the inscription
on the counterguard "PRESENTED TO / BRIG. GENL.
WM. A. PILE / BY THE / NON. COM. / OFFICERS
AND PRIVATES / OF THE 68TH / U. S. INFTY. COLD. /
TEN THOUSAND FREEDMEN SPEAK HIS PRAISE."
Length of blade: 33 in. (83.9 cm.). Mark:
TIFFANY & CO., N. Y. and COLLINS & CO., HARTFORD,
CONN. *(Collection of Jay P. Altmayer)*.

226

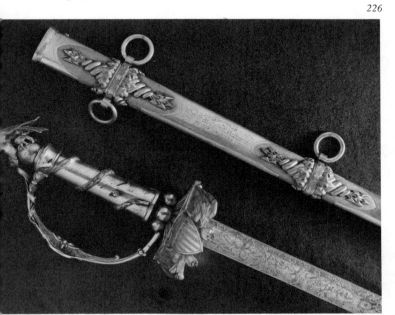

227

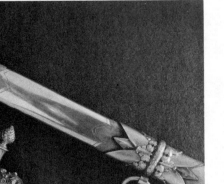

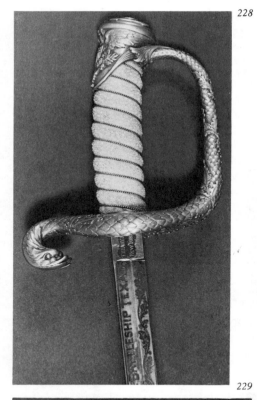

worthy of being shown with Tiffany's Civil War swords. The sword in Figure 228 was given to Captain John W. Philip who commanded the battleship *Texas* during the War. The fact that this symbol of war was presented by the Sunday school children of the state of Texas seems odd and rather incongruous to us. The presentation of the sword was accompanied by an elaborately adorned copy of the Bible designed by Paulding Farnham and made by Tiffany.

The Philip sword has the ubiquitous eagle and shield on the pommel, and a serpent forms the knuckle guard with its head terminating the quillon. The grip is wound with twisted silver wire.

The more ornate sword in Figure 229 was presented to Commander Richard Wainwright in 1898. The Wainwright sword has a mermaid mounted on the knuckle guard, a star-studded pommel, and a grip with a strip of leaves wound around it.

Wainwright had been executive officer of the battleship *Maine* when she was destroyed in Havana Harbor in 1898. The event commemorated by the presentation sword was when he commanded the *Gloucester,* a poorly armed vessel that had been J. P. Morgan's yacht, and he vanquished the Spanish destroyers *Furor* and *Pluton* off Santiago de Cuba.

Tiffany made only a few presentation swords after the Spanish-American War. They made more use of enamels and less use of rich castings. They were colorful but perhaps not as interesting as the earlier swords. The presentation sword disappeared along with the sword as a weapon.

Guns

Tiffany was associated with three gun manufacturers in the nineteenth century: Deringer, Colt, and Smith & Wesson.

Tiffany & Co. never made guns but they sold both handguns and rifles from the early days of the Civil War. Some of these guns were decorated by Tiffany and were marked by them. It would also appear that some guns might have been decorated and sold by them without their usual marks.

The following advertisement in the *Army and Navy Journal* (December 26, 1863) spells out clearly that Tiffany was primarily a reseller of Deringer's pistols:

We were not able to find any mention of Deringer guns in the Tiffany plant records and we know of no Deringer guns with silver-decorated handles with the Tiffany mark.

There exists today a group of Colt pistols of the Civil War period with so-called "Tiffany" grips. For some time these pistols were attributed to Tiffany, although none of them bore the Tiffany & Co. mark. The problem of these Colt pistols, with handsome, elaborately decorated silver handles, is an interesting one. Sutherland and Wilson in *The Book of Colt Firearms*[5] say that the name Tiffany was applied to grips on early Colt arms of the 1863–1873 period quite arbitrarily by early arms' collectors. There were three types of "Tiffany" grips: (1) the American eagle, 1863–1869 and the Mexican eagle ca. 1873; (2) the Civil War battle scene (Fig. 230); and (3) the Missionary and Child 1864–1870 designed by the American sculptor John Quincy Adams Ward.

Sutherland and Wilson believe that Tiffany & Co. were not involved in the making of these grips. They attribute them to the New York dealers, Schuyler, Hartley & Graham; "some factory engraved, but mostly done to order by L. D. Nimscke." They sum up their position with the statement "To factually place Tiffany into the picture has completely eluded the authors, except as a usable label developed by arms collectors starting in the 1920s, identifying them in name as 'Tiffanys,' but credit the source as Schuyler, Hartley & Graham."[6]

Jinks and Wilson in an article on "Tiffany Stocked Firearms" attribute the "Tiffany" grip pistols of Colt to the Ames Sword Company of Chicopee, Massachusetts.

228 Hilt of sword presented to Captain John W. Philip in 1898. The inscription reads: "FROM THE SUNDAY SCHOOL CHILDREN OF TEXAS TO CAPTAIN JOHN W. PHILIP, COMMANDER OF THE BATTLESHIP TEXAS, IN RECOGNITION OF HIS BRAVERY AND ACKNOWLEDGEMENT OF ALMIGHTY GOD." Mark: TIFFANY & CO / NEW YORK. (*United States Naval Academy Museum*).

229 Presentation sword given to Commander Richard Wainwright in 1898. The inscription reads: "TO COMMANDER RICHARD WAINWRIGHT, USN, FROM HIS FELLOW CITIZENS OF WASHINGTON, D. C., IN RECOGNITION OF HIS BRILLIANT VICTORY OVER AND SINKING OF THE SPANISH TORPEDO BOATS FUROR AND PLUTON WHEN COMMANDING THE USS GLOUCESTER, JULY 3, 1898, OFF SANTIAGO DE CUBA." Mark: TIFFANY / & / CO. (*United States Naval Academy Museum*).

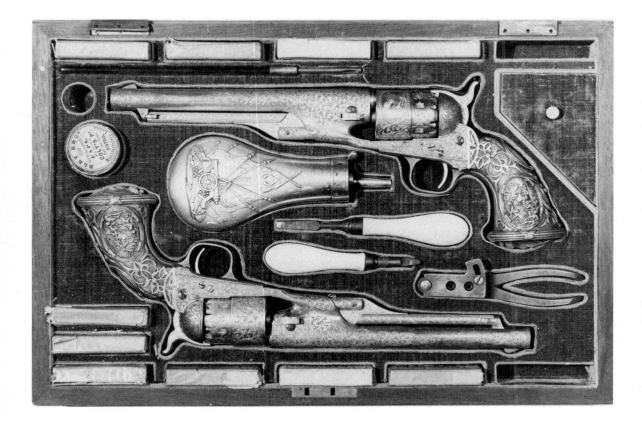

230 A pair of Model 1860 Army Colt presentation revolvers in display case lined with maroon velvet, with green velvet trim. Accessories include silver-plated flask, silver-plated iron bullet mold, two ivory handled screwdrivers, cleaning rod, Eley Brother caps, and several packages of skin cartridges. The pistols have the so-called "Tiffany" type grip with a battle scene motif, and an American eagle butt. Length of pistol: 13 1/2 in. (34.3 cm.). *(The Smithsonian Institution).*

"Although it appears probable that Tiffany and Company cast some of the deluxe metal grips on a limited number of Colt revolvers in the period c. 1860–c. 1875, the authors are of the opinion that most of this work was done by the Ames Manufacturing Company."[7]

The authors of this book have searched Tiffany records and found one item which indicated Tiffany *did* make pistol mountings for Colt guns during the Civil War. The Tiffany plant journal No. 1 covering the period 1851 to 1870, lists, in entry No. 1304, dated Jan. 6, 1863, a "Pistol Mounted Colts Navy size A. W. Spies." It lists a plant cost of $7.00 each. The plant cost would have been doubled at the retail level, and to this must be added the value of the silver, indicating that the work on the Colt pistol would have cost the Tiffany store customer about $25.

We have already pointed out in note 1 of this chapter that we have found no plant records of the Civil War presentation swords (with the exceptions noted) and suggested there may have been a separate account book for such items. We also cannot rule out the possibility there was a separate account book for guns, although we have no evidence that one ever existed.

A third group of late nineteenth-century arms has been rather fully documented. These are the silver stocks made by Tiffany & Co. for certain Smith & Wesson and Colt revolvers of the 1890s and early 1900s, and for at least one Winchester rifle. From 1890 to 1909 the Tiffany *Blue Books* advertised under the heading "Pistols": "Revolvers of the most improved types, mounted in silver, carved ivory, gold, etc. with rich and elaborate decorations, $50.00 to $300.00. Cases, boxes, belts and holsters made in appropriate styles for presentations."

The largest group of firearms decorated by Tiffany during this period was for Smith & Wesson. Many were used by Smith & Wesson as exhibition guns at the Columbian and Pan American Expositions. Jinks and Wilson explain how the Tiffany silversmiths decorated the Smith & Wesson guns:

When a firearm is decorated by an engraver he lays out a design and then proceeds with hammer and gravers to cut the intricate motifs into the steel surfaces. This was not true on the weapons executed completely by Tiffany. Here the craftsmen fitted silver sheaths to the frame of the gun, and if necessary even cut or reshaped the frame at the grips so that the handle could be formed in the desired design. The silver sheaths were fastened to the front of the frame by small pins on solid framed guns, or by the barrel hinge screw on a top break revolver. . . .

231 Smith & Wesson .38 Single Action Third Model revolver decorated in silver by Tiffany ca. 1892. Mark: TIFFANY & CO/ T/ STERLING. *(Collection of Roy G. Jinks).*

The decoration of the silver itself was generally done by relief stamping or hammering. This method differs from engraving, in that the soft silver is embossed to form the design, instead of the metal being cut away. The Tiffany craftsmen also used acid etching and (rarely) engraving to form the smaller lines of shading used to accent the major design. In the decoration of guns having grips of wood or ivory, the silversmith occasionally used lattice work of silver, skillfully pierced and decorated, then fitted over the grip so the wood or ivory showed through.[8]

We illustrate two of the Tiffany decorated Smith & Wesson pistols made in the 1890s. Several of this type were displayed by Smith & Wesson at the 1893 Chicago Exposition. Figure 231 is of the type mentioned above with a silver lattice applied over a wooden handle. Figure 232 shows a gun with a solid silver handle which has been etched with a hunting scene. Both of these guns were decorated for Smith & Wesson by Tiffany and were sold by Smith & Wesson.

232   Smith & Wesson .32 Hand Ejector First Model revolver with a solid silver handle made by Tiffany ca. 1892. Mark: TIFFANY & CO MAKERS STERLING. (*Collection of Smith & Wesson*).

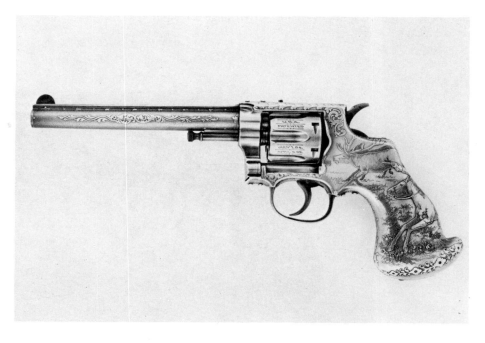

9. Yachting and Other Sporting Trophies

ALTHOUGH yacht racing dates back at least to the seventeenth century, it was not until the middle of the nineteenth century that it really took hold in America. The New York Yacht Club was organized in 1844, the first yacht club on the east coast and the second in America to survive more than a year or two.[1] The first record of a silver trophy rewarding the winner of a New York Yacht Club race was in 1845, when "the prize was a silver cup of the value of the entrance fees, which was five dollars, actually a sweepstake."[2] The practice of giving the winner a silver trophy caught on and is a tradition today.

Yachting Trophies

The great period of yachting trophies was the second half of the nineteenth century, when they were made by almost all the leading silversmiths. In the 1850s trophies were modest in size and design, but in the 1870s they became larger and more spectacular. They were described in detail and often illustrated in the newspapers and magazines of the day and were treated seriously as works of art.

The finest collection of nineteenth-century yachting trophies in the United States is that of the New York Yacht Club.[3] Half of the Yacht Club's collection of forty-two nineteenth-century trophies were made by Tiffany & Co., most of these being from the period 1855 to 1890. During that period Tiffany practically had a monopoly on trophies bought by the club. We illustrate a number of the Tiffany trophies from the club's collection to show the range of styles in which these objects were made. The trophies reflect the taste, inventiveness, crafts-

233 Vegetable dish with cover made by Moore for Tiffany about 1857. Inscribed "NEW YORK YACHT CLUB/ 1ST CLASS/ ANNUAL REGATTA JUNE 4TH 1857/ SLOOP JULIA." Height: 6 in. (15.2 cm.). Length: 11 in. (27.9 cm.). Mark: NO. 11 (2727). (*New York Yacht Club*).

234 Yachting trophy made about 1871. Inscribed "COMMODORE'S/ CHALLENGE CUP/ FOR SCHOONERS/ 1871." First won by *Tidal Wave* on June 22, 1871. Thirteen other winners inscribed to 1901. Height: 23 3/4 in. (60.3 cm.). Mark: TIFFANY & CO UNION SQUARE N.Y. (*New York Yacht Club*).

233

234

manship, and, most of all, the exuberant energy of the Tiffany silversmiths. One has only to compare them with the cool, restrained, and frankly, almost uniformerly dull trophies of the twentieth century to realize how much we have lost.

Before discussing the Tiffany trophies we should note that the most famous of the New York Yacht Club trophies, in fact, probably the most celebrated of all sporting trophies, the America's Cup, was *not* made by Tiffany, but by an English maker, Robert Garrard, Jr. This grand old cup was originally known as the Hundred Guinea Cup, and it was only after the yacht *America* won it in England in 1851 and brought it to this country that it received its name.

The least ornate of the Tiffany trophies, and the earliest, is the vegetable dish in the Classical Revival style in Figure 233. The merman handle is removable so that the cover can be used as a separate serving dish. This delightful trophy was won by the sloop *Julia* in the club's annual regatta in 1857.

After the Civil War yachting trophies were larger and more ornate. The two-foot high cup in Figure 234 topped with a goddess and two sea horses was donated by one of the great yachtsmen of the nineteenth century, James Gordon Bennett, Jr. Bennett had received international fame at the age of twenty-one by winning the first transatlantic race in 1866 with his yacht *Henrietta*. In 1871, at the age of twenty-six, Bennett became Commodore of the New York Yacht Club. In the annual regatta of 1871

170

235

235 Silver trophy on marble base, made in 1872. The engraved inscription reads: "CAPE MAY/ CHALLENGE CUP/ PRESENTED BY THE/ COMMODORE OF THE N.Y.Y.C./ OCTOBER 10TH 1872." The winners' names are engraved on the far side of the silver base. Height including marble base: 28 1/4 in. (71.8 cm.). Width: 16 1/2 in. (41.9 cm.). Mark: NO. 16 (3144/4822). *(New York Yacht Club).*

236 Detail of the cup in Fig. 235. The die-rolled anchor border was also used on the trophies shown in Figs. 237 and 238.

236

he gave two trophies, one for schooners and one for sloops. There were eighteen schooners in the 1871 race which was won by *Tidal Wave,* 85 tons, owned by W. H. Langley.

The Cape May Challenge trophy illustrated in Figure 235 shows a sure hand in the modeling of the two sailors (see Fig. 236). The symmetry of the sailors is mirrored by the wings of the eagle on top and the tusks of the walrus on the base. This cup was in Tiffany's exhibit at the Philadelphia Centennial Exposition in 1876.

Unlike the America's Cup, which has remained in American hands since 1851, the Cape May Challenge Cup has twice been lost to English yachtsmen. Sir Richard Sutton won it with his yacht *Genesta* in 1885 and the Prince of Wales won it in 1893 with his yacht *Britannia.* The club's records indicate the Prince of Wales never defended the cup but had it returned to the club in 1897.

Tiffany made a number of yachting trophies in what they called their Japanese style in the 1870s and early 1880s. The Japanese style is discussed at length in chapter 10, and there we illustrate the great Buck Cup (Fig. 271)

237 Punch bowl trophy in the Japanese style made in 1875. The engraved inscription reads: "NEW YORK YACHT CLUB/ ANNUAL REGATTA/ JUNE 16, 1875/ PRIZE FOR FIRST CLASS SLOOPS/ WON BY VISION." The fish and other ornaments are applied; the seaweed is engraved. Height: 11 3/4 in. (29.8 cm.). Width: 17 1/4 in. (43.8 cm.). Mark: NO. 19 (4060/888). (*New York Yacht Club*).

238 Chafing dish trophy made about 1875. The engraved inscription reads: "NEW YORK/ YACHT CLUB/ ANNUAL REGATTA/ JUNE 1878/ WON BY TIDAL WAVE." The finial on the lid in the form of an applied anchor with rope is cast. The Japanese-style fish are applied; the seaweed is engraved. The applied decorations over the hoofed feet comprise leafy branches entwining a crossed oar and trident. Height: 9 3/4 in. (24.8 cm.). Diameter: 12 1/2 in. (31.7 cm.). Mark: NO. 19 (4058/7085). (*New York Yacht Club*).

which we feel is the masterpiece of this style. In the first phase of the style Japanese motifs were used as decorative elements on conventional forms. Examples are the punch bowl won by *Vision* in 1875 (Fig. 237) and the chafing dish won by *Tidal Wave* in 1878 (Fig. 238).

The baroque, curling handles surrounding flying fish of the bowl in Figure 237 add an Art Nouveau touch to this very marine-oriented object. The chafing dish in Figure 238 has similar applied fish and engraved seaweeds and die-rolled border of anchors. In both objects we are conscious of the fact that Japanese-inspired decorative motifs have been added to conventional western objects—a punch bowl and a chafing dish.

The 1881 cup for schooners shown in Figure 239 is a fine example of Tiffany's Japanese silver. The applied, raised lettering above and below the realistically etched schooner fits well enough into the undulating, organic design of the cup and with the boldly scaled water lily on the reverse side with feet fashioned of horse chestnuts, but the schooner itself looks like an afterthought. On the other hand, the cup *is* a yachting trophy as well as a work of art.

It is interesting to note that two of the finest Tiffany trophies in the Japanese style, the Buck cup and the 1882 cup for schooners, were won by the same yacht, the schooner *Halcyon*. *Halcyon* belonged to General Charles J. Paine of the Eastern Yacht Club of Marblehead, Massachusetts, who also managed the Boston syndicate headed by J. Malcolm Forbes which built *Puritan,* the successful America's Cup defender in 1885. In addition, Paine owned *Mayflower* and *Volunteer,* the cup defenders in 1886 and 1887.

The ship-model trophy (Fig. 240) was made in 1884, only five years after the Japanese cup in Figure 239, but is utterly different in style. The trophy, with its exaggerated Neptune figurehead, is derived from seventeenth-century and eighteenth-century ship models. Stylistically it is a tour de force.

The 1886 Goelet Cup for schooners shown in Figure 241 is obviously not from the same hand that designed the Tiffany Japanese pieces. The churning complexity of this huge repoussé trophy is more related to such Art Nouveau designs as the Berlin Vase in Figure 42, or modern abstract expressionist painting, than to the ordered, poetic simplicity of the company's silver in the Japanese style. Nevertheless, its whirling, swirling depiction of wind and ocean does evoke those two constants of the yachtsman's world. Although there is no winner's name on the cup, we know from the records that it was won by *Grayling,* owned by Latham A. Fish.

The rather bizarre Morgan trophy in Figure 242 combines a silver top, base, and handle with a section of elephant tusk. Tiffany made other objects, particularly

239 Parcel-gilt cup made in 1881. The applied inscription reads: "N.Y. & E.Y.C. RACES. 1882/ CUP FOR SCHOONERS/ WON BY/ HALCYON." The body is hand hammered; the schooner is etched. Height: 10 in. (25.4 cm.). Width: 14 3/4 in. (37.5 cm.). Mark: NO. 19 (6419/6152/1709), plus "9 1/2 pts." *(New York Yacht Club).*

240 Trophy made in 1884. The engraved inscription on the stern reads "THE GOELET CUP FOR SCHOONERS 1884/ WON BY GRAYLING." Height: 18 3/4 in. (47.6 cm.). Length: 22 in. (55.9 cm.). Mark: NO. 20 (7891/4766). *(New York Yacht Club)*.

vases, which combined elephant tusks with silver in the 1880s and 1890s, and some of these have handles cast from the same dragon mold as the handle of the stein. The Morgan trophy was won by General Paine's *Volunteer,* the great sloop which successfully defended the America's Cup in 1887, defeating the Scottish entry *Thistle* which was racing for the Royal Clyde Yacht Club.

The 1888 Goelet Cup for sloops (Fig. 243) was also won by *Volunteer*. It was one of the most admired of the

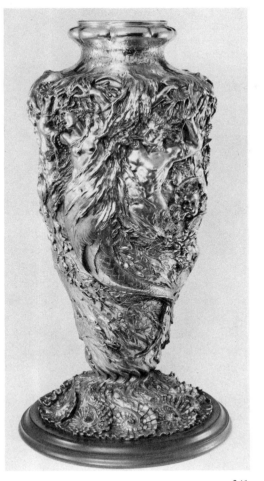

241

241 Vase-shaped trophy made about 1886. This massive object weighs 39 pounds. The florid chased inscription around the neck reads: "GOELET CUP 1886." Deep repoussé chasing depicts a mermaid and figures representing the winds and the sea. Height including the base: 28 1/2 in. (72.4 cm.). Mark: TIFFANY & CO MAKERS STERLING SILVER. *(New York Yacht Club)*.

242 Stein with lid. The body of the stein is of elephant tusk. Top, base, and cast handle are silver. The engraved inscription on the base reads: "MORGAN CUP WON BY SLOOP VOLUNTEER/ AUG. 8, 1887 VINEYARD HAVEN TO MARBLEHEAD/ PRESENTED BY J. PIERPONT MORGAN." Height: 17 in. (43.2 cm.). Mark: NO. 20 (5828/7896). *(New York Yacht Club)*.

242

Goelet cups and was considered one of Tiffany's best efforts at the time. A contemporary account said this about the cup:

The decorative design is in every sense one for yachtsmen to appreciate and admire. A female figure emblematic of the winds is driving before her a pair of snorting sea horses, dimly discernible through mist and spray. The two handles are spouting dolphins, and various sea grasses help embellish the scene.

On the side opposite the cup bears the inscription, "Goelet Cup, 1888," boldly etched in an odd but pleasing design representing a breaker, which at one end tapers off into a wave curl. A silver tablet on the base is intended for the name of the cup's lucky possessor, and the silver palm leaves on each side of it are emblematic of his victory over the other contestants.[4]

175

243

244

243 Amphora-shaped trophy made in 1888. The engraved inscription on the reverse side reads: "GOELET CUP/ 1888/ WON BY VOLUNTEER/ C. J. PAINE/ OWNER/ NEWPORT, AUG. 10, 1888." Height: 17 1/2 in. (44.4 cm.). Mark: NO. 20 (9918/ 1656). (*New York Yacht Club*).

244 A drawing from *Harper's Weekly,* August, 1888, showing the Goelet Cup in Fig. 243 with its original turned ebony base and silver tablet for the winners' names.

Figure 244 shows an engraving of the cup with its original ebony base. The base improved the proportions of the trophy since, without it, it looks somewhat top-heavy. Today the 1888 Goelet Cup seems very much a period piece and it is hard to take the scantily clad sea nymph and her sea horses very seriously.

Yachting trophies of the size and elaborateness of those shown in this chapter almost vanished with the end of the nineteenth century. They were no longer made because of the higher cost of silver, changes in taste, and vastly increased wages that had to be offered to the ever diminishing number of silversmiths who would undertake commissions of such size and ambition.

Other Sporting Trophies

In addition to yachting trophies Tiffany & Co. made a large number of trophies for a variety of sports from billiards and baseball to tennis and horse racing. Many of them were illustrated in the newspapers of the time and they unquestionably gave Tiffany considerable publicity. Even today (1978) the Tiffany Superbowl trophy with its silver football mounted on a pedestal has been widely reproduced in the press.

We show four trophies of the 1869–1904 period from four different sports, each quite different stylistically. The Belmont Cup in Figure 245 is one of the largest and most ambitious of Tiffany's sporting trophies. It was first awarded in 1869 to August Belmont for his winning horse, Fenian.

The Belmont Cup uses the motif of the acorn and the oak to symbolize the origins of the bloodlines of modern racehorses. Every thoroughbred in the world today traces

245 The August Belmont Memorial Cup first awarded in 1869. Height: 17 1/2 in. (44.5 cm.). *(The New York Racing Association).*

directly in tail-male (the top line of the pedigree) to three horses, the Darley Arabian, the Byerly Turk, and the Godolphin Barb, all of them Eastern sires imported into England in the eighteenth century from Arabia, Turkey, and Persia. The line of each was carried on by just one of his descendants, so every thoroughbred today traces back to one of these three: the line of the Darley Arabian is carried on through Eclipse (1764), that of the Byerly Turk by Herod (1758), and that of the Godolphin Barb by Matchem (1748).

The three sires on the Belmont cup are Eclipse, Herod, and Matchem.

The modest, appealing cup in Figure 246, decorated with applied trout and a fishing basket, for many years graced the dining room table of the Southside Sports-

246 Three views of a goblet-shaped trophy made ca. 1884. The engraved inscription on the bowl reads: "AWARDED BY THE/ NEW YORK FANCIERS CLUB TO THE/SOUTH SIDE SPORTSMEN'S CLUB/ OF LONG ISLAND, FOR THE/ BEST EXHIBITION OF LIVE TROUT/ JANUARY 23, 1884." On the foot is engraved "PRESENTED BY JULES REYNAL." Height: 10 3/4 in. (27.3 cm.). (*The New-York Historical Society*).

men's Club. The Club had the largest fish hatchery on Long Island.[5]

One of the most handsome of Tiffany's tennis trophies is the one shown in Figure 247 with its swirling Art Nouveau form and Art Nouveau lettering around the top of the cup. This doubles cup was retired in 1901 by Dwight F. Davis (who donated the Davis Cup) and H. Ward.

The Vanderbilt Cup in Figure 248 is the most important of the early automobile trophies. It was first given in 1904 by William K. Vanderbilt, Jr. to bring the best of foreign cars to the United States for observation. It has been said that the trophy contributed to the development of the automobile in the United States in the pre–World War I era. The Vanderbilt Cup races were the most colorful of the early racing events but they were marred by many accidents. Run more or less regularly between 1904 and 1916, these contests were under the supervision of the American Automobile Association.

The first Vanderbilt Cup race on October 8, 1904 was run on public roads outside Westbury, Long Island. George Heath, an American residing in Paris won, driving his 90-hp French Panhard 284 miles in 5 hours, 26 minutes, averaging 52 miles per hour. By 1916 the winning speed was 87 miles per hour.

247　Tennis trophy (one of a pair). Etched around the top in Art Nouveau lettering: "USLTA THE CHAMPIONSHIP'S FOR PAIRS—NEWPORT PRESENTED BY THE NEWPORT CASINO." First won by Valentine G. Hall and Clarence Hobart, August 1890. Trophy was retired in 1901 by Dwight F. Davis and H. Ward. Height: 10 1/2 in. (26.7 cm.). Mark: NO. 19 (10599/574). (*The National Lawn Tennis Hall of Fame, Newport, R. I.*)

248　Challenge Cup presented by W. K. Vanderbilt, Jr. in 1904 for auto racing. Engraved with winners, dates, times, and distances of races 1904–1916. Weight about 40 pounds. Height: 23 in. (58.4 cm.). Mark: TIFFANY & CO. 35 PINTS. (*The Smithsonian Institution*).

10. The Japanese and Other Exotic Influences

THE ARTS of the Orient, particularly those of China, have fascinated the West for centuries, and have had a profound influence on Western art. Although a trickle of Chinese silks and ceramics had come out of China since Roman times it was only in the sixteenth and seventeenth centuries, when the Portuguese, the English, and the Dutch started their East India Companies, that quantities of Chinese art had become available to the West. By 1700 things Chinese became a craze. Chinese art was avidly collected and Western copies and derivations in silver, ceramics, textiles, furniture, painting, and architecture were widespread. We now use the word "chinoiserie" to describe those Western arts derived from the Chinese, although in the eighteenth century chinoiserie was used indiscriminately to describe both Chinese art and its copies. Chinese art has continued its hold on the West to this day and chinoiserie decorations are still being used in wallpapers, furniture, ceramics, textiles, and other decorative arts.

In this chapter we discuss the influences of exotic arts, particularly the arts of Japan, on Tiffany silver, not as isolated "eclectic" influences, but as part of a continuing tradition of Western art renewing and revitalizing itself by using arts from outside the traditional mainstream.

The Japanese Style

From its opening in 1837 Tiffany & Co. handled Oriental art. We know from their earliest advertisements that a variety of Chinese objects were sold in the store. George Frederic Heydt, in his history of Tiffany & Co. published in 1893, mentions that "Japanese papier-mâché and terracotta wares" were sold from the beginning.[1] We question this statement since very little was coming out of Japan before Admiral Perry's famous visit in 1854. It is unlikely that sufficient quantities of art objects of Japanese origin could have been available in New York in 1837 to have established a viable commercial line.

Although Tiffany sold Chinese bronzes, ceramics, furniture, and silks from the beginning these wares had little effect on their silver designs. Chinese motifs were occasionally used, such as Chinese floral borders, Chinese frets and dragons (etched dragons on bowls and dragon-handled cups), but there was little "Chinese" Tiffany silver as such. A beautifully made example of chinoiserie sold by Tiffany, Young & Ellis is the repoussé chased pitcher in Figure 249 made about 1850 (see also Fig. 4). The trees, buildings, and Chinese figures are deeply and crisply repousséd. There is a vast amount of hand work on this piece. The body is entirely hand raised and hand chased. A punch, making a $\frac{1}{16}$-inch circle, was used to chase all background areas and tiny dots were chased *inside* these circles.

Chinoiserie had been around for a long time in Western art—since the late seventeenth century. It had been around for so long that as a style it had become completely conventional and westernized. Chinoiserie had long since lost any real feeling of excitement for Western designers.

Japanese art was different. When it first became widely known in the 1860s and 1870s it had a tremendous effect on the avant-garde art of the time. After Japan was really opened to the West by Admiral Perry's 1854 visit, art objects soon started pouring out of the country. These were primarily products of the artisans of the day, certainly none of Japan's great national treasures. First came the Japanese wood-block prints. These prints were inexpensive and widely available, particularly in France and England. Their flat patterned surfaces were very different from Western art. They showed a whole new way of depicting the visual world. The prints of Ando Hiroshige and Katsushika Hokusai and other Japanese artists began to have a profound influence on French modernist artists, an influence that was to last into the twentieth century. In the 1860s the whole direction of such major artists as Edouard Manet and Edgar Degas and James Abbott McNeill Whistler was strongly influenced by Japanese wood-block prints. Later Monet and Toulouse-Lautrec and, in fact, most of the great French

249 Chinoiserie pitcher made about 1850. Height 10 in. (25.4 cm.). Mark: TIFFANY, YOUNG & ELLIS. *(Collection of Mr. and Mrs. Cruger D. G. Fowler).*

181

artists of the late nineteenth century came under the spell of the arts of Japan.

The influence of Japanese art on nineteenth-century painting is well known and is beyond the scope of this book. This influence has been documented by a number of articles, books, and exhibitions in the post–World War II era. The Japanese influences on nineteenth-century decorative arts is less well known and only recently has been the object of rather widespread study.

Although the Tiffany plant records indicate that a mounting was made for a "Japanese Mug" in 1864 it was not until 1869 that the firm began to deal in Japanese art. A New York newspaper advertisement dated April 13, 1869 announced that "Tiffany & Co. have just received a few choice and very rare pieces of JAPANESE BRONZE and Porcelain Lacquered Vases of large size."

One would guess that Edward C. Moore, as Tiffany's chief designer, first really became aware of Japanese art in Paris about 1867. The 1862 Exposition in London had the first comprehensive showing of Japanese art in the West but it is doubtful whether this was much noticed in America. The War Between the States was raging and Tiffany was not making much household silver. Tiffany & Co. showed their silver for the first time at the 1867 Paris Universal Exposition where they won a medal. The Japanese government sent an exhibit to that Exposition which included a wide variety of decorative arts. Edward C. Moore was undoubtedly a visitor to the Exposition and it is possible that his collection of Oriental art was started at that time.

Edward C. Moore's Sketchbook II of the 1865 to early 1870s period, which we discussed in Chapter 2, contains many design ideas for silver in what Tiffany called the Japanese style. Figures 250 and 251 show typical pages from the sketchbook. The drawings of birds, leaves, flowers, gourds, and winding tendrils were to appear again and again in Tiffany's silver in the Japanese style.

Edward C. Moore's collection of Japanese art was unquestionably a prime source of design ideas for Tiffany's silver in the Japanese style. The collection, bequeathed to The Metropolitan Museum of Art in 1891, had almost 900 items of Japanese art. These included a large group of textiles (there were many magnificent brocades), Japanese pottery of the sixteenth to nineteenth centuries, metal works (bronzes and iron, sometimes inlaid with gold and other metals), baskets, lacquer and papier-mâché,

250–251 Pages from Edward C. Moore's Sketchbook II, 1865 to the early 1870s, showing "Japanese" sketches. Page size: 9 1/4 x 12 1/4 in. (23.5 x 31.1 cm.). *(Tiffany & Co.)*.

ivories, and large groups of sword guards, daggers, and swords.

Moore's Japanese collection could have come from several sources—dealers in London and Paris, from the Expositions in Paris, London, and Philadelphia, and of course, from Tiffany & Co.

In 1877 Tiffany exhibited and sold a large collection of Japanese items brought from Japan by Christopher Dresser. Dresser, an English enthusiast for Japanese art, made a three-month trip early in 1877 to Japan to make collections for two dealers, Londros & Co. of London and Tiffany & Co. of New York. The arrangement for Dresser to buy for Tiffany was probably made through Londros & Co. Londros was a well-known English dealer in Oriental art in the 1860s and 1870s. (They may have been a wholesale source for Tiffany.) The actual arrangements for Dresser to represent Tiffany in Japan were almost certainly made in England since there is no record of Dresser ever being in New York.

Dresser arrived in Japan on December 26, 1876. He visited artists and factories and shops wherever he went. He observed the making of pottery, textiles, and bronzes, and later wrote about the processes used in making these objects. His descriptions of these manufacturing operations were distinctly those of a layman. There is no hint that Dresser found anything that was later used in the actual making of Tiffany's silver in the Japanese style.

When Dresser returned to London in 1877 he sent to Tiffany's in New York their part of the Japanese collection. He says:

I had made my collection of typical ware, some of which went to Messrs. Tiffany of New York, who, I believe, after they had gathered the information that they desired, with the authority that they kindly considered my researches gave them, sold what they did not care to retain under the auction hammer; the other part is now doing its tutorial work, and as it is finished with will come into the possession of our museums or great houses.[2]

The auction which Dresser speaks about took place at Messrs. Leavitt in the Clinton Hall Salesrooms in New York in June, 1877. There were 1,902 lots in the sale and they covered a bewildering variety of artifacts, from a $3,000 pea-green jade jar which became a "most exquisite pink" when a lighted candle was placed in it, to a Japanese bronze firebox, with handle, for $5.50. Tiffany &

Co. apparently lost money on the sale, with many items going for a fraction of their cost. There were probably too few knowledgeable collectors and dealers at that time to absorb such a large collection at one auction. Tiffany no doubt kept the best pieces and the sale certainly created a great interest in Japanese art and gave the store much favorable publicity.

The Tiffany designers used Japanese artworks both as models and as points of departure in design. At first the tendency was to copy and adapt. The Japanese brush holder in Figure 252, which was in Moore's collection, was obviously the prototype for the Tiffany vase in Figure 253. The configurations of the spider web and the bamboo rim around the top are similar in both pieces. The Japanese bronze has a pebbly, sand cast background which the Tiffany piece translates as a hand-hammered surface. But the cast Tiffany base (whose form derives from Chinese and Japanese carved-wood pedestal stands) is far more elegant. The overall effect of the Japanese bronze is one of a rather casually made production item of folk art, while the Tiffany vase has an almost jewel-like perfection. The Tiffany piece is far more carefully

252 Bronze brush holder, Japanese, nineteenth century, with spider and web, and bamboo shaped rim. This was the model for the Tiffany silver vase in Fig. 253. Height: 6 3/4 in. (17.1 cm.). *(The Metropolitan Museum of Art, Bequest of Edward C. Moore, 1891).*

253 Tiffany vase with hand-hammered background. The spider web is engraved and the spider and the dragonfly are mountings. Elaborate base. Made in 1873. Numbers: 696/2991. *(From a Tiffany photograph of the 1870s.)*

252

253

made, more studied, and is exquisitely finished. This is not a value judgment, but only a description of how Tiffany used one of their Japanese models.

The first works of Tiffany silver in the Japanese style were the flatware patterns, *Japanese* (Figs. 254 and 255), first made in 1871, and *Vine* (Fig. 256), first made in 1872. The *Japanese* pattern was designed by Edward C. Moore. His patent No. 4831 for the pattern, issued on April 18, 1871, describes the handle design as having "branches and twigs with leaves, buds, and flowers of a peculiar kind. Among these branches, twigs and flowers is a bird."

254

255

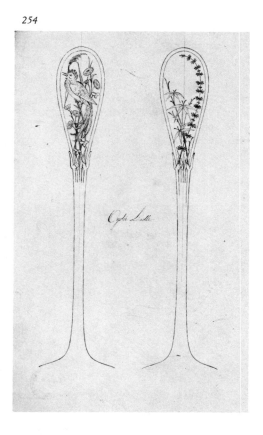

254 Original Tiffany drawing for an oyster ladle in the *Japanese* pattern, dated March 6, 1871.

255 Oyster ladle in the *Japanese* pattern (back view). Length: 10 3/4 in. (27.3 cm.). Mark: m TIFFANY & CO STERLING PAT. 1871. *(Private Collection)*.

Different pieces of the *Japanese* pattern had different designs and the back side of the oyster ladle in Figures 254 and 255 shows the first use of the stylized seaweed that appeared on so many pieces of the hollow ware in the Japanese style. The seaweed on the back and the exotic bird with its long plumed tail on the front of this *Japanese* pattern were entirely different from anything in American silver of the time.

The carrying of the design from the top part of the handle of the ladle in Figure 255 by means of reeding through the shank or straight part of the handle to the base of the ladle cup where it terminates "in a circular form with a frill of leaves" is a formal device much used later by Louis Comfort Tiffany, particularly in his table and floor lamps. These turn-of-the-century lamps have reeded shafts which tie the design of the base to the top, giving an organic unity to the objects.

The *Vine* pattern had all the elements of the mature hollow-ware forms made in the late 1870s. The undulating vine and trailing spiral tendrils and hanging gourds are all motifs of Japanese origin that were used often in Tiffany's hollow-ware pieces in the Japanese style. The stippled background of the *Vine* pattern corresponds exactly to the hand-hammered surfaces of the later hollow-ware pieces.

The Japanese style first appeared in flatware patterns instead of hollow ware probably because of the momentum of Tiffany's introduction of a whole new line of flatware patterns in the 1869–1872 period. In looking for new ideas for flatware Moore undoubtedly drew on his new-found love of Japanese art. The *Japanese* and *Vine* patterns became so successful that it was natural to extend the idea to hollow ware.

Tiffany's hollow ware in the Japanese style can be well documented from the Tiffany plant records. Many of the original working drawings, plus what are called "Hammering" or "Engraving Designs," are still in the files, and the plant journals have details of specific pieces, when they were made, their weight and cost. The hammering and engraving drawings have a variety of labels including "Hammering and Mounting Designs" and "Hammering and Engraving Designs." Like all of the Tiffany plant working drawings, the drawings are in the same scale as the finished piece of silver. Many of the designs are dated —those now in the files being dated from 1873 to 1882. These designs are beautifully drawn, often in color. The areas to be hand-hammered are designated by a hammering number which is coded to the size and shape of the hammer indentation. These drawings are particularly interesting documents of nineteenth-century silvermaking

256 Spoon in the *Vine* pattern, first made in 1872. Length: 6 1/8 in. (15.5 cm.). Mark: NO. 39.

187

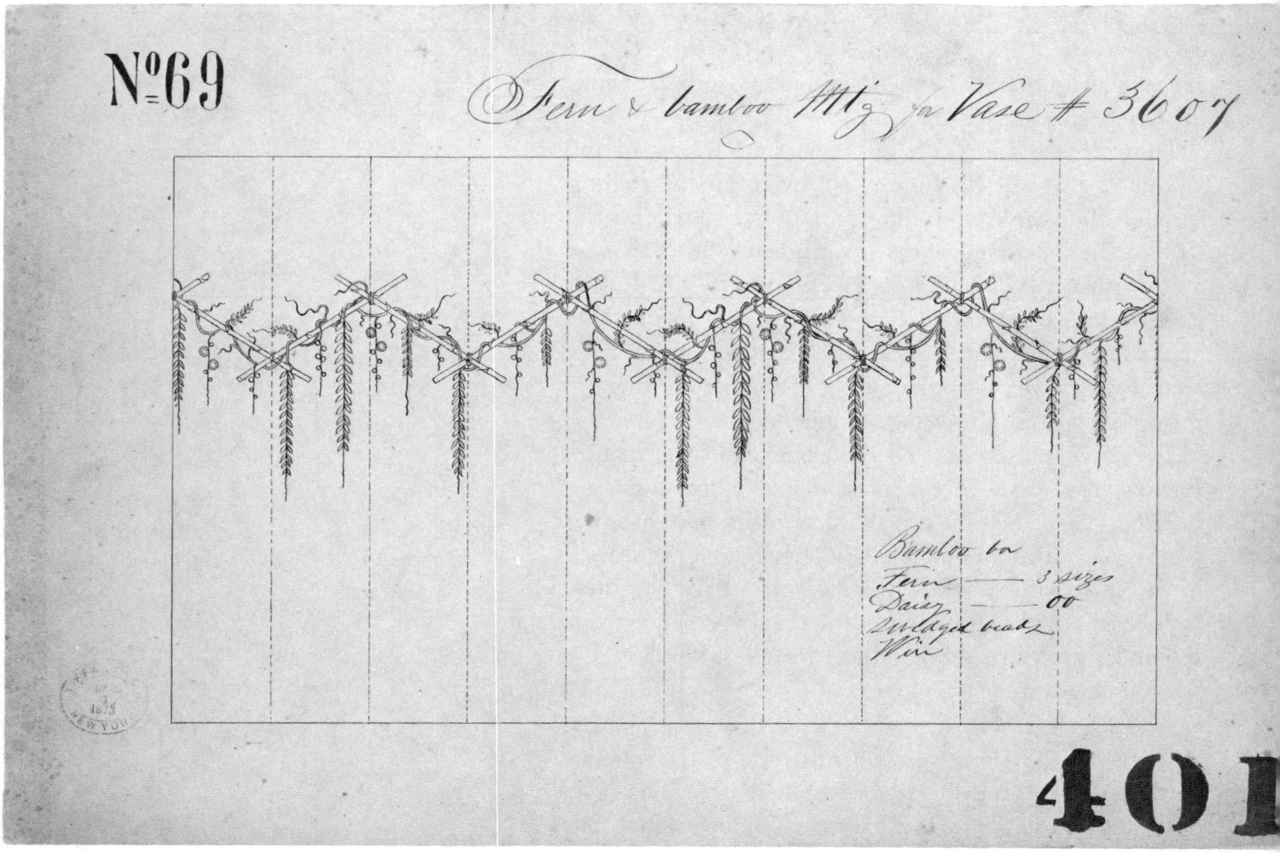

Fern & bamboo Mtg for Vase # 3607

Bamboo on
Fern ———— 3 sizes
Daisy ———— oo
Wedged made
Wire

401

257 Tiffany & Co. working drawing for mounting design on a vase. Dated December 6, 1873. Height of vase: 7 3/16 in. (18.3 cm.). (*Tiffany & Co.*).

and they are in themselves interesting as works of art.

Figure 257, a working drawing dated December 6, 1873, shows a stylized, rhythmical fern and bamboo mounting design for a vase. The flowers are the "peculiar kind" mentioned in Edward C. Moore's patent application for the *Japanese* flatware designs.

The use of hand-hammering was introduced in about 1876 and most of Tiffany's silver in the Japanese style was hand-hammered from that date. The hand-hammered surfaces caused much comment when Tiffany showed this silver in the 1878 Paris Exposition. The French critics in particular were struck with what they called the *martelé* finish. The hand-hammered look became very popular among artisans and was almost *de rigueur* for arts and crafts silver (and other metals for that matter) by the turn of the century.

The handsome and vigorous drawing of a spring bell in Figure 258 (dated March 24, 1879) uses abstract cloud, wave, and flower motifs. The mounting design for the tiny coffee pot in Figure 259 is typical of Tiffany's Japanese silver in the mature phase of the style.

Figures 260 through 271 are examples of Tiffany hollow ware in the Japanese style in approximate chronological order.

258 Working drawing for mounting design on spring bell. Dated March 24, 1879. Height of bell: 3 3/8 in. (8.6 cm.). *(Tiffany & Co.)*.

259 Working drawing for a small coffeepot with engraved and mounted leaves and copper beans. Dated February 4, 1880. Height: 4 1/8 in. (10.5 cm.). *(Tiffany & Co.)*.

258

259

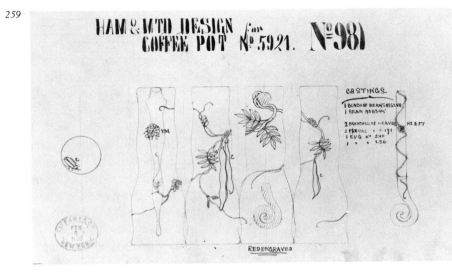

There is a maturing and a progression of the style idea during this period. Tiffany silver in the Japanese style can be divided into two phases:

(a) *The First Phase,* 1871 to 1876/77. In this early phase, Japanese motifs were applied to conventional silver forms. Sometimes decorative elements from other "exotic" cultures were mixed with the Japanese motifs.

(b) *The Mature Phase,* 1877 to 1882. The best pieces of this phase show that the Japanese influence had been assimilated and absorbed, creating a coherent and unified new style.

This classification is arbitrary, but we have found that most pieces fall naturally into their time categories.

The First Phase

As mentioned previously, the 1871 *Japanese* flatware pattern of Edward C. Moore was the real beginning of Tiffany's silver in the Japanese style.

Based on a study of the plant records we believe that the first piece of hollow ware in the Japanese style made by Tiffany is the covered canister in Figure 260. This piece, made in 1873, is called in Tiffany's records a "Tea Caddy—Japanese Box." The applied cherry blossom sprays, the compass ornaments on the lid, and the handle on the lid are common Japanese design elements. The engraved monogram (ELR) disguised as Japanese calligraphy is an amusing touch.

The peppers in Figure 261 show the design elements that were most often used in the first phase of Tiffany's Japanese style: applied fish and worms swimming among the (engraved) seaweeds. Note that the border around the bottom of these peppers makes use of the same compass ornaments used on the lid of the tea caddy in Figure 260. The peppers were made in 1874. Tiffany's records indicate that in the years 1873 and 1874 the following kinds of pieces were made in the Japanese style: vases, porringers, cups, salts, chatelaines, perfume bottles, bells, tea caddies, mustards, bowls, cream and sugars, butter dishes, pitchers, and sporting trophies.

The Tiffany plant journal indicates that the creamer and sugar bowl in Figure 262 were made as a separate pair and not as part of a tea set. The sugar and creamer have what the plant journal calls "ear handles." The two pieces, which were made late in 1873 or early in 1874, are

260 Tea caddy with lid. Gold lined. Applied cherry blossom ornaments. The engraved monogram ELR is in mock Japanese calligraphy. This piece, which was made in 1873, is apparently the earliest piece of Tiffany hollow ware in the Japanese style. Height: 4 1/4 in. (10.8 cm.). Mark: NO. 19 (2555/3908). *(The Preservation Society of Newport County, Rhode Island).*

190

261 Pair of pepper shakers with applied silver fish and worms and engraved seaweed. Pagoda-like finials. Engraved C.T.V.W. Made in 1874. Height: 5 1/2 in. (14 cm.). Mark: TIFFANY & CO / 3551 M 6613 / STERLING SILVER. (*Museum of the City of New York, Bequest of Miss Katherine Van Wyck Haddock*).

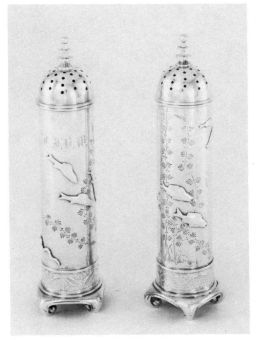

261

engraved with a number of unrelated Japanese motifs undoubtedly copied from Japanese prints or books. The creamer (on the right) shows a Hagoita (paddle), and a ball with feathers (shuttle cock) used by girls in a famous Japanese New Year's Day game. Also shown is a cicada. On the reverse side of the creamer are engraved sea shells, teapot, and cup. There is an engraved monogram on the front. The sugar bowl (on the left) illustrates a story from Japanese folklore. It shows two figures, perhaps carpenters, with their arms around a giant wooden pillar from the Todaiji Temple in Nara which was completed in 751 A.D. According to the story, the original mortice for a crossbar was made in the wrong size, so the column was installed upside down, thus placing the rectangular-shaped mortice hole near the ground. The legend is that if a person can squeeze through the hole he will surely go to heaven. On the rear of the sugar bowl around the monogram are engraved a swallow in flight, a string-held ball floating on water, and a Raidan, a Buddhist ceremonial hibachilike burner. At the base of

262 Sugar bowl and creamer with engraved decorations, die-rolled borders, and cast handles with geometric piercings. Both pieces have engraved monogram in a circle LHB. Gilt interiors. Height of sugar bowl: 5 5/8 in. (14.3 cm.). Mark on both pieces: NO. 16 (3205/1797). (*Private Collection*).

262

the handles of both pieces are triangular areas of geometric Japanese brocade designs. The die-rolled border around the tops of the bodies is similar to the border on the peppers in making use of arclike compass ornaments and stylized flowers. The geometric borders, which make up the feet of the sugar and creamer, picture at regular intervals cranes with spread wings. The cast handles have cherry sprays on one side and pine boughs with cones on the reverse side. The handles are pierced with round, triangular, and arc shapes.

The Mature Phase

In 1877 Tiffany's Japanese silver subtly changed and matured into a full-blown style. In most cases the designs were simplified, becoming unified and complete within themselves. The origin of the designs in Japanese art was clear, but the influence had been absorbed and the designs gained that necessary inner logic which any distinct style must have.

There are several characteristics of the second or mature phase of Tiffany's silver in the Japanese style:

(a) Hollow-ware pieces such as coffeepots and pitchers tend to have organic, gourdlike shapes.

(b) Much use was made of applied metals, such as gold, copper and copper alloys, and of course silver. When mounts of metals other than silver were used the pieces were marked:

STERLING-SILVER

— AND —

OTHER METALS

(c) Much of the ornamentation was derived from nature (through Japanese art). The Japanese influence brought back a new interest in nature as a design source.

(d) Hammered surfaces. Almost all of the best pieces were hand-hammered with the hammer marks left in. Different-sized and different-shaped hammer heads gave a wide variety of hand-hammered surfaces.

(e) Mat finishes. Most pieces were given a frosty or non-shiny surface.

One of the most admired pieces at the Paris Exposition was the water pitcher in Figure 263. Drawings of this piece were reproduced in publications all over the world, giving wide publicity to the Japanese style. Tiffany's

263 Water pitcher with applied decorations on a hand-hammered body, made in 1877. From a Tiffany photograph of the 1870s. Numbers 683/4706.

192

264

264 Water pitcher with applied ornaments on hand-hammered body, made in 1878. From a Tiffany photograph made in the 1870s.

265 "Composite" vase with red, gold, and niello decorations. From a "Photochromie" by Leon Vidal, 15, Quai Voltaire, Paris, 1878.

265

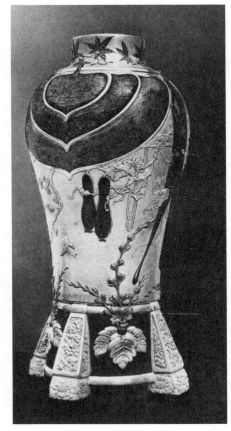

plant records show that several dozen versions of this pitcher were made in the 1870s and 1880s. One is owned by The Baltimore Museum of Art and another was sold in the Mentmore sale in England in May, 1977. The water pitcher in Figure 264 has an Art Nouveau feeling with its organic forms and relatively large-scale decorations. The decoration is pictorial rather than abstract, with the flowers, the water, the frog, and the dragonfly being treated quite realistically.

One of the most ambitious pieces in the Paris Exposition was the large "composite" vase in Figure 265. The red and gold highlighted vase was a *tour de force* in silvermaking even though its ornamentation is excessive by today's taste. Edwin C. Taylor, writing in the *National Repository* in 1879, said this about the vase:

The composite vase is a characteristic example of the new school, the tendrils, leaves and hanging gourds being formed partly of silver and partly of the new metallic alloy I have mentioned ["a new metal or alloy susceptible of assuming almost any color"]. These enrichments are applied on the surface and fused with a blowpipe. The two broad bands at the side below the neck are formed of laminations of different metals and alloys, and produce an effect like the graining of rare wood and a harmonious play of color.

193

266 Cream pitcher with cast handle and applied ornamentation on hand-hammered body. Height: 4 in. (10.1 cm.). Mark: NO. 20 (5048/3005/741). *(Museum of Art, Carnegie Institute, Pittsburgh. Gift of David T. Owsley).*

267 Coffeepot, sugar, and creamer with silver, copper, and gold ornaments applied to the hand-hammered bodies. Made about 1877. Height of coffeepot: 8 1/2 in. (21.5 cm.). Mark: NO. 30, pot 3401/441/447; creamer 4759/438/534; sugar bowl 3401/438/388. *(Bethnal Green Museum, London, England).*

266

267

The delightful small cream pitcher or jug with short spout (Fig. 266) has a massive look in spite of its four-inch height. It has silver mountings of vine and pendant gourd on the hand-hammered background. The vine and gourd design is identical to the design of the 1872 *Vine* flatware pattern (Fig. 332). They both have the same leaves, meandering vine, trailing tendrils, and pendant gourd. The artist simply changed the scale of the ornamentation and fitted the pattern to the body of the jug.

Many of the best pieces in the Japanese style were small and unpretentious. This relative restraint is very much in the Tiffany tradition. It is only in the large "important" pieces, as the composite vase, that the decorative elements seem overdone.

The pieces of silver in Figure 267 and Plate IV are first-rate examples of Tiffany's Japanese style. The tea set in Figure 267 is superb. The individual pieces of the set are small and the forms relatively simple and conventional. Even the Islamic-shaped coffee pot with its long thin spout had by 1878 become a conventional form. However, even though the forms are conventional, the shapes are free and spontaneous. The gourd shape of the coffee pot is echoed by the shape of the pendant gourd in the decoration on the pot. The subtly undulating vine mountings meander gracefully around the full organic forms of the pieces. The touches of gold and copper alloy of the mounts heighten the decorative effect, and the hand-hammered surfaces add life and vitality to the forms.

The small one-quart pitcher or jug in Plate IV and Figure 268 (the Tiffany plant records call it a "cream pitcher") was made in 1878. This unique, hand-wrought piece has an interesting history. It was sold at the Mentmore sale in Buckinghamshire, England in 1977 when the estate of the sixth Earl of Roseberry was auctioned. It was first exhibited at the 1878 Paris Exposition and it was purchased from the Exposition, probably by a Rothschild (the 1879 Tiffany *Blue Book* listed nine members of the Rothschild family as purchasers from the Exposition) as a wedding gift to Hannah Rothschild and the fifth Earl of Roseberry. This wedding, one of the great social events of 1878, united the heir of a famous English family with the "richest woman in England," Hannah, only daughter of Baron Meyer de Rothschild.

The Mentmore pitcher has a hand-hammered, organic-shaped body which is related to the gourd shape of the

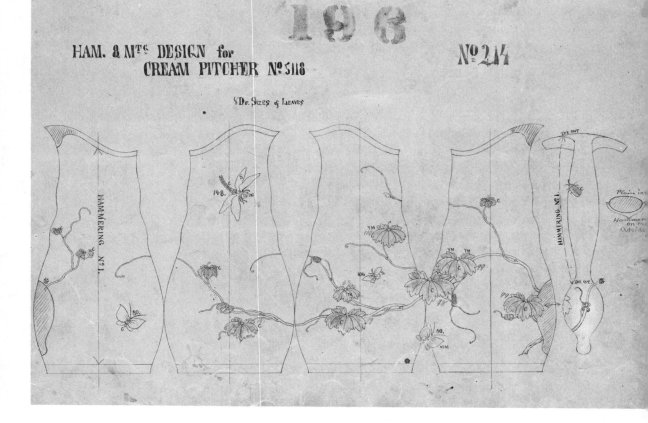

HAM. & Mts DESIGN for
CREAM PITCHER No 5118

No 214

8 Dif. Sizes of Leaves

HAMMERING No 1.

HAMMERING No 1.

268 Working drawing for the hammering and mounting design of the pitcher in Plate IV. The date stamp is almost illegible. It could be July 12, 187[6?].

coffee pot in Figure 267. The sixteen mounts on the pitcher are beautifully placed. There are leaves in copper and gold, a silver dragonfly, silver moths with copper bodies, a butterfly whose wings are striated with gold, copper, and silver, and a copper beetle on the handle. The meandering engraved tendrils carefully tie the design together. The handle, swelling in the middle, flows easily into the gentle S-curve of the top of the pitcher. The hammered surface of the piece is frosted.

It was these small, hand-hammered pieces inlaid with other metals that so entranced visitors and critics alike at the 1878 Paris Exposition. Tiffany & Co. received the Grand Prize at Paris for their silverwares in the Japanese style and Edward C. Moore received a gold medal. Charles L. Tiffany, the firm's founder, was made a Chevalier of the Legion of Honor of France.

The pieces in Figure 267 and Plate IV are the kind of thing that could have been "cute" and overdone in lesser hands. But the Tiffany silversmiths, with their basic conservatism and thorough knowledge of design, never went too far. These quiet pieces *are* pretty but they are also strong and vital. They are little masterpieces.

The Cleveland Museum owns a handsome coffee set (Fig. 269) similar to the Bethnal Green Museum set. The scale of the flower ornamentation of the Cleveland set is larger, and it is one of the few pieces of silver in the Japanese style of the second period that is not hand-hammered, the pieces being smoothly finished before the ornamentation was applied.

The round tray in Figure 270 has a powerful, simple design showing the copper sun rising out of the sea and two cranes, one awake and one still sleeping. The large-scale hand-hammering in this tray gives the appearance of water shimmering and glittering in the morning light: a lovely and very Japanese design.

The large punch bowl in Figure 271 with its rhythmical frieze of dolphins is certainly one of the most remarkable pieces of silver of Victorian America. It has great architectural strength and unity. The vigorous dolphins, the water bug and crab, and the deeply chased, curling tendrils are all in perfect scale and feel, as formal elements, to the hand-hammered surface of the piece. The punch bowl form is conventional and functional, but this

269 Coffeepot, sugar, and creamer inlaid with gold and copper. The petals of the large blossom on the pot are striated with copper while the filaments of its stamen are terminated by small gold balls. Ears and leaves of wheat decorate the cream pitcher, and the sugar bowl has the blossom, bud, pod, and leaves of the lotus. Made in 1879. Height of pot: 8 7/16 in. (21.4 cm.). Mark: NO. 30, pot 5401/441/907; creamer 401/2987/909; sugar bowl 5383/2087/908. (*Cleveland Museum of Art, Norman O. and Ella A. Stone Memorial Fund*).

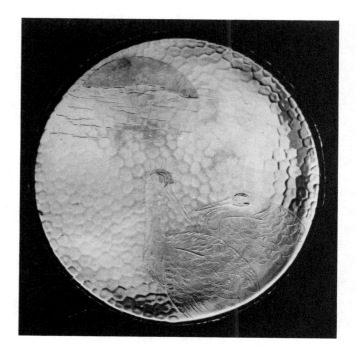

270 Hand-hammered tray with copper sun inlay and yellow gold alloy inlays in the heads of the two cranes. Inscribed on the bottom: "A TESTIMONIAL OF GRATITUDE / FROM / W.H.S. / TO / DR T.H. BUCKLER / APRIL 1880." Diameter: 10 in. (25.4 cm.). Mark: NO. 30 (5767/1480/169). *(Baltimore Museum of Art).*

bowl is a far cry from the usual punch bowl of the time. It is pure sculpture. We know that the motifs had their origin in Japanese art but these motifs are used so abstractly that the bowl is not really Japanese in feel. It is perhaps the masterpiece of Tiffany's silver in the Japanese style.

Japanese Metalworkers at Tiffany's

The story of Japanese metal workers being brought over from Japan to work in Tiffany's Prince Street silver plant has been mentioned by a number of writers in recent years. It was assumed that they were involved in the making of Tiffany's silver in the Japanese style. But the details of the story are elusive. We have been unable to pin down any specific facts. The only contemporary accounts of such Japanese workmen are brief mentions in French publications of the 1880s and 1890s.

The first mention of Japanese workmen at Tiffany's was by L. Falize (writing under the pseudonym of M. Josse) in an article, "L'Art Japonais," published in the *Revue des Arts Décoratifs* in 1883.[3] Falize stated that Tiffany & Co. had sent an associate to Japan who brought back a group of chasers *(ciseleurs)* to work in their silvermaking plant in New York where he said they were

198

given relatively free reign except that they were restricted to conventional silver forms. G. de Leris, writing in the *Revue des Arts Décoratifs* a few months later, also mentions, probably as a result of Falize's article, that Japanese workmen were brought over from Japan by Tiffany.[4]

Samuel Bing in his book *Artistic America*, first published in 1895, wrote:

Moore had invited teams of Japanese craftsmen to America, under whose guidance tonalities of every kind were mixed with silver. The effect of these inlays, to which niello had already been added, was burnished still further by other coloring methods. Experiments with enamels followed, in which, by alternating muted, sombre tones with brilliant, translucent areas, a maximum degree of technical skill and ingenuity was attained. And finally, to be sure that every resource had been exhausted and to obtain the last work in splendor, precious stones were added.[5]

271 Large parcel-gilt punch bowl, hand hammered with applied dolphins around the top, water bug and crab applied to base. Deeply chased tendrils on base. Engraved with the inscription: "BUCK CUP FOR ALL SCHOONERS OF NYYC / AND EYC. NEW BEDFORD, AUG. 5, 1881 / WON BY HALCYON." Height: 12 in. (30.5 cm.). Diameter: 17 in. (43.2 cm.). Mark: NO. 19 (6175/2977). (*New York Yacht Club*).

These French references have created a problem. At the time of this writing (1978) we have not been able to find a single reference to these Japanese workmen in any contemporary American publication. The volumes of Tiffany & Co.'s clipping files, which go back to the 1840s, appear to have no mention of the employment of Japanese workmen by Tiffany. None of the dozens of plant working drawings of the silver in the Japanese style have any Japanese names or Japanese notations of any kind on them, all pencil notes being in English. A promotional brochure issued in 1877 by Tiffany was rather emphatic about their silver being made by Americans. In describing the first floor of the store they noted:

Passing still onward, the cases to left and right contain gold and silver plate, both in plain forms for ordinary table use, and also in every variety of costly pieces for decoration. Among these things it will be found that the spirit of Japanese Art has been largely utilized, while at the same time it has been so modified as to be brought into full harmony with the requirements of American and European civilization; and to afford, *in the hands of American workmen* [our italics], results of the most striking kind.

Edwin C. Taylor, writing in *The National Repository* in 1879 about Tiffany's Japanese silver, said that Tiffany had created a "new school" of decorative art:

The forms of some of the articles of daily use—the tea pots and the water jugs—follow nature very closely, and the gourd forms and modifications of vegetable life are used with admirable effect. These, too, are suggested by the familiar works of the Japanese, who show a rare sympathy with nature in their employment of decorative figures; but technically they have advanced far beyond their Japanese models, and they were regarded with astonishment by the clever Orientals at the Exposition, the Japanese commissioner purchasing characteristic specimens for his government.

The actual techniques of making silver in the Japanese style would have been familiar to the Tiffany silversmiths—except perhaps those operations involving the use of metal mixtures and alloys of copper, gold, and silver. The earlier pieces of silver in the Japanese style, where such silver mounts as fish and insects were applied directly to the body of a piece, made use of casting and soldering techniques well known at the time. The idea of applying and inlaying one metal onto a different kind of metal had been used in Near Eastern and Far Eastern art for centuries. Moore's workmen undoubtedly studied the many pieces of Islamic metalwork from Moore's collection, where silver and gold were inlaid in brass and copper.

If Japanese workmen were employed in Tiffany's Prince Street works (and one assumes Falize and Bing had some basis for their statements) there is the question of when they worked in New York. It must have been after 1877 and possibly it was in the 1880s, since the objects employing techniques described by Bing were almost all made in the 1880s and 1890s.

Tiffany continued to make silver in the Japanese style until the end of the nineteenth century, mostly based on designs of the 1870s. The *Jewelers Circular* in reporting on the 1889 Paris Exposition noted that Tiffany showed "many specimens in the Japanese style." However, there was no evidence of Japanese silver in Tiffany's exhibit at The Columbian Exposition in Chicago in 1893, only four years later. The style, insofar as Tiffany was concerned, seems to have ended with Edward C. Moore's death in 1891.

It is clear that the Japanese influence was beneficial to Tiffany silver and the decorative arts in general. It was a breath of fresh air that led artists back to nature as a prime source of artistic ideas. Tiffany made unusually intelligent use of the arts of Japan and opened up entirely new ways of making old commonplace objects. It certainly led to some of the most beautiful silver Tiffany ever made. In retrospect we realize it didn't last very long: a dozen creative years—1871 to 1882.

Other Exotic Influences

Islamic art, particularly the art of Persia and Turkey, was a continuing influence on Tiffany silver throughout the latter part of the nineteenth century. But it was never as all-pervasive at any one time as the Japanese influence and there was never a cohesive Islamic or Persian or Turkish "style" in Tiffany silver. The long-necked and long-spouted Islamic coffeepot was a popular and long-lasting stylistic influence, being used with all kinds of related and unrelated styles.

Moore's sketchbooks have a number of Islamic notations but there are far fewer Islamic drawings than those pertaining to Japan. Perhaps, as in the case of Chinese art mentioned earlier in this chapter, it was *too* familiar. Islamic art was well known and accessible through books

272 Coffeepot, sugar, and creamer from a six-piece service in heavy niello work with Indian and Islamic design motifs. The set was presented at Christmas 1879 to Superintendent of Schools Henry Kiddle by the teachers of the public schools of New York City. Made in 1874. Height of coffeepot: 10 1/8 in. (25.7 cm.). Mark: NO. 19 (3650/8920). (*Museum of the City of New York*).

273 Teapot, sugar, cream pitcher, and sugar tongs in hand-raised silver, gilded, with colored enamels. Carved ivory finial on teapot lid. Made in 1885. Length of teapot: 11 in. (27.9 cm.). Mark: NO. 19 (8473/8147 [teapot 8148]). (*The Metropolitan Museum of Art*).

and magazines. Many nineteenth-century travelers visited the Islamic art centers in Spain, North Africa, and the Near East. Although Islamic art was studied and collected and admired throughout the nineteenth century, it never at any one time led to a burst of interest comparable to the wave of enthusiasm that Japanese art created in the 1860s and 1870s.

Nevertheless Islamic art was an influence and some fine examples were made by Tiffany. The niello coffee service in Figure 272 is related to Islamic metalwork. The Tiffany designers have taken the overall decorative effect of Islamic pieces such as the jug from Edward Moore's collection in Figure 29 and stylized the design. This was done by clearly compartmentalizing the floral motifs into distinct vertical panels with decorative horizontal bands above, a dense but beautifully realized design. The coffeepot is a standard Islamic shape with its sensitively curved handle and spout.

The enameled tête-à-tête set in Figure 273, which is also Islamic in origin, was made in 1885. The pieces are entirely handmade. They are enameled, etched, and gilded both on the outside and the inside. These pieces were no doubt influenced by Russian and French enameled silver. In them, silver becomes a kind of jewelry. They are magnificently crafted, but they are art objects to be admired rather than to be used. This precious jewellike quality is very much apparent in the inlaid wood cup in Figure 274. The lift of the smooth, carved, cutout handles, the graceful vertical ribbing with beads, and the delicate inlays of silver, mother-of-pearl, and turquoise give this piece a buoyant opulence that was very much in tune with the late nineteenth century.

Just before and after the turn of the century, Tiffany made several exhibition pieces specifically for the world's fairs of the times. Pieces were made for the World's Columbian Exposition in Chicago in 1893, the Exposition Universelle in Paris in 1900, and the Pan-American Exposition in Buffalo in 1901. The silver made for these expositions had a special mark in addition to the usual Tiffany mark (see Chapter 13).

The Viking Punch Bowl in Figure 275 was, along with the Magnolia Vase (Fig. 37), the most talked about and ambitious Tiffany work of "silver" shown at the Columbian Exposition in Chicago. It was, perhaps, more restrained and formal in design than the Magnolia Vase, but every bit as spectacular. The design is pure Tiffany

274 Two-handled loving cup of amboyne wood mounted with a die-rolled border of grape leaves and grapes and a cast base of grape leaves with rams' heads and feet. Silver mounting strips and silver lining and inlays of mother-of-pearl and turquoise. Made ca. 1893. Height: 9 in. (22.9 cm.). Mark: NO. 21 (11184/3195) plus mark for the world's Columbian Exposition. (*The Metropolitan Museum of Art*).

275

276

275   The Viking Punch Bowl made of decarbonized iron inlaid with gold and silver. There
is a plain silver lining and a detachable
base. Made in 1892. Diameter: 20 1/4 in. (51.4
cm.). Mark: TIFFANY & CO 11171 MAKERS, plus
mark for The World's Columbian Exposition.
(*The Metropolitan Museum of Art, Edgar J.
Kaufmann Charitable Foundation, 1969*).

276   Tiffany called this a "New Zealand Love
Cup," basing the design on Maori motifs.
Height: 14 3/4 in. (37.5 cm.). (*From a Tiffany
photograph of about 1901*).

even though the decorative elements derive from medieval manuscripts and Viking artifacts. The bowl itself is not actually silver but "decarbonized iron" which has been etched and inlaid with gold and silver, with a plain silver lining. The handle shapes piercing the rim of the bowl symbolized the prows of Viking ships.

The handmade and hand-chased cup in Figure 276 was shown at the Pan-American Exposition. Tiffany called it a "New Zealand Love Cup." It is based on Maori wood carving forms and motifs.

Indians, Indians

American Indians were not exactly "exotic" to Americans of the last quarter of the nineteenth century. There were still Indians living in close proximity to white men in the East, and the struggle for the West was still going on—Custer made that stand in 1876. However, Indians were treated romantically (as if they were exotic) by Tiffany's artists. The Tiffany silversmiths often depicted the frenzied world of ritualistic Indian dances rather than the quiet, dignified, and infinitely sad world Edward S. Curtis gave us in his photographs of actual American Indians. American Indian design was never a major influence on Tiffany silver and it was only the Indian spoons of the 1880s and 1890s that received much recognition.

That Edward C. Moore was thinking of Indian spoons and other things Indian at a fairly early date is shown by the pages from Sketchbook II in Figure 277. We do not know of any actual pieces of Tiffany silver based on these sketches.

One of the widely publicized pieces of Tiffany silver of the 1870s was a fantastic pair of "Indian" candelabra (Fig. 278). The candelabra were praised by critics in America and Europe. One glowing 1879 account said:

A feature of the display of American plate at the Paris Exposition, and one that we might wish had been more conspicuous and found more numerous examples, because it was essentially and wholly American in design, was embodied in a single pair of candelabra (an engraving of which is given on this page) ornamented with implements and adornments of the North American Indian. The fitness of these primitive ornaments for decorative purposes of the very highest order was clearly shown in the sole example, which also presented the only piece of true metal sculpture, *per se,* in the display

277 A page of drawings from Sketchbook II showing designs for Indian spoons and the prow of a "Celtic" ship.

of American plate. This was the representation of two Indians, one at the base of the candelabrum peacefully paddling his canoe; the other surmounting the whole design, and in an attitude of victory, waving above his head the bloody trophy of victory. The execution of these figures called forth flattering comments from the *Gazette des Beaux Arts,* and as they represent a field of art that has been less diligently worked in America than some others, the success should encourage greater effort and the expectation of grander results.

The typical American ornament which formed the subordinate decoration of these candelabra possesses as pure a nationality as the everlasting Pyramids, and when developed in coming years it will insure a style of decoration as dis-

206

tinctive and as rich in artistic effectiveness as that of Egypt, Greece, or Japan.

These decorative forms are fine examples of metal sculpture—that is, they are cast and then finished by chasing tools in the hand of a skillful artisan, so that indeed they are as much works of art as though chiseled from a shapeless block of metal.

The attitude of the exultant chief that surmounts the candelabrum tells its own story, but the delicate tooling of the features—so fine as to show the pores of the skin, cannot be shown in a small engraving. The height of the originals is 35 inches; they weigh nearly 500 ounces and cost $3000, it is needless to add that they were executed by Messrs. Tiffany & Co., of New York. They were purchased by Mr. James Gordon Bennett, Jr. of the New York *Herald*.[6]

The first of Tiffany's Indian spoons were designed and made in 1884. Charles T. Grosjean, who designed most of Tiffany's flatware of the 1880s, obtained two design patents for the Indian spoons:

	Patent No.	Date Filed	Date Issued
Large Indian spoons	15,785	Oct. 14, 1884	Feb. 10, 1885
Small Indian spoons	15,831	Dec. 31, 1884	Feb. 17, 1885

Both patents showed actual photographs of the spoons indicating they were made and ready for sale in 1884.

The large Indian spoons have cast finials which have sculptured figures on the front side and are flat on the back. The backs are engraved and chased with appropriate designs. The large cast finials are about 2⅜ inches (6 cm.) long with the overall length of the spoons being about 8 inches (20.3 cm.) to 9½ inches (24.1 cm.).

The large spoon finials all depict ritual Indian dances:

Scalp dance	Pipe dance
Chief dance	Beggar dance
Slave dance	Ball dance
Bear dance	Discovery dance
Coon dance	Medicine dance
Buffalo dance	Eagle dance

The small Indian spoons were after-dinner coffee spoons whose bowls were plain inside but decorated on the back. The decorated shafts were topped by the Indian "statuettes." These statuettes were small sculptures in the round, about 1¼ inches (3.2 cm.) in length. There were twelve subjects indicated for the handles:

278 Drawing of one of a pair of candelabra made by Tiffany about 1876. They were 35 inches high and weighed "nearly 500 ounces." They were purchased by James Gordon Bennett of the New York *Herald* and were exhibited at the 1878 Paris Exposition.

Full dressed warrior	Pipe dance
Lacrosse player	Bow dance
Indian maid	Club dance
Bear dance	Discovery dance
War dance	Medicine dance
Buffalo dance	Coyote dance

These small spoons are related to English apostle spoons, as was noted by several contemporary writers.

William Randolph Hearst acquired a large flatware service from Tiffany's in the 1890s decorated with the above mentioned Indian motifs. Figure 279 shows typical pieces of the service. The knife handles are decorated with gilt and copper roundels. When the Hearst service was sold at Sotheby Parke Bernet in 1975, it comprised: 30 soup spoons, 36 dessert spoons, 23 bouillon spoons, 29 cocktail forks, 30 lunch knives, 29 dinner forks, 29 lunch forks, 24 butter spreaders, 19 dinner knives, 29 teaspoons,

279 Part of a service with American Indian motifs acquired by William Randolph Hearst in the 1890s. The original set had well over 300 pieces. Mark: M TIFFANY & CO STERLING PAT 1884. The individual pieces are marked with pattern numbers, the large spoon on the left is marked "608." (*Sotheby Parke Bernet*).

15 serving pieces, and a 4-piece carving set. This 297-piece service weighed 532 ounces.

The William Randolph Hearst collection also included some interesting "Aztec" silver made by Tiffany's. The large plateau in Figure 280 is a spectacular example. The circular tray decorated with the Aztec Calendar design is raised on eight step supports, with openwork apron, each support headed by a polished agate in the form of a scallop shell.

From 1885 to the early 1900s Tiffany made a number of pieces of hollow ware based on Indian motifs. Figure 281 shows a chalice or cup decorated with bas-relief designs of three George Catlin drawings: "Sundance Shield," "Bear Dance," and "Scalp Dance." The photograph in Figure 281 shows the Scalp Dance. The Tiffany artist simplified and condensed Catlin's design, making a

280 Plateau with etched Aztec calendar design, raised on eight step supports, with openwork apron, each support headed by a scallop shell shaped agate. Made about 1892. Diameter: 21 in. (53 cm.). *(Sotheby Parke Bernet).*

strong compact image. The cup's feet are three massive buffalo heads and buffalo hoofs.

Around the turn of the century a few hollow-ware pieces were made which were almost direct copies in silver of Indian forms. The bowl in Figure 282 is copied from a Zuni Indian basket. It has copper colored designs and turquoise set in the top. This piece, which was shown at the 1900 Paris Exposition, is the most successful of several Tiffany pieces based on Indian baskets. This was the great period of Indian basket collecting and there was widespread interest in all kinds of Indian artifacts.

Tiffany's excursions into Indian designs were relatively limited with only the Indian spoons reaching a degree of popularity. Their Indian designs never had the influence and critical acclaim that the silver in the Japanese style had, but they have a continuing interest, particularly to Americans.

281 Three-handled cup with repoussé bas-relief designs from George Catlin's drawings, with *Scalp Dance* being shown. Handles are in the form of buffalo horns and the feet are buffalo heads and buffalo hoofs. Copper insets. Height: 10 5/16 in. (26.2 cm.). Mark: NO. 19 (8648/1197) plus "11 1/2 pts." *(Courtesy of Christopher Webster)*.

282 Silver bowl with copper and turquoise inserts, in the form of a Zuni Indian basket. Height 3 1/4 in. (8.2 cm.). *(From a Tiffany photograph of about 1900)*.

281

TIFFANY & CO. EXHIBIT
PARIS EXPOSITION 1900
BOWL, ZUNI INDIAN BASKET, SILVER AND TURQUOISE
NEG. NO. 1943   HEIGHT 3¼

282

11. Electroplated Silver

This CHAPTER deals with electroplated silver hollow
ware and flatware sold by Tiffany & Co. Electroplated
silver, which is much more widely owned because of its
lower cost, has, when new, the glitter and appearance of
sterling even though its composition is quite different.
Electroplated silver is made by depositing thin layers of
pure silver on the surface of such metals as copper, nickel,
and "German silver." (Incidentally, German silver contains no silver but is an alloy of copper, zinc, and nickel
with a silverlike appearance.) We use the term electroplated silver so as to distinguish it clearly from the
earlier Sheffield plate. Both terms electroplate and Sheffield plate refer to silver-plated objects but their origins
are quite different.

The term electroplate was regularly used by Tiffany.
Their 1879 catalog had a long listing of articles under the
heading of HARD-METAL ELECTRO-PLATED WARE. The modern usage of the term old Sheffield plate refers to those
objects, mostly from Sheffield, England, made of copper
coated with silver by fusion. In Sheffield plated ware two
thin sheets of silver were laid on the two sides of a
thicker sheet of copper, making a sandwich of silver outside and copper inside, which was heated and then rolled
in a mill, fusing the metals together. Also two-component
laminates of one thin sheet of silver and a thicker sheet
of copper were used, resulting in a sheet with silver on
one side and copper on the other. The silver-clad copper
was made into objects of all kinds by silversmiths using
the same techniques as with sterling metal. The introduction of Sheffield plate in the eighteenth century greatly
broadened the market for silversmiths' goods, since the
then new wares were much cheaper than sterling. Shef-

field plate was also able to replace many pieces that were formerly made in pewter.

The introduction of electroplated silver in about 1840 in England by the firm G. R. & H. Elkington of Birmingham revolutionized the plated silver business. The object to be plated was placed in a solution ("bath") containing the proper chemicals, usually cyanides. The object was attached to an electrical circuit which included a power source, such as a battery, and another electrode, usually pure silver. In the solution the silver metal electrode acts as the anode and the electrical current causes atoms of silver to leave the silver anode and migrate through the solution to the cathode, the object being plated. The amount of silver deposited on a piece is a function of the amount of electrical current, the composition of the solution, and the plating time.[1]

The use of electroplating soon finished the old Sheffield process. It was cheaper and involved less labor. Instead of making a laminated silver and copper sandwich and *then* making the desired object, the new process involved making an object first of copper or other metal and then depositing a thin layer of silver on it. The electroplating process involved less wastage of silver, and, in addition, thinner layers of silver could be used. Of course much of the new electroplated ware did not have the durability of old Sheffield plate, but its appearance when new was as good as or better than the old Sheffield plate. Inevitably the old process was superseded.

Elkington immediately tried to sell their process in America but at the beginning there was little interest. However, several electroplating shops were opened in America in the mid-1840s and by the end of the decade silver electroplating had become an established industry, first for flatware and then for hollow ware. Electroplated wares had one advantage over sterling—they were cheaper and remain cheaper.

Although there is evidence from Tiffany plant records that a few pieces of electroplated ware were made by them in the 1850s, it was only after the Civil War that they began to promote electroplated silver actively.

It should be noted that the Sheffield plate mentioned in the advertisement at right was electroplated silver, not the old Sheffield plate. The American electroplate that Tiffany sold came from the Thomas Shaw Company of Providence, Rhode Island.

Thomas Shaw, founder of the company with his name,

213

PLATED WARE

—

TIFFANY & CO.,

Union Square, New York,

Having completed their new works for the manufacture of Plated Ware, are now producing, by improved processes, ware superior to any before offered.

Being made of the best hard white metal and SILVER, SOLDERED IN EVERY PART, it is almost indestructible by use.

The forms are designed with reference to real service, and the ornamentation is free from the showiness that usually distinguishes plated from silver ware, the greatest care having been taken to produce articles to meet the wants of the best City trade.

In order to make room for a complete stock of the above goods, their stock from English and other makers will be sold at reduced prices.

TIFFANY & CO. also call attention to their stock of TABLE CUTLERY from the best Sheffield makers.

was a talented English silversmith who was first apprenticed to Elkington of Birmingham about 1850. He was skilled both as a designer and silversmith and was highly knowledgeable about electroplating. It is this latter skill that drew him to the Gorham Company in Providence, Rhode Island. Shaw came to America right after the Civil War in 1865 and was, no doubt, instrumental in helping Gorham start up their electroplating operation in that year. Gorham had experimented with electroplating in the 1850s but it was 1865 before they were in commercial production.

In about 1868 Shaw left Gorham and formed Thomas Shaw & Company in cooperation with Tiffany & Co. Tiffany probably furnished the capital for the new company since Charles L. Tiffany was its treasurer. In about 1874 Mr. C. C. Adams resigned from the Gorham Company where he had been in charge of manufacturing and joined Thomas Shaw, the company name becoming Adams & Shaw. A Nov. 24, 1874 advertisement suggests that the formation of the new company, Adams & Shaw, coincided with a new manufacturing plant (left).

Tiffany never referred to Thomas Shaw or Adams & Shaw in their advertisements and promotional literature. The Tiffany brochure for the Philadelphia Centennial in 1876 only noted that they (Tiffany & Co.) were "Makers of Electro-plated ware, Works, Providence, R. I." In 1877 Adams & Shaw moved their manufacturing facilities to Newark, New Jersey at the corner of Park Street and Mulberry. Adams & Shaw, who had an office at 692 Broadway in 1870, made both sterling and electroplated wares for the trade in general. The Adams & Shaw operation was absorbed into Tiffany & Co., probably in the 1880s, with Mr. Shaw becoming superintendent of the Tiffany plant.

Possibly one of the reasons that Thomas Shaw sold out to Tiffany & Co. was the loss of his son in 1885. Frank Shaw, the son, had learned the silversmithing trade under the guidance of his father. Frank was a talented designer and no doubt his father was thinking in terms of his taking over the business. But this was not to be. Frank was found to have tuberculosis. He went to Denver, Colorado, for his health in 1885 but he soon died there at the age of twenty-four. He wrote his father from Denver the following letter referring to the drawing in Figure 283. It is a peculiarly poignant letter showing clearly how much his mind was on his beloved silver-smithing:

214

Denver Feb. 25th 1885

Dear Father

I send with this a drawing for that pattern you sent and I think it will look nice. It can be made to miter, and I intend the scrolls on the spout and handle to mitre [sic] those on the body so when they are put together it will look like one thing and not look put on like most handles and spouts do. It is not a finished drawing but I guess you can see what I mean. I dont know that the scrolls will come out all right round the body. (I mean those I have drawn).

I could fix it all right if I had a body made. Do you like the idea of the scrolls overlaping each other? For the nob I think a scroll will look good coming out of the others on the cover like I have shown. I suppose Mr Allen will be here tomorrow. It is a splendid day.

If you want me to chase a body why I will. I dont know whether the drawing is a good size or not. The box has not come yet so I will make another drawing.

From your Son

Frank

If you send a body to be chased send the drawing too. If you had a wooden model made I could model on it and it would be better than chasing. Also send that box of wax in

283 Pencil and ink sketch for a teapot by Frank Shaw, made for his father Thomas Shaw, in 1885. *(Newark Museum)*.

215

284 Electroplated sugar bowl made by Adams and Shaw for Tiffany about 1875. Height: 3 9/16 in. (9 cm.). Mark: NO. 41 (24). (*Gebelein Silversmiths*).

285 Electroplated coffeepot made about 1890. Reeded lid and base, engraved designs on body and spout. Ebony handle and finial. Height: 10 1/2 in. (26.7 cm.). Mark: NO. 42. (*Newark Museum*).

284

285

the book case. Do you intend to stamp the cover at the same time? or spin it. You cant stamp it all at once for it wont leave.

Tiffany sold a very complete line of electroplated wares. They stressed quality and emphasized the fact that their hard metal plated wares were silver soldered in every joint. An 1875 Tiffany & Co. advertisement noted: "Tiffany & Co. were the first to discard entirely the use of soft solder in soldering joints, and no weak spot or defect can be found in any piece of ware made by them." The 1878 Tiffany catalog noted that their plated wares were "in use at the Baldwin, the new hotel in San Francisco, Delmonico's, The Union Club, the Brunswick, and many other public houses and private families."

The Tiffany catalogs of the 1870s and 1880s show that they sold plated wares in almost every form available in sterling. The 1880 catalog listed items in almost a hundred categories ranging from "Ale mugs with glass bottoms" to "Waiters, round and oval." Of course many people bought both sterling and electroplate. It is not at all unusual to find a sterling tea and coffee service with a plated tray. Many serving dishes were electroplate and electroplated flatware was popular for hotel and club use and everyday family use.

Tiffany did not use the same designs for both sterling and electroplate. Many of the designs are similar, with the electroplate designs often being simplified versions of the sterling designs.

Plated tea sets were popular items. In the 1879 catalog five-piece tea sets with teapot, coffeepot, sugar bowl, slop bowl, and cream pitcher were listed at $85 to $175. A similar tea set in sterling would have cost from $250 to $2,500. Figure 284 shows a sugar bowl of a tea set from about 1875. The design is related to those of sterling tea and coffee services of the time. The detail is a little coarser, particularly the handles, but the overall effect is one of restraint and good taste at a time when some other makers were selling the most outlandish and overdecorated electroplate designs.

The coffeepot in Figure 285 is a first-rate piece whose quality is equal to the best of Tiffany's sterling of the time. The coffeepot descended in the family of Thomas Shaw and the design has been attributed to him. The chaste and beautiful lacelike engraving on the body and the spout are balanced by the fluting on the lid and the

216

286

base. Islamic in shape, it is full and graceful.

The teapot in Figure 286 is a lovely example of Tiffany's electroplate made about 1905. To the traditional classical shape has been added a handsome repousséd floral border. The repoussé work fills the space completely but the design is so well integrated and so orderly that there is no sense of crowding. Every flower and every leaf is clearly and distinctly delineated and yet there is no feeling of fussiness.

The turn-of-the-century candelabra in Figure 287 in the perennially popular rococo style shows a particularly appropriate use of electroplate. This kind of object gets a

286 Electroplated teapot made about 1905. Reeded lid and base, engraved designs on lid. Ebony handle and finial. Height: 6 in. (15.2 cm.). (*The New-York Historical Society*).

287 Electroplated candelabra with removable sockets. Rococo style with C-scroll arms. Height: 10 3/16 in. (25.9 cm.). Mark: 984 / TIFFANY & CO / MAKERS / SILVER-SOLDERED—E.P. / 151 / W. (*Hilbert Brothers*).

287

217

288 Electroplated coffee or hot water urn with lid, stand, and lamp, made about 1910. Ivory spigot handle. The urn locks onto the stand. Height: 13 in. (33 cm.). Mark: NO. 43 (180/ 7378). (*Private Collection*).

289 Electroplated portable stove consisting of a cup with folding handles and lid, alcohol reservoir and lamp. The stove pieces fit into the leather carrying case. The wind shield was not made by Tiffany. Height in case: 4 3/4 in. (12 cm.). Mark: TIFFANY & CO / MAKERS / SILVER-SOLDERED / DOUBLE 269 260 C. (*Brooklyn Museum*).

288

minimum of wear and tear and the silverplate should hold up much longer than it does on such objects as trays.

The coffee or hot water urn in Figure 288 which was made early in the twentieth century is a fine example of those things for which Tiffany & Co. has become famous— taste and quality. The fluted panels of the full, ripe shape of the body are echoed in the fluting of the handles, the legs of the stand, and the lamp. It is a strong, simple design for a useful object. The quality of the workmanship is superb. The silver plating is intact and immaculate today—three-quarters of a century after it was made —indicating that the "Double" in the mark really did mean two complete cycles in the silver-plating operation. It was characteristic of electroplate makers of the time to talk of double, triple, and quadruple plate but with their usual reticence Tiffany seldom used the word "double" on its electroplate marks (Mark No. 43). This coffee urn certainly represents the best of Tiffany's electroplate.

The collapsible stove in Figure 289 is a most interesting object. The parts of the stove fit neatly in a leather carrying case from which they can be assembled into a stove unit for outdoor cooking or heating of soup or other liquids. The shield shown in Figure 289 (which was not made by Tiffany) would be useful in keeping the lamp lit on windy days. This is the sort of superb gadget for which the Tiffany silvermakers had an obvious fondness.

Tiffany's Electroplated Flatware

Tiffany did not emphasize their plated flatware and it was not featured in their catalogs. It was the kind of trade more adapted to the high volume companies such as Rogers Brothers than to the high quality (and high priced) sterling market where Tiffany was the leader. No doubt many of their customers used Tiffany electroplated flatware for everyday, for "second best," and in their summer houses. And it was used in hotels and clubs. But Tiffany electroplated flatware never was made in any great volume. It is seldom found in antique shops and shows.

Tiffany retailed other makers' electroplated flatware during the 1870s and the early 1880s. This must have included flatware from Adams and Shaw. During at least part of this period Tiffany also sold English electroplate, advertising it as "Sheffield plated ware." The 1880 Tif-

289

290

fany catalog indicates that a very complete line of "Hard-metal Electro-plated flatware" was available in everything from tablespoons to grape scissors. Essentially all forms of flatware serving pieces available in sterling were also available in electroplate: "Tiffany & Co. patterns of Forks and Spoons have a distinctive character that renders them equal to silver in everything but intrinsic value."

In 1885 Tiffany made the move to establish its own electroplated flatware line, and four designs, all patented by Charles T. Grosjean (p. 96) appeared in that year: *King, Regent, Floral,* and *Mt. Vernon* (Figs. 290 through 293).

The *King* pattern (Fig. 290) was remarkably similar to the traditional *King* or *Kings* pattern and one wonders how Grosjean was able to obtain a patent (No. 16,216) on his pattern as a new and novel design. The *King* pattern had first been used in France and England late in the eighteenth century and it remained one of the most popular flatware patterns, both in Europe and America.

290   *King* (plated), first made in 1885.

219

Many companies made a version of *King* in both sterling and electroplate. Tiffany offered their version in sterling in 1885 calling it *English King*.

The *Regent* pattern (Fig. 291), also introduced in 1885, is related to the *King* pattern, with the shell at the top of the handle being greatly diminished in size with only a small fanlike shell shape remaining.

The *Floral* pattern (Fig. 292) also patented by Charles T. Grosjean in 1885 is described this way in the patent application:

These flowers and leaves are as follows: In the upper part of the head of the spoon are leaves and buds interspersed, with daisies and other conventional field flowers immediately beneath them. Beneath these latter-mentioned flowers are roses, rose-buds, and rose-leaves extending partly into the shank. In the shank are placed forget-me-nots and other conventional buds and leaves, interspersed, down to the bowl of the spoon.

The *Mt. Vernon* pattern (Fig. 293) is a version of the Tiffany sterling pattern *Antique* (Fig. 128) with discreet reeding on the handle.

The *Old French* pattern (Fig. 294) was designed by Edward C. Moore. His patent for the pattern (see p. 97) was issued in 1889—thirty-eight years after he joined forces with Tiffany in 1851.

Three electroplate patterns were added in the twentieth century, *Norman* in 1904 (Fig. 295) and *Stuyvesant* (Fig. 296), a traditional eighteenth-century form, in 1915. The date of the introduction of *Whittier* (Fig. 297) is unknown.

The End of Tiffany Electroplate

Tiffany stopped making electroplated wares in 1931. In that year the price of silver had dropped to an all-time low of twenty-nine cents per ounce (it was $4.90 per ounce in January 1978), and the profit margin on electroplate had disappeared. There was almost as much labor involved in the production of electroplated hollow ware as there was for similar objects made of sterling which meant that the electroplated wares should have been priced not too far below sterling. This was, of course, commercially not feasible. It is ironical that the depressed price of silver metal was able to drive the more inexpensive electroplated wares of Tiffany off the market.

291 *Regent* (plated), first made in 1885.

292 *Floral* (plated), first made in 1885.

293 *Mt. Vernon* (plated), first made in 1885.

294 *Old French* (plated), first made in 1889.

295 *Norman* (plated), first made in 1904.

296 *Stuyvesant* (plated), first made in 1915.

297 *Whittier* (plated).

12. The Making of Tiffany Silver

ONE OF THE PLEASURES of writing this book was in finding out more about the actual processes involved in the making of silver. We have studied present-day silvermaking practices at the Tiffany & Co. plant in New Jersey and have compared them with those described in the published accounts of silvermaking at Tiffany's Prince Street works in New York in the 1870s and 1880s. The making (silversmiths always refer to *making* rather than to *manufacturing*) of silver by Tiffany has changed remarkably little in the last one hundred years. Process controls are better, some of the equipment is more mechanized, but their silversmithing today remains very much as it was in the nineteenth century—essentially a hand craft.

Nineteenth-century Americans were fascinated with how things were made. Newspapers and magazines often had breezy accounts of visits to manufacturing plants of all kinds; several of these accounts were of Tiffany's Prince Street operations. We have used engravings from two of these 1870s articles to illustrate this chapter.[1] These hundred-year-old prints not only clearly illustrate the various silvermaking processes, they also give a flavor of the times.

Tiffany's silvermaking processes, which were considered highly modern in the nineteenth century, are good examples of the mechanization of earlier hand tool silver production methods. By present twentieth-century standards of computerized and automated manufacturing equipment, the Tiffany machinery of the nineteenth century was pretty primitive—really just power driven extensions of the old hand tools. However, the fact that power machinery was used at all has created a prejudice against late nineteenth-century silver among some writers, collectors, and curators.

The cutoff date of about 1830 to 1840 had been, until comparatively recently, almost universally accepted as the end of "good" silver in America. After that time, it was said, the quality went downhill. Fashionable antique and silver dealers rarely handled this "late" silver; serious collectors did not acquire it, and it was seldom shown in museums with the exceptions already noted in Chapter 1. Most of the literature on American silver and silversmiths ends at or about 1840, and, until recently, there has been little attention paid to American silver made since that time. One reason was that the silver was not old enough. It was still being used. It was not "antique." Another reason was stylistic. We have already noted in Chapter 1 how the taste of the twentieth century rejected most Victoriana. Conventional wisdom blamed the machine for much of the problem with "late" silver. Too often writers and antiquarians with insufficient knowledge of industrial America in the nineteenth century said that silver (and furniture for that matter) made by machines in factories just was not as good as older completely handmade objects. The following quotations expressed the mid-twentieth-century viewpoint: "Design started on its downward path in the nineteenth century soon after the machine became important."[2] "The craft flourished until about 1840 when the factories with their machinery for stamping and spinning silver came into general use and the silversmith as a craftsman disappeared."[3] We believe this machine-made theory has been, and continues to be, one of the principal reasons for ignoring or downgrading the silver and other decorative arts of the last half of the nineteenth century.

There is no question that by early eighteenth-century standards of silvermaking (using only hand tools) Tiffany silver can be said to have been partially machine made. But the part played by hand operations plus those processes using relatively simple power-driven tools make us reconsider the whole problem of what is "handmade." Remember that the so-called handmade silver of the eighteenth century and earlier used a myriad of specialized hand tools and that several of the machine processes we usually associate with the nineteenth century (such as rolling and stamping) were already well developed in England in the eighteenth century.[4]

In addition, it should be noted that the specialization of silvermaking processes into a kind of assembly-line production was not an invention of the nineteenth century. For example, the silver works of Matthew Boulton, the Birmingham, England, silversmith, in 1782 employed (in addition to silversmiths and apprentices) platers, spoonmakers, chasers, finishers, mounters, piercers, stampers, gilders, and candlestick makers.[5] Tiffany used the same kind of specialization even though they, like Boulton, had silversmiths fully capable of making by hand all of the traditional silver forms.

Specialization, of course, does not necessarily result in a lowering of quality. It was quite the contrary with Tiffany. Their standards and quality controls were legendary. Sloppy and second-rate work was not acceptable. Below standard pieces were either reworked or scrapped to be made again.

Even today Tiffany and some of the other leading makers of sterling silverware in the United States consider their manufacturing methods, particularly for hollow ware, to be essentially hand operations. A recent survey at Tiffany's Newark, New Jersey plant indicated that about 85 percent of their total labor time could be classified as hand operations.

Mr. Roger H. Hallowell, president of Reed and Barton, wrote in the 1960s:

Sterling silver holloware manufacturing in the modern day and age has its problems. Those in the business consider it as one of the last "craft industries" in existence. The actual operations differ little from that of ancient times. Hand methods have been converted to mechanical methods. Power in one form or another has replaced the hammer. Steel tools have replaced wooden ones. Electricity and gas have replaced charcoal for heat, but still the metal is worked in approximately the same manner.[6]

Unquestionably the number of skilled man-hours it took to make a silver coffeepot was greater in the first part of the eighteenth century than in the last half of the nineteenth century. The use of the spinning lathe alone was a great time and labor saver over the older traditional method of "raising" the body of a coffeepot by means of a long series of blows of the silversmith's hammer. Incidentally, Moore and Tiffany's have been credited with the invention of the spinning lathe,[7] but our research has not supported this claim. Metal spinning with a lathe was in use in the 1830s and possibly as early as the 1820s.[8] Moore made efficient use of the spinning lathe in his shops at a time when its use was becoming widespread, but he did not invent the process.

In summary, we do not think that the method of manufacture is the problem with late nineteenth-century silver. There had been shoddy, poorly designed silver made in all ages. There *was* probably more silver made in the nineteenth century than ever before, or since, for that matter, partly because of these improved manufacturing techniques. We must finally judge a piece of silver for what it is rather than how it was made.

Before describing the silvermaking processes used by Tiffany in the nineteenth century, we would like to say something of the metal used by the silversmiths—sterling.

What is Sterling?

Fine[9] or pure silver is too soft to be used in ordinary silverware where strength and resistance to wear are desirable and necessary. From the earliest times copper has been used to harden and strengthen silver. Examples of Roman silver in the British Museum have approximately the same analysis as our present-day sterling.[10] The English standard for silver coinage, sterling, came into use in the twelfth century during the reign of Henry II (1133–1189). The standard has been maintained since then for coinage and silverware in England, where careful governmental surveillance guarantees the maintainance of quality standards.

Sterling is defined as a metal alloy containing 92.5 percent (925-1000ths) silver and 7.5 percent (75-1000ths) copper or other base metals. The usual designation for sterling was and is 925-1000. Sometimes 925 is used alone as a shorthand designation. We often see the term *sterling silver* used although the term *sterling* is quite sufficient to describe the alloy.

Early Tiffany silver was marked in such a way as to make very sure the buyer knew he was receiving real sterling. From 1854 to 1870, centered in the Tiffany mark was:

ENGLISH STERLING
925-1000

After 1870, the term was changed to:

STERLING SILVER
925-1000

When Tiffany and Moore made their exclusive arrangement in 1851, they immediately adopted the English standard for sterling and soon showed it on their marks. There was good reason for Tiffany using the term ENGLISH STERLING, since sterling was well above the average quality of silver used by most American silversmiths of the time.

In the second quarter of the nineteenth century, just before Tiffany's entrance in the silver market, it was often customary in this country to mark silver: COIN, PURE COIN, COIN SILVER, DOLLAR, STANDARD. However, these terms could be misleading since the coins used were usually foreign and of uncertain silver content. The American coin standard from 1792 to 1837 was 892.4-1000 silver. The act of January 18, 1837 raised the U. S. standard to 900-1000 silver. Thus, even the use of American coins by silversmiths would not have produced silver of sterling standard.

In recent years the laboratories of the Henry Francis du Pont Winterthur Museum in Wilmington, Delaware have analyzed a large number of pieces of American silver by means of X-ray fluorescence spectroscopy, a nondestructive method of analysis.[11] Most silver, marked COIN, etc., shows a silver content of 850 to 900-1000ths which of course is below the sterling standard.

It is interesting to note that continental silver makers in the nineteenth century and before used a variety of standards for silver quality. Dutch silver had two standards for large pieces: a 934-1000 standard (marked Lion in shield) and an 833-1000 standard (marked Lion in hexagon). Russian silver marked 84 has led many people to erroneously conclude that it means 84 percent or 840-1000 silver. Actually the 84 designates a standard of 875-1000 silver. German silver made for the German market was only 800-1000 silver while German silver made for foreign markets used the sterling standard and was so marked.

Although Tiffany adopted the sterling standard in 1851 when Moore and Tiffany joined hands, the actual term STERLING was first used on a Tiffany mark in about 1854 (see Chapter 13). The influence of Tiffany and others led to a federal law in 1868 defining sterling.

The Tiffany Factory

Tiffany was proud of their silver workshops and often referred to them in their newspaper advertisements in the 1860s and 1870s. An advertisement in 1871 noted (Fig. 298):

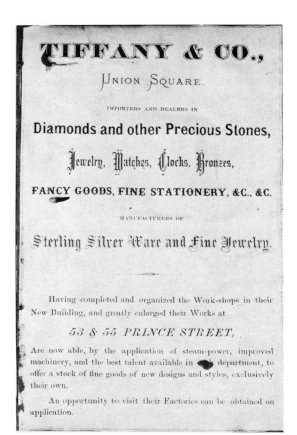

298

299   The Prince Street Silver Shop, looking west.

We do not know how many of Tiffany's customers accepted the invitation noted in the ad to visit the Prince Street factories,[12] but we do know from the newspapers and magazines of the 1870s that a number of journalists did make the visit and recorded rather extensive descriptions of the Tiffany operations. These contemporary accounts, combined with a knowledge of present-day Tiffany operations, enables one to draw a fairly accurate picture of how Tiffany made their silver in the nineteenth century.

During most of the last half of the nineteenth century Tiffany made their sterling flatware and hollow ware in their five-story Prince Street building (Fig. 299).

The Prince Street factory in its heyday of the 1870s and 1880s employed a total of 500 workers. Apprentices started at $4.00 a week. The six-day work week was the standard ten-hour day, sixty-hour week of the nineteenth century. The higher paid workers, such as designers, made up to $60 per week. This was at a time when farm

227

laborers were receiving a dollar a day, and average union "lower skilled" laborers in the United States were receiving sixteen to eighteen dollars per week.[13] The Tiffany workers were well paid according to the standards of the times.

The position of women in Tiffany's was probably normal for the time. There were no women in the sales force in either the Broadway or the Union Square stores. There were a few women employed at the Tiffany plant at wages varying from four to twelve dollars per week. An 1883 anonymous account in *Harper's Bazaar* described at some length, and in not too flattering a light, women's work in the Prince Street plant of Tiffany.[14] The article complained that women wanted to advance too rapidly and that they occasionally talked back to their foreman and refused to do certain jobs because the physical task was too heavy for them. The author did admit that women were more dependable: "Girls are regularly at their places on Monday morning whereas men are not."

The *Harper's Bazaar* article ends on an upbeat note by pointing out that women should have a good future in silversmithing as finishers, engravers, chasers, and particularly as designers:

Any woman possessing ability as a designer can earn from twenty to sixty dollars a week; and "I don't know," remarked a silversmith recently, "why a woman should not fit herself for that specialty rather than go and daub up a lot of canvas." But to become a silversmith a woman must be willing to enter a workshop, to obey rules that sometimes seem hard and be in dead earnest.

The Designing Room

The "designing room" (Fig. 315) as it was called, was the nerve center of the Prince Street works. The two dozen or so designers and their apprentices worked in a well-lit, art- and book-lined room. A journalist described Tiffany's designing room in 1878:

Our first impression as we enter is that we have strayed into the Museum of Natural History. All around are well-preserved counterfeits of birds and smaller animals, as also gourds, ears of corn, etc., all of which have already served, or will serve, as studies. Running back the entire length of the long light room are drawing boards, at which sit busy designers, while above them hang plaster casts, models and electrotypes of designs which have graced work previously done.[15]

The Prince Street works had a collection of classical and Oriental objects which were used for study purposes and models and objects from Edward C. Moore's collection were also available to the Tiffany designers. An 1878 account referred to these objects in Tiffany's designing rooms:

The Designing Room is extensive, and we saw many bright-looking youths working assiduously with paper and pencil.

A number of competitive prizes of cash were lately offered by Messrs. Tiffany & Co. for the best designs and the best specimens of repoussé, chasing and engraving. They were competed for by all the apprentices in the employ of the house, and the result was a very interesting display of students' work.

The young men who are engaged in this department of the silver works have the advantage of careful and intelligent instruction and access to an extensive art library and a *collection of classic models of great variety and value,* [our italics] and they also feel the daily pressure and influence of the most refined public taste.

It is natural then, that they should develop into skillful art workers, and that their work should be not only correct as the result of this training, but far advanced as the result of their intercourse with the ripe judgement of the times.[16]

The Prince Street Library

The art library referred to above was extensive for its time. It contained a remarkably catholic collection of books, monograms, and periodicals covering a variety of art, nature, and scientific subjects. There were books on classical art and contemporary (nineteenth century) art, Oriental art, and books on design and classical ornamentation, plus books on metallurgy and nature books of all kinds. Each of the books had a small bookplate with an identification number:

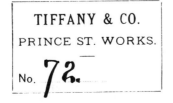

TIFFANY & CO.
PRINCE ST. WORKS.
No. 72.

There were long runs of periodicals such as *L'Art Pour Tous, The Practical Magazine, The Art Journal,* and *Scientific American.* There were many publications in French and German, with perhaps a third of the books being in French. In addition to the books and periodicals there were scrapbooks covering a wide variety of subjects: ferns, flowers, birds, Indian architecture, Japanese and Chinese pottery, Oriental metal works, classical ornaments, and so on.

There are still dozens of the original volumes in the present Tiffany plant. A few titles are:

BOOKS FROM TIFFANY'S PRINCE STREET SILVERWORKS

The Arundel Society, *Designs for Silversmiths,* London, 1871.
The Arundel Society, *Ecclesiastical Metal Work of the Middle Ages,* London, 1868.
Audsley, George A. and Bowes, James Lord, *Keramic Art of Japan,* London, 1875.
Blondel, Spire, *L'Art Intime et Gout en France,* Paris, 1884.
Ebell, Adrian J., *The Classification of Insects,* New York, 1872.
de Genouillac, H. G., *L'Art Héraldique,* Paris (no date).
Hulme, F. Edward, *Plant Form,* Stratford, Essex, England, 1867.
Jones, Owen, *Examples of Chinese Ornament in the South Kensington Museum,* London, 1867.
Lièvre, Edouard, *Les Arts Décoratifs a Toutes les Epoques,* Paris, 1870.
Meehan, Thomas, *The Native Flowers and Ferns of the United States,* New York, 1880.
Mesnard, Jules, *Les Merveilles de l'Exposition Universelle de 1867,* Paris, 1867.
Moore, Thomas, *British Ferns,* London, 1871.
Oeuvre de Jacques Androuet Dit Du Cerceau, Paris (no date).
Les Palmiers, Histoire Iconographique, Paris, 1878.
Pfnor, Rodolphe, *Ornementation Usuelle,* Paris, 1867.
Rothschild, J., ed., *Les Fougères,* Paris, 1867.
Rouaix, Paul, *Dictionnaire des Arts Décoratifs,* Paris (no date).
Sebah, P., *Musée Arabe,* Paris, 1878.
Williamson, John, *Fern Etchings,* Louisville, Kentucky, 1879.
Wornum, Ralph N., *The Characteristics of Styles,* London, 1856.

The Processes Used in Silvermaking

In the remainder of this chapter we describe briefly the processes of making and rolling the sterling metal, the conversion of the rolled sterling stock into flatware and hollow ware, and the finishing of these products.

SILVER MELTING: Measured amounts of fine silver, copper, and materials called deoxidizers (for removing impurities) were placed in the ceramic crucibles (shown on the steps in Fig. 300). The mixture in the crucible was then melted in a gas-fired furnace (in the eighteenth century, a charcoal-fired furnace with hand bellows would have been used in this operation). After about an hour and a half in the furnace the metal mixture became completely molten at about 1800° F. (980° C.).

After the silver had been in the molten state long enough to become completely mixed with the copper, the crucible was removed from the furnace with metal tongs. Before pouring, small pieces of hard wood were thrown on top of the molten metal. The wood burned immediately and formed a protective layer of carbon dioxide to prevent oxidation during pouring. Oxygen in the silver causes fire scale, a gray oxide layer on the silver which has to be removed by buffing or by a nitric acid dip.

The molten sterling metal was poured into cast iron ingot molds. The size of the mold depended on what was to be made from the silver ingot. The ingot or "skillet" for flatware was 20 inches long, 1¼ inches wide, and ¾ inch thick. The skillet for hollow ware was 10 inches long, 6 inches wide, and 1½ inches thick.

The metal cooled and solidified quickly and in a few minutes could be removed from the mold. After complete cooling, the skillet was "pickled" in an acid bath and the surface of the skillet was scraped on all sides to remove impurities and was then ready for rolling.

ROLLING THE SILVER INGOTS: The steam driven rolling mill shown in Figure 301 was typical of the mills used in the larger silversmithing shops to reduce the size of the sterling ingot to a dimension convenient for further fabrication. This type of rolling mill for silver slabs came into use in the eighteenth century. Before the introduction of the rolling mill, it would have been necessary to reduce the size of the silver ingots by the slow, laborious process of beating with a sledge hammer.[17]

For hollow ware, the larger 1½-inch thick sterling skillets were rolled in the two-roll mill until the slab was about .036 to .045 of an inch thick. The reduction of the thickness of the slab by rolling caused corresponding increases in length and width.

For flatware the ¾-inch thick ingot was put through the two-roll mill for several passes until the stock was reduced to a quarter-inch thickness. The rolling process caused "work hardening" which meant that it was necessary to anneal the metal to a cherry-red heat and cool

300   The Melting Room.

301   Rolling the Silver.

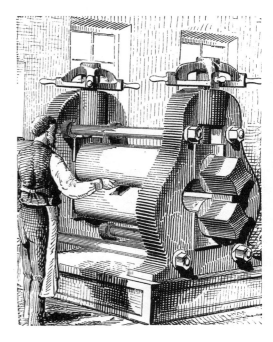

231

302 Photograph of "Silversmiths, Fourth Floor, EAST" in the Prince Street works. Note the gas and compressed air pipes in front of each workman for annealing. Some of the young apprentices look to be no more than 14 or 15 years old. *(Photograph ca. 1885 from Tiffany & Co. files).*

303 Spoon blanks. A shows rough blanks with bowl part to the top rolled thin. B shows blank ready to receive a pattern.

304 Drop Press.

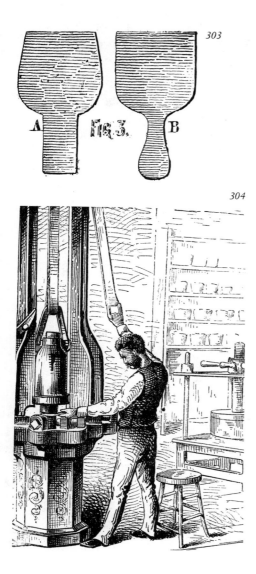

303

304

before further working. The softening of sterling by annealing was repeated many times throughout the whole silvermaking process. In annealing the silversmith had to be careful not to heat the metal too high or too long because of the danger of oxidizing the metal to form fire scale. A contemporary newspaper account went into Tiffany's annealing process in some detail:

Annealing was formerly done with charcoal fires, and soldering with whale-oil lamps; they were slow, and clumsy, and dirty processes then. The dust and ashes of the charcoal and the filthy soot and gurry of the lamps begrimed rooms and workmen alike. Now the rooms are as clean as a first-class laundry, and the workmen—well, the workmen are considerably cleaner than most washerwomen. By the side of the solderer lies a pipe composed of two parallel tubes attached to flexible hoses; through one hose pours gas, and through the other condensed [compressed] air; a stop-cock turns on both, the gas is lighted, and the air rushing out beside it projects the long flame upon any desired part with an intense heat, which quickly does the work. [See Fig. 302] This system, invented by this house, has been partially copied by others; but this is the only house where it can be said that no charcoal whatever is used. One of the many advantages of this is the lessened danger of fire. TIFFANY & CO. now pays much less insurance than they did under the old sperm and charcoal system.[18]

THE MAKING OF FLATWARE: The bar of silver, which had been rolled to a quarter-inch thick strip, was ready to be made into forks and spoons. Ponderous shears first cut the strip into suitable lengths for the individual articles to be produced. The ends of these pieces were then rolled in a transverse direction which flattened that part which was to form the bowl of a spoon or tines of a fork, until such parts were about 2½ inches in width. The blank, as it was termed, was in the shape of A in Figure 303. This piece was then placed in a die in the drop press (Fig. 304) where it was cut into the required shape, rounded at the shank as shown in B of Figure 303.

The "blank" was then ready to receive the pattern, which was imparted in one of two ways. The first involved the use of flat steel dies in a drop press. The second method, which was the one most commonly used by Tiffany in the nineteenth century, involved the use of die rolls. The pattern was impressed on the blank by passing it through a hand-engraved case-hardened roll (Fig. 305). In operating the machine, the rolls were set

302

in motion, and the workman inserted blanks for the articles desired, as the respective dies rotated in front of him. As the metal entered the rolls it was caught by the deep notches made beside the pattern, and was thus prevented from slipping. On emerging, a blank appeared as in Fgure 306.

The pattern was perfectly formed but the bowl was flat, and around the spoon now outlined was a large amount of superfluous metal "flash," which was clipped off by hand shears, the pieces falling into a lock box. Then a file wheel was used to remove all excess material

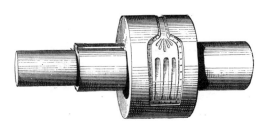

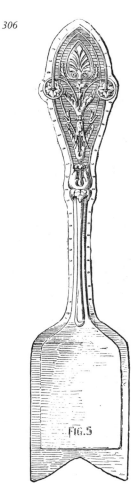

305 Fork Roll.

306 Spoon blank after design had been rolled on. Excess silver around the handle shows raised dots which acted as grips in the rolling operation.

233

307 Tin die for the forming of fluted sugar spoon bowl.

308 Polishing Room.

307

308

close to the edge of the pattern, and if a fork was being made, a rotary file cut the space between the tines.

The nineteenth-century method of rolling patterns on spoons and forks had a disadvantage. The lengths of the finished pieces varied slightly. For example, spoons of the *Japanese* pattern made in rolls would vary as much as a quarter of an inch in length. The reason for these variations was the slight differences in the silver blanks. A thicker piece woud be extended into a longer spoon (or fork). For this reason this type of roll is no longer widey used. The flat dies now used enable the silver-smith to reproduce pieces of flatware of uniform length.

The next operation was forming the bowls of spoons or the curved portions of other objects. This was done in the drop press using steel "punches" which forced the portions to be curved into matrices of tin. Tin was used because it was softer than the sterling alloy and yielded to the raised portion of the ornamentation on the under-side of the object as the blow was delivered by the drop press. If the matrix had been of steel, the ornament would of course have been flattened out. A tin die for a fluted sugar spoon bowl is shown in Figure 307.

The proper curve to the handle of a spoon or fork was imparted by "setting" with a wooden mallet. Then fol-lowed smooth filing and weighing of the object, previous to polishing. As a rule, about one-third of the metal in the original piece cut from the bar remained in the spoon. The waste pieces were remelted. The buffing and polish-ing of flatware was done on wheels rotating up to 2,000 revolutions per minute, oil and sand being first used and then ordinary rouge powder. Figure 308 shows the polish-ing room. The polished flatware was then ready for packing.

THE MAKING OF HOLLOW WARE: We will outline the steps in making a water pitcher since this involved operations typical to the making of many kinds of hollow-ware pieces. The parts of the water pitcher in Figure 309 are shown in the "exploded" drawing in Figure 310.

SPINNING: The rounded body parts of the pitcher (parts No. 2, 4, and 6) in Figure 310 were made on a lathe by a process known as spinning (Fig. 311). Spinning began to be used about 1830 for the production of teapots, coffeepots, pitchers, creamers, sugar bowls, etc. It was also used for metals other than silver such as Britannia, cop-

234

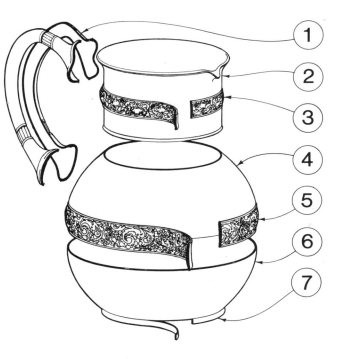

309 Water pitcher with applied die-rolled borders designed and made in 1877. Engraved on the front is the inscription "MARY LEE/ FROM/ SAMUEL HAND/ DEC. 27 1877." Height: 7 9/ 16 in. (19.2 cm.). Mark: NO. 19 (4706/9032). (*Private Collection*).

310 "Exploded" drawing of the water pitcher in Fig. 309. There are seven separate parts in the pitcher: (1) Handle cast in two mirror-image parts. (2) Neck of the pitcher. (3) Die-rolled decorative band. (4) Top half of the bulbous base. (5) Die-rolled decorative band. (6) Bottom half of bulbous base with flat bottom. (7) Narrow ring applied to bottom which acts as foot to the pitcher. (*Drawing by George Reed*).

311 The Spinner at Work.

per, brass, and white metal. Spinning was and is one of the great labor savers for the silversmith, enabling him in less than an hour to make shapes which would have taken days using only hand tools.

In forming each of the body parts of the pitcher a flat round disk of sterling was placed in a lathe against a wooden form or chuck, which was in the exact shape of the piece to be made. By applying pressure to the rotating silver with a polished steel spinning tool, the metal was formed over the chuck in stages, just as in the hammering operation. The spinner gained power and control by using a movable pin as a fulcrum, as shown in Figure 311. It is almost magical to watch an expert spinner literally flow the fast spinning metal over the chuck form. One of the tricks of the trade is not only to flow the metal upward on the chuck, but also to flow it back towards the bottom in order to maintain uniform thickness in all parts of the piece. Chucks in the nineteenth century were made of well-seasoned dogwood or rock maple, and were usually made by the spinner himself. Modern chucks are commonly made of steel or nylon. When the desired form had a smaller diameter at the top than in the body, such as with a narrow-necked vase, the spinner used a sectional chuck which could be taken apart to be removed from the inside of the finished article of silver. Spinning speeds varied from as high as 3,600 rpm for small lightweight objects to about 600 rpm for large shapes.

In all three of the parts which the spinner made for the pitcher in Figure 310, the chucks were bowl shapes with flat bottoms. The bottoms were cut out of the upper pieces, parts No. 2 and 4, since only the walls of these two pieces were used in the actual pitcher. The two pieces with curved sloping sides were soldered together to form the bulbous bottom part of the pitcher while the vertical piece for the neck was hammered to produce the pouring lip.

The decorative bands of silver were made using rolled steel dies similar to the fork roll in Figure 305. After the bands were formed they were cut to the required length, formed into a hoop, and the ends soldered together. Great care was taken to make the design continue around in an unbroken manner. There were a large number of possible decorative bands, from simple Greek key types to complex, rococo borders containing flowers, animals, cherubs, nymphs, or fruit along with a variety of abstract

236

design elements. Sometimes these bands were further embellished with hand chasing.

CASTING THE HANDLE PARTS: Handles and spouts for tea and coffeepots, feet, finials and decorative elements such as masks, ram's and bear's heads, were cast using age-old techniques whereby molten silver was poured into sand and/or plaster molds or by the use of the lost-wax process. The two mirror-image parts of the handles were cast hollow to be subsequently soldered together to make the hollow handle for the pitcher (1. in Fig. 310). The handle parts, as cast, usually have rough edges that must be filed by hand before being soldered together.

ASSEMBLING: The various parts of a hollow-ware object such as the water pitcher were assembled or put together in the "making department." All the pieces were fitted together in preparation for soldering, rough edges being filed for perfect fitting. Silver solder was used with melting points from 1100° to 1450° F. (593° to 790° C.). The solder was melted by means of a blowpipe which was handily located in front of each silversmith (Fig. 302). Body pieces were often held together with fine soft iron wire during soldering. After all rough places were smoothed out, the object was ready for further surface decorating, if any, and finishing.

PROCESSES FOR DECORATING SILVER SURFACES:

Mounting. The application of applied bands and pieces such as fish, buds, flowers, or abstract decorative elements, to the surface of a piece of silver by means of soldering was known as mounting. Mounts were made of silver or other metals such as copper, bronze, or gold. Mounts could be either castings, stampings, or rolled pieces. Decorative applied edges and bands were usually rolled.

Chasing. To ornament metal by indenting with a hammer and other tools without a cutting edge is known as chasing. No metal is removed in chasing and the indentation of the design can be seen on the reverse side. Flat chasing results in relatively shallow indentations on a flat surface while repoussé chasing is usually much deeper.

Repoussé Chasing. Repoussé work was an important part of the silversmith's art in the nineteenth century. The term repoussé means "repulsed"—or "pushed back" —work. Some writers on English silver prefer the term embossed.[19] The term repoussé is applied because the metal is raised by hammering on the object from within, that is, it is dented outward. As it would be literally impossible to insert a hammer in many small narrow-necked vessels, or to use it in almost any hollow article with any convenience, the snarling iron is employed (see Fig. 312).

The snarling iron is simply a metal bar having one end bent and secured in a vise and the other end turned upward and tapered to a dull point. The piece to be chased was slipped over the snarling iron, so that the vertical end of the iron came just under the portion to be raised. The workman then tapped lightly on the snarling iron close to the vise. The resiliency of the vibrating bar caused the blows to be transferred to the silver, slowly forcing the surface out into lumps of the desired size and shape. As soon as the entire pattern was raised, the vessel was annealed because the hammering hardened the silver, and for subsequent operations the silver had to be completely ductile.

The vessel was then filled with a hard, resilient, low melting point resin pitch which made a solid foundation for the chaser's work. The chaser, working on the outside of the piece, used a series of different small steel punches which literally pushed the metal into the called for designs (Fig. 313).

To make a raised flower he had first to bulge out the surface by means of the snarling tool. Then, working on the outside with his little punches, he pushed certain parts of the metal under the edges of the protrusion, threw up other portions, and finally the shapeless swelling was converted into delicate flower petals in full relief from the surface (Fig. 314).

Embossing. The raising of surface decorations from the back was usually called repoussé or repoussé chasing, but shallow raised designs were sometimes spoken of as embossed. Many decorative edges for dishes, etc., were made by rolling. The dish was rotated between the matching hard steel rolls, transferring the decorative design to the plate.

Engraving. As opposed to chasing in which the design was dented into the surface from either the outside or inside with no loss of metal, the engraver *cut* the design from the surface with sharp gravers or hardened steel tools. Metal was actually removed from the surface in the engraving operation.

312

313

312   Repoussé Work—Snarling.

313   Repoussé Work—Chasing.

Tiffany had its own engraving styles. Tiffany's engraving, particularly where it involved lettering, was so characteristic that it can serve as an autograph, identifying the engraving as Tiffany's (Fig. 114).

Engine-Turning. The tracing of delicate patterns and lines on silver by a process known as engine-turning used a rather complicated machine. In front of the operator was a stationary steel-pointed graver, while the article to be decorated was placed in front of it and fastened in a movable frame which passed up and down in contact with the point of the graver. The frame, which held the work, had at one side an iron point which was pressed by a spring on the other side of the frame against an upright brass cylinder; on this were indentations, suggestive of the notes on a cylinder of an antique music box. The principle was the same, for, as the frame was moved up and down, and the movements of the work against the cutting tool were guided by it, the result was that the pattern was cut or scratched in wavy lines.[20]

Etching. Coats of arms, illustrations and patterns of many kinds were etched on the silver surface by use of acid. The surface was entirely covered with wax or asphaltum paint and the design scratched through the paint. Thus the acid attacked only the scratched places

314 Detail of teapot in Figure 66 showing repoussé work.

on the surface. After etching, the wax or asphaltum was removed by heating.

Oxidizing. Oxidizing consisted of selective blackening of the surface by exposure to a sulfurizing agent, the black color being due to silver sulfide and not silver oxide.

Niello. Here, a chased or engraved decorative pattern was filled with an alloy in powder form of silver, copper, and lead sulfide, which was melted and later polished. The lines show up as gray-black. This ancient art is still practiced in the Middle East.

MIXED METALS: In the 1880s Edward C. Moore experimented with metal mixtures (not alloys) made from copper, silver, and gold. The metal mixtures were obtained by hammering the different metals together. Objects made of these metal mixtures were shown at the 1889 Paris Exposition where they were admired by Samuel Bing.[21]

A note found in Mr. Moore's files explained how the metal mixtures were made.[22]

It consists of Fine Gold, Fine Silver, Pure Copper, Shakudo (Copper and Gold) Shibu-ichi (Copper and Silver).

These five layers of metal are soldered together making a block about three-fourths of an inch thick. This is beaten and rolled out making it thinner. When it is reduced to about one-fourth of an inch in thickness, it is folded together, three parts making fifteen layers. This again is reduced and again folded double, making thirty layers. A sterling silver backing is now added and the process or variegation begins by cutting figures and spots through the outer metals and then by beating and forcing the under metals through and up to the surface. This goes on until the desired fineness, effect and thinness is produced.

It is now ready to be hammered into the shape designed, then smoothed and the colors of all the metals developed by chemicals producing the patina of each.

ENAMELING: The term "enamel" may be used to describe a hard glossy material, usually glass fired on to a metal base, or a hard durable paint suitable for application to metal. The fired enamels were made by applying a glass paste to the metal base and then firing at a sufficiently high temperature to melt the paste and cause it to adhere to the metal. The enamel becomes a form of colored glass which ornaments the surface of silver or gold with jewellike brilliance.

240

GILDING: The covering of all or part of a piece of silver with a thin coating of gold was done for both decorative and practical purposes. The gold layer prevented tarnishing and the attack of acids on such items as berry spoons. The gold was put on silver electrolytically. The old highly toxic mercury process of gilding had practically gone out of use by Tiffany's time. The mercury process used a gold-mercury amalgam which was applied to the silver surface and then fired to volatilize the mercury, leaving a deposit of gold. This is the reason for the term "fire gilt." The French word "vermeil" is also often used to describe gold-plated silver, but in this book we have generally used the word gilt which is the word usually used on Tiffany's nineteenth-century working drawings for silver.

POLISHING AND FINISHING THE SILVER: The amount and type of polishing a piece of silver received depended on the condition of the surface before polishing and the final type of finish desired. If the surface condition was rough and many file marks were to be removed, more polishing was required. The final finish could vary from mat-dull to mirror-bright. It was a matter of taste. In the 1870s Tiffany widely promoted their satin finish. Today, a hundred years later, most fine silver has a bright, glittering mirror finish. A matter of taste.

The first polishing step was sand bobbing, or sand polishing, which used a walrus hide "bob" wheel and finely ground pumice. It was used to remove file and fire marks.

The next step involved a brush buffing wheel using tripoli to remove the pumice scratches made in sand bobbing.

Final finishing was accomplished with soft wool cloth buffs and rouges of varying finenesses depending on the brilliance of finish desired.

A bright buff finish was obtained with tripoli and green rouge on a fast moving cloth buffing wheel.

MAT FINISHES: In the 1870s Tiffany developed a series of nonshiny, nonreflective finishes. These finishes not only set off decorated areas such as the copper and gold mounts on the silver in the Japanese style, they also made the silver less glittery and less subject to finger printing from handling. The surfaces ranged from the velvety *Satin Finish* (patented by Tiffany in 1875) to mat fin-

241

ishes with microscopic pin holes (from sand blasting) to a *milk white finish* obtained by the use of pulverized pumice. Mat surfaces were also obtained by hand chasing backgrounds with thousands of small indentations. (See the Ivy Chased service, Fig. 70.)

A butler finish was a dull polished finish.

A steel brush finish was used on the *Japanese* pattern flatware. The fast moving steel brush gave a soft mat finish not unrelated to the scratch patina of old silver. After the steel brushing, the birds and other high places in the Japanese pattern were hand buffed to accentuate the forms against the soft mat background.

Hand finishing was used for special pieces, particularly for chased work. In the first step the craftsman, wearing soft white gloves, rubbed the piece with tripoli. After extensive rubbing, the piece was washed and dried. A second thorough rubbing was made with lime cake and new white gloves. Then the piece was again washed and dried and given a final polish with a soft dry cloth.

315   Designing Room. *(Photograph ca. 1885 from Tiffany & Co. files).*

13. Tiffany Marks

AMERICAN SILVER made before 1850 was inadequately marked when compared with English silver. The rigorous hallmarking system that has been used for several hundred years in England is a guarantee, protected by law, that silverware made there is truly of the quality specified. The Worshipful Company of Goldsmiths of London has administered the assaying and hallmarking of silver and gold in England since 1327. The English system of hallmarking has made frauds rare.

At one time, in England, to forge plate was punishable with death, although we do not understand that this penalty was ever enforced. However, we do know that in 1597 two goldsmiths who produced some counterfeit silver were put in the pillory, and each had one ear cut off.[1]

In modern times fines have replaced these ancient Spartan penalties.

English silver of the nineteenth century often had five marks. For example, a piece with the mark:

conveyed the following information: The first mark

is the maker's mark (or touch mark) of W. Hattersly. The second mark, a "lion passant," represents the standard or quality of the silver, indicating it is sterling of 925 parts silver plus 75 parts copper totaling 1000 parts alloy. The third mark,

the leopard's head, is the city mark, in this case, London. The fourth mark,

called the date letter, indicates the piece was made in 1858. The fifth mark,

the sovereign's head (Queen Victoria), or duty mark, was so called because it represented the payment of a tax. The duty mark was discontinued in 1890 when the tax was abolished.[2]

The English silversmith placed only the maker's mark on his silver before sending it to the Goldsmiths' Company for assay. If the assay showed the piece was qualitatively satisfactory hallmarks of the type mentioned above were stamped on the piece. If the piece did not come up to the sterling standard, it was not marked but smashed to pieces or cut up in the presence of witnesses and returned to the maker.

The fact that American silver was not hallmarked in the English manner (with the exception of silver in Baltimore from 1814 to 1830) does not mean that early American silversmiths cheated their customers. Their wares were made of the raw materials at hand, old silverware and silver coins, usually foreign, to be melted down. This meant that the quality of silver varied. As noted in Chapter 12, American silver of the second quarter of the nineteenth century marked COIN or COIN SILVER or PURE COIN was no guarantee of quality because of the varying silver content of the coins used.

Tiffany almost from the beginning adopted hollowware marks which conveyed several precise pieces of information: the full name of the company, the store's address, the maker of the silver, the silver content, the pattern number, the order number, and sometimes the patent date. However, as can be seen in the list of marks, not all marks had all of this data. The only significant piece of information not included in the Tiffany mark is the year the piece was made. Although the date of making can be estimated from the mark and from the pattern number, dates of making were never part of Tiffany marks. On small pieces, particularly flatware, the marks tend to be more abbreviated. On sets, such as tea and coffee services, not all pieces of the set were always completely marked.

As we have noted earlier in this book, in the period 1851 to 1869, Tiffany had much of their hollow ware made by the Moore Company. John Chandler Moore is listed in the New York City Directory in 1832–3. At that time his mark was star — M — anchor. In the 1835–6 Directory he is listed with Garrett Eoff as Eoff & Moore; from 1836 until 1851 he is listed alone. At various times during this period Moore worked with M. B. Dixon (Moore & Dixon) and Henry Hebbard (Hebbard & Moore). During the 1840s Moore's mark was JCM or an old English 𝔐 in an oval:

It is probable that Moore's silver with these marks was sold at Tiffany's in the 1848–1851 period. The Moore old English 𝔐 was incorporated into Tiffany marks after 1851.

245

In 1851 the active management of the Moore firm passed from John C. Moore to his son, Edward C. Moore. In the 1848–1851 period the firm was known as John C. Moore & Son. The presence of the two Ms on Tiffany silver marks from 1854 to 1870 refers to the two Moores— John C. and Edward C.

As we have noted earlier (p. 26) the Moore Company was bought out by Tiffany & Co. in 1868.

Applying the Mark to the Silver

The mark is hammered onto the silver with a steel marking die or stamp. There are two kinds of marking stamps. The first type is flat on the marking side and is applied by means of one sharp blow of a hammer. The second is a roller type, the marking surface of which is rounded, and the mark is applied by striking the stamp with a series of hammer blows as the stamp is rolled or rotated through about a forty-five degree arc. The roller type tends to produce a more uniformly distinct mark.

Pattern numbers and order numbers are applied separately and an individual marking stamp is used for each digit in the number.

Tiffany Sterling Hollow Ware Marks 1848–1978

The following Tiffany marks are those used on sterling hollow ware made by Tiffany as well as sterling hollow ware made by other makers and sold by Tiffany. The list is by no means complete since there are a number of minor variants of most of these marks.

The marks for gold, silver-and-other-metals, flatware, and electroplated ware follow the list of sterling hollow-ware marks.

1   1848–1852. Tiffany, Young & Ellis. Made by the John C. Moore Co.

2 1848–1852. Tiffany, Young & Ellis. Made by Wood & Hughes. (The Wood & Hughes mark is upside down.)

3 1848–1852. Tiffany & Co. Made by Moore.

4 Ca. 1853. Tiffany & Co.

5 Ca. 1853. Tiffany & Co. Made by Moore.

6 Ca. 1853. Tiffany & Co. Made by Moore.

7　Ca. 1853. Tiffany & Co. Made by Grosjean & Woodward.

7A　1853–1865. Tiffany & Co. Made by Grosjean & Woodward.

8　1854–1865. Tiffany & Co. Made by Grosjean & Woodward.

9　1854–1855. Made by Moore.

10   1854–1870. Made by Moore.

11   1854–1870. Made by Moore.

12   1860–1865. Made by William Gale.

13   Ca. 1865. Tiffany records (from about 1900) indicate made by Bogert, Newburg.

14 1865–1870. Made by Moore.

15 1865–1870. Made by Moore.

On certain pieces the standard marks were "expanded" to better fit the space. An expanded version of mark No. 16 appears on the creamer of the Chased Ivy service (see Fig. 70).

16A

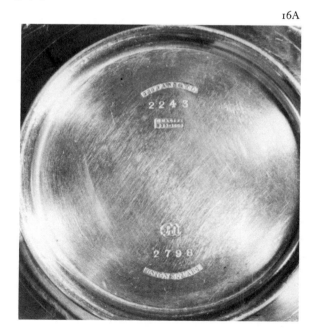

16 1870–1875.

17 1870–1875.

18 1870–1875.

19 1873–1891. The M in the mark refers to Edward C. Moore, head of Tiffany's silver operation until 1891.

20 1873–1891.

21 1891–1902. After Moore's death in 1891, the custom of including the initials of the surname of the president of the firm was originated. In this case it was Charles L. Tiffany, the founder.

251

22 1902–1907. Charles T. Cook was Tiffany's president during this period.

23 1907–1947. John C. Moore, Edward C. Moore's grandson, was president from 1907 to 1938 and chairman to 1947.

TIFFANY & C?
MAKERS
STERLING SILVER
12345
M
★

24 1943–1945. This mark with the star was used on silverware made of *domestically produced silver* placed on sale April 17, 1943.

TIFFANY & C?
MAKERS
STERLING SILVER
12345
M

25 1947–1956. Louis deBebian Moore, son of John C. Moore, was actually president from 1938 to 1956.

TIFFANY & C?
MAKERS
STERLING SILVER
12345
L

26 1956 to about 1965. The L was for William T. Lusk, great-grandson of the company's founder. After 1965 the practice of including the president's initial was discontinued.

Silverware made for international expositions bore the following special marks in addition to the usual one:

LINEAR MARKS: Pieces were sometimes marked in one continuous line, usually because of space limitations. An example is the mark on the card case in Figure 182.

27

Occasionally a hollow-ware piece was marked in one line even when there was no problem of placement.

28

GOLD MARKS: The marks for pieces made of gold are similar to sterling marks except the word SOLID GOLD replace STERLING-SILVER. The pattern numbers and order numbers are stamped in the usual place to the left and right of the word MAKERS on the mark. A typical gold mark is the one on the pieces of a gold tea service (not illustrated), now in the Museum of the City of New York, given in 1897 to Samuel Sloan, president of the Delaware, Lackawanna & Western Railroad, by his employees:

29   TIFFANY & CO.
    13416   MAKERS   9360
            SOLID GOLD
              18 KT.

SILVER AND OTHER METALS: When Tiffany made their silver in the Japanese style with copper, brass, and gold mounts, it created a problem in marking. They could not truthfully call it sterling because of the added metal mounts. In fact, in England, it would have been against the law to mark such wares as sterling. Tiffany acknowledged the difficulty and marked such pieces: STERLING-SILVER/AND/OTHER METALS. A typical example is the mark on the Mentmore pitcher in Plate IV:

30

In mark No. 30, 5118 is the pattern number and 148 is the order number. The number at the bottom of the mark, 214, is the hammering and mounting design number (see Fig. 268).

31

EUROPEAN SILVER SOLD BY TIFFANY & CO.: Tiffany sold European-made silver in both their Paris and London stores and also in New York. The usual practice on such wares was to include both the maker's mark and TIFFANY & CO. A twentieth-century English tea caddy (not illustrated) has the complete English hallmarks prominently stamped on its side and the Tiffany mark on the bottom.

Flatware Marks

From about 1850 to 1869 Tiffany retailed the flatware of other makers (see Chapter 5). The flatware of this era usually bears both the mark of the maker *and* Tiffany, Young & Ellis before 1853 or Tiffany & Co. after 1853. Occasionally in this period Tiffany sold flatware with only its own mark and no maker's mark. In such cases the actual maker can sometimes be identified by a characteristic pattern, but with such common patterns as *Fiddle and Thread* it may not be possible to make a positive identification. This is the case with a ladle which is marked:

32

254

The next mark on the crumber in Figure 103 has an unidentified pseudo-hallmark in addition to the firm's mark:

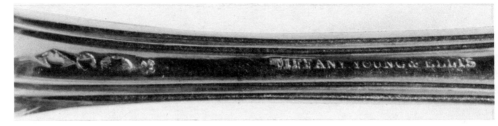

33

The next two marks have both the maker's mark and the Tiffany mark. Number 34 shows the mark on a ladle with John Polhemus's mark:

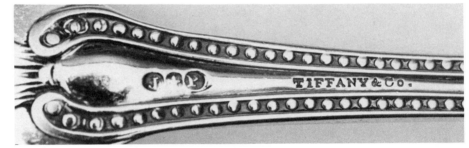

34

Mark No. 35 is on a ladle by Henry Hebbard:

35

In 1869 Tiffany began making its own flatware and their marks usually included the company name TIFFANY & CO. and STERLING and the appropriate initial for the time period:

1869–1891	M	For Edward C. Moore (In the early 1870s a small case m was sometimes used.)
1891–1902	T	For Charles L. Tiffany
1902–1907	C	For Charles T. Cook
1907–1947	m	For John C. Moore
1947–1955	M	For Louis deBebian Moore
1955 to about 1965	L	For William T. Lusk

The practice of using an initial on the Tiffany mark was discontinued after 1965.

Sometimes a patent date was a part of the mark. This date is of course the year the design patent was issued, not when the piece was made, which could have been years later. Pattern numbers were only very occasionally marked on flatware and these were usually on special pieces such as Indian spoons (Fig. 279).

There are two methods of marking Tiffany flatware. The first uses individual dies or stamps while the second has the mark incorporated in the die used to make the object. In the former the mark was stamped on the flatware by means of a steel marking die or stamp *after* the piece was made. Examples of stamped marks are:

36   Mark on *Antique Ivy* fork of the 1870s.

37   Mark on *Lap Over Edge* fish fork in Fig. 123.

Note that the C in mark No. 37 indicates the piece was made in 1902–1907 even though it bears the patent date 1880 and the patent had expired.

38 Mark on Columbian Exposition souvenir spoon in Fig. 178.

A die mark is an integral part of the die used to stamp the flatware and both are created in the same step. Examples of die marks are:

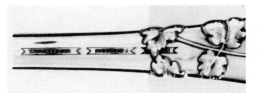

39 Mark on *Tomato Vine* pattern ladle.

40 Mark on Searles private pattern flatware in Fig. 110.

Electroplate Marks

Traditionally makers of electroplated silver have tended to be circumspect about the marking of their wares. They have used such euphuisms as "silver-soldered" on their marks or abbreviations as "E. P." (for electroplated) or sometimes only the name of the company. The silverware makers made certain their sterling pieces were so marked, but they sometimes seemed reluctant to point out in their marks that electroplated wares were *not* sterling. The term silver-soldered has of course nothing to do with electroplated silver as such but only means the maker used silver solder in the making instead of softer lead solder.

Tiffany at one time or another used a variety of marks on their electroplated wares—from a simple designation TIFFANY & CO/MAKERS—to a complete sterlinglike mark which includes the straightforward words: SILVER PLATED. Tiffany electroplate marks were often more casual than their sterling marks. Tiffany records of electroplated wares are much less complete than those for sterling and the available records are not as detailed as the sterling records. Pattern numbers do not appear to be chronological, particularly in the nineteenth century. There are still many electroplate drawings in the Tiffany files but there is less information on the drawings—sometimes only the descriptive name of the piece without any pattern number.

We show some typical Tiffany & Co. electroplate marks below. The list is not complete since there are many variants:

41 Mark on a card tray made by Tiffany's affiliate Adams & Shaw, Newark, N. J., about 1885.

42 Ca. 1890.

43 Mark on coffee urn in Fig. 288, about 1910.

44 Mark on tea and coffee service, about 1910.

A typical piece of Tiffany silver-plated flatware is marked:

45

Pattern Numbers and Dates of Issue—Hollow Ware

On most Tiffany hollow-ware marks there are two numbers: the pattern number and the order number. The pattern number is the number on the original drawing or pattern for a particular piece or related pieces of hollow ware. It does not refer to the type of decoration which was later added to a piece. The order number is an assigned number for a particular order and is primarily used for identifying a particular piece or group of related pieces or pieces ordered at one time.

The pattern number is usually on the upper side or left side of the mark, while the order number is usually below or to the right of the pattern number on the mark:

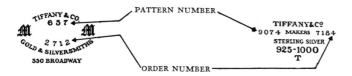

The pattern numbers which we discuss below refer only to those used on pieces made by Moore for Tiffany from 1851 to 1869 and Tiffany pieces made after 1869 when Moore's operations were absorbed into Tiffany. The significance of numbers on the marks of such makers as Grosjean & Woodward are not known at the present writing.

259

The pattern numbers are roughly consecutive from 1851 for Moore hollow ware. Plant records are available from the beginning of the Moore-Tiffany relationship in 1851 but not many of the journal entries are dated so we must deal with approximations, particularly before 1875. Based on our present knowledge we estimate the pattern numbers in the 1851 to 1876 period to be approximately as shown at left.

YEAR	PATTERN NUMBERS
1851–1855	1– 300
1856–1859	301–1000
1860–1864	1001–1550
1865–1869	1551–2250
1870–1874	2251–3800
1875–1876	3801–4500

It should be emphasized that these numbers are approximations based on available records and a study of dated pieces. One problem is that on some early pieces the pattern number and the order number are apparently reversed. That is, the pattern number is below or to the right of the order number instead of in the position originally described.

The dates represent the year when the pattern number was *originally* assigned. The same pattern may have been made over a period of time which in some cases stretched over several decades. Thus the pattern number may be misleading in that it could indicate a date earlier than the piece was actually made. However, our experience with dated pieces indicates that most pieces were made within a relatively few years of the date that is indicated by the pattern number.

Another source of error in dating from Tiffany pattern numbers is that in some cases old numbers were held open or simply not used in correct sequence. Sometimes such numbers were assigned in later years. However, such out-of-place pattern numbers are exceptional, and only occasionally were the pattern numbers issued in later years than indicated.

The following table shows the pattern numbers of Tiffany hollow ware from 1876 to 1950. The pattern numbers represent the first number used in January of the year noted:

HOLLOW WARE PATTERN NUMBERS AND DATES OF ISSUE, 1876–1950

Pattern No.	Year	Pattern No.	Year
4545	1876	6260	1881
4620	1877	6760	1882
5050	1878	7300	1883
5370	1879	7840	1884
5910	1880	8340	1885

260

HOLLOW WARE PATTERN NUMBERS AND DATES OF ISSUE, 1876–1950

Pattern No.	Year	Pattern No.	Year
8800	1886	19460	1918
9260	1887	19521	1919
9660	1888	19683	1920
10120	1889	19831	1921
10400	1890	20021	1922
10820	1891	20160	1923
11140	1892	20296	1924
11520	1893	20470	1925
11940	1894	20664	1926
12220	1895	20845	1927
12600	1896	21177	1928
13040	1897	21352	1929
13510	1898	21470	1930
13900	1899	21724	1931
14250	1900	21855	1932
14650	1901	21950	1933
15145	1902	21987	1934
15550	1903	22100	1935
15943	1904	22280	1936
16356	1905	22360	1937
16555	1906	22575	1938
16849	1907	22650	1939
17103	1908	22850	1940
17272	1909	22950	1941
17596	1910	23140	1942
17880	1911	?	1943
18190	1912	23164	1944
18395	1913	23177	1945
18601	1914	23204	1946
18808	1915	23238	1947
18996	1916	23250	1948
19193	1917	23274	1949
		23310	1950

FLATWARE PATTERN NUMBERS AND DATES OF ISSUE[1]

Pattern No.	Year	Pattern No.	Year
1	1869	761	1887
125	1874	767	1888
192	1876	879	1889
212	1877	928	1891
368	1879		
434	1880	1249	1901
438	1881	1304	1904
602	1884		
682	1886	1356	1911

[1] Only a relatively few pieces of flatware are marked with pattern numbers.

14. The Twentieth Century—A Postscript

T HE PRECEDING CHAPTERS on the making of Tiffany silver and Tiffany marks essentially end our story of the silver of Tiffany & Co. of the nineteenth century. We did not attempt an exact cutoff date of 1900. We have included a number of examples of early twentieth-century silver in the book, primarily because of their relationship to nineteenth-century examples. In this chapter we take a look at Tiffany silver of the first three-quarters of the twentieth century, not as a formal study, but as a brief, preliminary and very personal look of what is really the silver of our time.

In Chapter 1 we discussed the rather quick disappearance of Victorianism after the turn of the century. However, residuals of Victorianism continued for many years in the twentieth century. Rococo and colonial revival silverware continued to be made until the 1950s and there are still pieces sold by Tiffany's that would have been perfectly at home in the 1870s. But today is like the past—there are, and have been, a multiplicity of artistic styles coexisting more or less comfortably together. A store like Tiffany's must deal with realities. They must maintain a level of quality and style but they must also have objects people will buy. Their "public" has always included a wide spectrum of people whose taste and knowledge ranged from the uneducated and the unknowing to highly sophisticated and knowledgable people who appreciate the best. This same public includes (and still includes) a wide economic range, from the not-so-affluent to the very rich. And of course there is no direct correlation between taste and money.

We have not tried to be tasteful in this chapter. We picked a number of objects we liked and a couple we didn't, but felt they should be shown. We show new

262

forms and new ideas and old ideas dressed in new ways. Forms *did* become simpler in the twentieth century and in some cases they became tamer. For example, there is nothing in the twentieth century to compare with the great yachting trophies of the nineteenth century.

In this chapter we show a few examples of colonial revival silver. Tiffany first made these free interpretations of early American silver in the early 1870s. The "style" was particularly strong in the 1910–1925 period. This era more or less coincided with the beginnings of antique collecting on a really widespread basis in America. There was an ever-deepening interest in the past. This interest led Tiffany silvermakers to make some first-class reproductions of the works of such early silversmiths as Paul Revere and Ephraim Brasher. In the 1930s Tiffany made some particularly attractive Art Deco silver and we show pieces which were exhibited at the 1939 World's Fair in New York. Finally, we show a couple of post–World War II objects.

Gadgets always have a fascination, particularly when they are beautifully crafted in such a metal as silver. We start and end this chapter with two: first a jelly dish with a clever mechanical device for opening the silver lid, and finally a pocket electronic calculator, a truly characteristic object of the 1970s.

The jelly glass with sterling lid and handle in Figure 316 opens when the handle is pressed down (Fig. 317). It was designed about 1904 when Louis Comfort Tiffany was artistic director of the company and examples are known with Tiffany Studios opalescent or Favrile glass instead of the clear glass we show.

In Chapter 3 we noted that Tiffany made only a relatively few examples of Art Nouveau silver and these were usually quite restrained. The graceful water pitcher in Figure 318 is a chaste, late example of the style. The chasing and engraving is clear and simple with large unadorned areas. The floral motifs echo Louis Comfort Tiffany's ideas which are quite different from Tiffany silver of the 1880s and 1890s. It is easy to see how such designs led into the Art Deco silver of the 1920s and 1930s.

The round waiter in Figure 319 is a most interesting example of nineteenth-century revivalism. The waiter form itself is an 1879 design and the die-rolled border had been used in Tiffany silver since the 1870s. But the etched floral decoration on the flat center part of the

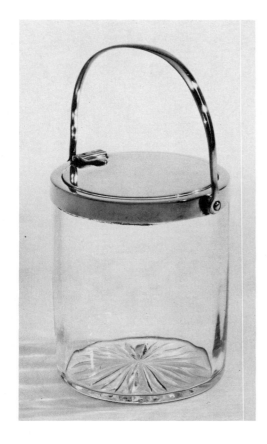

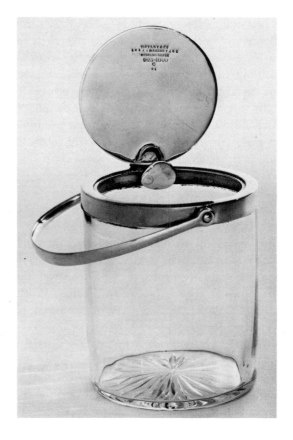

316 Jelly glass with sterling lid and handle.
Made about 1904. Height through handle:
6 1/4 in. (15.2 cm.). Mark: NO. 22 (16111/
7160/61). *(Private Collection)*.

317 Jelly glass in Fig. 316 showing mechanism
which lifts the lid when the handle is lowered.

waiter is definitely of the period of the piece, about 1910.
This heavy waiter (33 oz.) was *en suite* with the Tiffany
Studios tea and coffee service in Fig. 47 with the initials
"EFW" engraved in exactly the same manner as the
Tiffany Studios service in an engraving style character-
istic of Tiffany Studios.

Louis Comfort Tiffany had close connections with both
Tiffany & Co. and Tiffany Studios at this time, and it
would have been perfectly natural for him to order a
waiter from Tiffany & Co. stock to be engraved at Tiffany Studios. The waiter is etched with the same kind
of floral device as was used on the tea and coffee service:
stylized flower forms viewed alternately from the top
and the bottom, tied together in a gently swirling Art
Nouveau design.

264

318 Water pitcher with repoussé chased decorations made ca. 1905. Height: 11 1/8 in. (28.2 cm.). Mark: NO. 22 (14068A/2215) plus "4 3/4 pints." *(Private Collection)*.

319 Round waiter with applied die-rolled border and center etched with flowers, showing alternate views of the tops and bottoms of stylized chrysanthemum ("football mums"). The engraved monogram EFW is for Emily Frances Whitney. This tray was *en suite* with the Tiffany Studios tea and coffee service in Fig. 47. The floral etching in the center could have been designed by Louis Comfort Tiffany. Diameter: 12 in. (30.5 cm.). Mark: NO. 23 (5765/4374). *(Private Collection)*.

318

319

320

321

The tea set in Figure 320 is made of plain squared cube forms with rounded edges and an Oriental fret gallery around the tops. It is related to the small-scaled services of the 1870s in the Japanese style.

The colonial revival silver of the 1910–1925 period was like the colonial revival furniture of the time, a free interpretation of the past, usually with added decorative touches and occasionally with hints of Art Nouveau motifs. The extra curve in the handle of the coffeepot in Figure 321 and the gently waving cherry boughs around the top and on the base bring classical forms up to date. The crisscrossing panels making flat diamond shapes on the body was a favorite decorative device of the 1920s. It was an interest in geometric design that led to Art Deco and "Modern" silver.

The candlesticks in Figure 322 are simplified versions of century-old designs. They are modest in scale in keeping with the smaller rooms and smaller dining tables of the time.

The presentation cup in Figure 323 for Henry J. Heinz of pickle fame has a simple classical shape and handles related to the coffeepot in Figure 321. The classical frieze is in the manner of the French neoclassic painters of the time and such American painters as Arthur B. Davies.

320 A three-piece tea set made about 1911. Height of pot through handle: 6 in. (15.2 cm.). Mark: NO. 23 (17143/8162). *(Courtesy of Dr. and Mrs. Edward H. Richardson, Jr.).*

321 Coffeepot made in 1910. Height: 9 3/4 in. (24.8 cm.). Mark: NO. 23 (2760/06417).

Reproductions of Early Silver

The "Paul Revere" creamer in Figure 324 is quite a different thing from the silver in the colonial revival style. The heightening interest and increased knowledge of objects made by the great craftsmen of the past created a demand for good reproductions. In the second and third decade of this century Tiffany & Co. helped Judge A. T. Clearwater form his great collection of American silver which he later gave to The Metropolitan Museum of Art. Many of the objects in the Clearwater collection were studied by the Tiffany silversmiths and a number were copied. These copies ranged from the Paul Revere creamer (and sugar) and a small bowl by Ephraim Brasher to copies of eighteenth-century flatware.

The copying of the Revere creamer was a true homage by the Tiffany silversmiths to their great predecessor. The working drawings for the piece indicate how carefully and thoroughly they worked. There were detailed full-scale drawings of the object from the side, the front, and the top and there were drawings of details of the foot, the handle, and the engraving on the piece. In addition a plaster cast of the original was made, together with photographs from all angles plus two electrotypes. The gauge of the metal in the body, the foot, the handle, and the top edge were carefully noted. The copy was then handmade using all the tools available in the Tiffany shop. And finally the carefully made copy was clearly and completely marked on the bottom:

TIFFANY & CO

19494   MAKERS   6863

925-1000

ORIGINAL IN THE

CLEARWATER COLLECTION

METROPOLITAN

MUSEUM OF ART

REPRODUCTION

ORIGINAL BY

PAUL REVERE

BOSTON

1735–1818

(The actual stamp marks are arranged in three places around the bottom.)

322   Pair of candlesticks made about 1915. Engraved GFL. Height: 7 1/2 in. (19.1 cm.). Mark: NO. 23 (18685/1998) and "weighted/15." *(Private Collection).*

323   Loving cup given to H. J. Heinz in 1909 on the fiftieth anniversary of the founding of the company.

322

323

267

324

The copies of objects such as the 7½-inch diameter bowl by Ephraim Brasher have less of the feel of the original than the Revere copies. The fact that the modern bowl was spun on a lathe gives it a more perfect surface than the original, whereas the Revere copies, being handmade, have a more handcrafted look.

Art Deco

The term Art Deco was not used in the 1920s and the 1930s when it was very much in fashion. It was called Art Moderne or the modernistic style to distinguish it from the severe international style which made no use of ornament as such. The term Art Deco, first applied to the style in the 1960s, is from the Exposition des Arts Décoratifs et Industriels Modernes held in Paris in 1925 where the style was codified for the first time. The style was successful from the beginning and was most influential during the 1925–1940 period.[1] It influenced everything from the decorative arts to architecture (in such buildings as the Chrysler Building in New York and the Koppers Building in Pittsburgh).

As a style Art Deco was a modern adaptation of various ornamental styles of the past, particularly classical. It has been said of Art Deco that "It created the last ornamental style known to Western Art by marrying the machine with the old handicraft tradition."[2]

The lovely mirror in Figure 325 has geometric blue and green enamel decorations and engraved lines in the silver. The coffee set and tray with simple vertical lines and stylized leaf decorations in Figure 326 was no doubt influenced by Scandinavian silver popularized by Georg Jensen and others in America. The massive, beautifully crafted cigar box in Figure 327 is high Art Deco, reflecting the kind of detail that was used in everything from furniture to office-building interiors of the 1930s. The place setting in Figure 328 has a square geometric Art Deco plate to match the *Century* pattern flatware. The *Century* pattern was first made in 1937 and it fittingly commemorated the one hundredth anniversary of Tiffany & Co.

All of the Art Deco objects in Figures 325 through 328 were designed in the 1930s by the late A. L. Barney and others at Tiffany's and were shown at the 1939 New York World's Fair. Tiffany designed their last souvenir spoon for this Fair, a severe, geometric depiction of its sym-

324   Handmade reproduction of a Paul Revere cream pitcher. Height: 6 3/4 in. (17.1 cm.). *(Gebelein Silversmiths)*.

325   Hand mirror with blue and green baked enamel and engraved lines ca. 1937.

326   Coffeepot, sugar bowl, cream pitcher, and tray made in 1939. Height of coffeepot: 9 3/4 in. (24.7 cm.).

327   Large cigar box made in 1939. A heavy carved ornamental band of scroll and leaf forms is across the center of the box. There are two large rectangular carved handles of leaves and rosettes. Length: 13 in. (33 cm.).

325

326

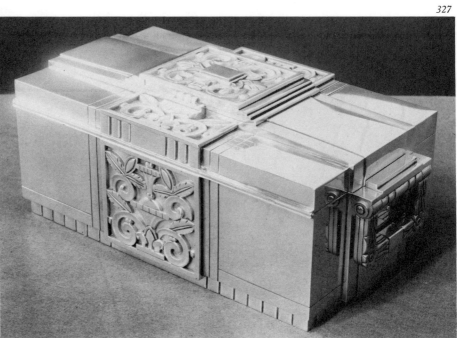

327

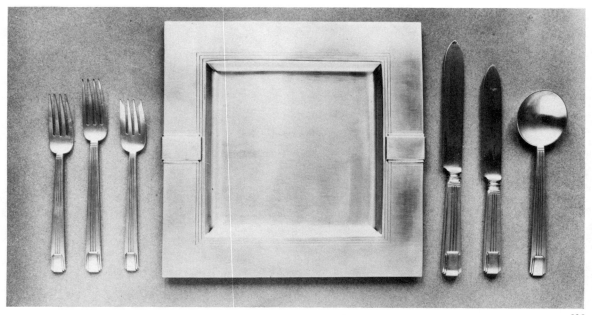

328

329

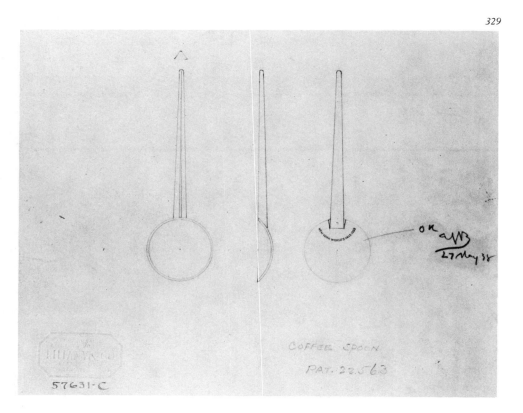

COFFEE SPOON
PAT. 22563

57631-C

bols, the Trylon and Perisphere (Fig. 329).

We show only two silver objects made after World War II. The graceful, sculptural yachting trophy in Figure 330 designed by Oscar Riedener in 1961, carries on the great Tiffany trophy tradition with a contemporary and imaginative solution of how to depict in silver the yachtsman's wind and ocean. The trophy conveys the taut tension of the sail and the gleaming hull slipping easily through the water.

We end our story of Tiffany silver with the illustration of an object that is very much a symbol of our times, an electronic calculator. If the period of this book, Victorian America, can rightly be called the age of silver, then the 1970s can be called the electronic age with the computer as king. Pocket calculators are everywhere. Almost every school child has one to do his math problems. They have

328 Square plate and *Century* flatware which was introduced in 1937 to commemorate the 100th anniversary of the founding of Tiffany & Co.

329 Original drawing for souvenir spoon for the 1939 New York World's Fair. Length of spoon: 4 1/16 in. (10.3 cm.).

330 Martini & Rossi trophy "for the foremost United States Racing Sailor of the year," first awarded in 1961 to Harry C. Melges, Jr. Height with base: 20 in. (50.8 cm.).

330

allowed engineers to throw away their slide rules. Housewives and husbands use them to balance their checkbooks. It's hard to realize that at the time of this writing (1978) the pocket calculator is only seven years old, the first one having been made in Boston in 1971. The technology of calculators and computers is changing so fast that today's marvel may be out of date tomorrow. Tiffany offered the silver-encased pocket-sized calculator designed by John Brown in Figure 331 for the first time in 1976, and it immediately became one of their most popular items. The *Wall Street Journal* advertisement of April 5th, 1976 shows a photograph of the calculator with the caption:

THE TIFFANY
COMPACT CALCULATOR

Slimmed down calculator folds up when not in use to conveniently fit pocket or purse. Handsomely encased in sterling silver by Tiffany & Co., the Sharp, four-function, battery-operated calculator is 3⅛ by 2⅞ by ¾ inches thick. $150, engraving extra.

Sharp, the maker of the calculator, is a Japanese firm. Japan and things Japanese have long fascinated Tiffany and its designers. The calculator was made just a century after Edward C. Moore's wonderful silver in the Japanese style. The sleek silver-encased electronic calculator pays homage to a great man and a great age.

331 Pocket calculator made by Sharp with Tiffany sterling case. *(Top)* calculator closed, *(bottom)* open. Introduced in 1976. Length: 3 1/8 in. (7.8 cm.).

A Note on the Care of Silver

The care of silver is a problem which must be handled with intelligence and restraint. It is not only a problem for individuals who worry about their tarnished silver and how best to polish it, it is also a problem for museums. With museums the problem has two facets: the housekeeping problem of polishing silver on exhibit, and how to prevent deterioration of the object. Museums have found that continued polishing tends to obliterate shallow engraved and chased lines.

Most silver objects made more than a hundred years ago show a measurable amount of weight loss since they were made. Typical is the well-known set of six tankards made by Paul Revere, Boston, in 1772 for the Third Church of Brookfield, Massachusetts, now owned by The Henry Francis du Pont Winterthur Museum. Revere's accounts of the weights of the tankards when they were made compared with their weights in 1968 indicate a consistent loss.

Weight in 1722	Weight in 1968*
24 oz., 13 dwt.	24 oz., 9 dwt., 13 gr.
25 ” 1 ” 12 gr.	24 ” 17 ” 22 ”
25 ” 3 ”	24 ” 18 ” 19 ”
24 ” 5 ” 12 ”	23 ” 18 ” 20½ ”
25 ” 1 ”	24 ” 15 ” 20 ”
24 ” 19 ”	24 ” 13 ” 12 ”

* Martha Gandy Fales, *Early American Silver for the Cautious Collector*, Funk & Wagnalls, New York, 1970, p. 233.

The weight losses average about one percent. This may not sound like very much but remember that most of this loss would have undoubtedly been from the *outside* surfaces of the tankards as a result of two centuries of cleaning and polishing. A comparable loss of silver from the surface of some objects could mean the wearing down of such engraved features as monograms, the loss of detail from raised parts of the surface and, in the case of plated wares, sometimes the complete loss of parts of the silver coating, exposing the copper or other base metal underneath.

A few years ago The Henry Francis du Pont Winterthur Museum conducted a series of carefully controlled tests on a number of commercially available silver polishes. The factors that were judged included: (a) the amount of silver removed by the polish and (b) the appearance of the silver from the time of polishing to six months after polishing.

The results were surprising. The worst of the polishes removed more than *forty* times the amount of silver than the best, and even the best removed silver at the rate of 1 mil (one thousandth of an inch) per century. The worst would remove the silver from ordinary electroplated wares in a few years.

These test results have not been published and there are no present plans for publication.

In view of the very real danger of damaging the surface of silver objects by overzealous cleaning and/or injurious polishes we recommend moderation. Do only what has to be done to preserve the object. Handle silver as little as possible. Keep fingers off plain surfaces. Wash objects frequently by hand, *not in a dishwasher,* with warm soft water and mild soap and dry immediately with a soft towel.

Use only a mild, nonabrasive silver polish and use it no more often than necessary. Follow directions and be sure to rinse thoroughly with warm water and dry immediately.

We personally use a silver polish that is not widely marketed, TS1-701, Testing Systems Inc., Glenside, Pennsylvania. We also have used *Haggerty Silver Foam,* 3-M's *Tarni-Shield* and *Twinkle.* We like all of these because they are mild and wash away easily leaving no deposits of solid polish in interstices.

Store silver in a dry place, preferably with each piece in a cotton flannel bag. If the silver is to be stored any length of time we suggest the flannel bags themselves be wrapped in plastic. *Do not wrap silver directly in plastic.* Certain plastic films can, after a time, disastrously mark silver. Such markings can only be removed with great difficulty.

We advise against the use of lacquers to preserve silver. Lacquers alter the appearance somewhat and after a time they usually darken, and in some cases bad corrosion occurs underneath the lacquer layer. Lacquer can usually be taken off silver by the use of paint removers. After the lacquer has been removed, the silver can be cleaned and polished with a silver polish.

We do not like the chemical dips that remove silver tarnish "instantly." The trouble is that they remove *all* of the tarnish even from the recesses. It gives silver with repoussé chasing a flat "skinned" look which we find unpleasant. And in certain cases it removes dark backgrounds from recessed areas that were originally put there by the silversmith to create a contrast. There is, however, one case where the use of chemical dips is acceptable: in the cleaning of the tines of forks. Tines tend to darken from contact with foods and they are difficult to clean with ordinary polishes.

Dents, bumps, cracks and other structural defects should only be repaired by a competent silversmith. If for some reason a piece of silver is to be repaired or cleaned by a professional we suggest that specific instructions be given not to overclean or "skin" the object and to use no buffing. Buffing removes too much silver and may completely destroy the soft patina of an old piece.

Notes

1. Changing Views on Victorianism

1. *The Connoisseur*, No. 1, Spring 1885, p. 5.

2. The Early Years: 1837–1867

1. George Frederic Heydt, *Charles L. Tiffany and the House of Tiffany & Co.* (New York: Tiffany & Co., 1893), p. 17.
2. Katherine Morrison McClinton, *Collecting American 19th Century Silver* (New York: Charles Scribner's Sons, 1968), p. 49.
3. Eric Delieb and Michael Roberts, *Matthew Boulton: Master Silversmith* (New York: Clarkson N. Potter, 1971), p. 84.

3. The Leading Silversmiths

1. "Report of Artisans Selected by a Committee Appointed by the Council of the British Society of Arts to Visit the Paris Universal Exhibition, 1867," p. 208.
2. Joseph Purtell, *The Tiffany Touch* (New York: Random House, 1972), p. 49.
3. Samuel Bing, *Artistic America, Tiffany Glass, and Art Nouveau*, Introduction by Robert Koch (Cambridge, Mass.: The MIT Press, 1970), p. 248.
4. Ibid., p. 121.
5. From "Illustrated America," August 29, 1891 as quoted in *The Magazine Silver*, July–August, 1971, p. 10.
6. *Harper's*, July 1876.
7. *To William Cullen Bryant at Eighty Years, From His Friends and Countrymen* (New York: Scribners, Armstrong & Co., 1876), p. 34.
8. Ibid., pp. 23–24.
9. This must have pleased Charles Tiffany and Edward C. Moore when they read the account of the presentation in the *New York World* (July 10, 1887).
10. Tiffany scrapbooks, no newspaper name given.
11. Robert Koch tells a story that when Louis Comfort Tiffany's second wife polished some silver and other metal objects in their house he became very upset. He obviously preferred tarnished surfaces.

4. The Sumptuous Table—1: Hollow Ware

1. *The Statistical History of the United States from Colonial Times to the Present* (Stamford, Conn.: Fairfield Publishers, 1965), p. 371.
2. Ellin Berlin, *Silver Platter* (New York: Doubleday & Co., 1957), pp. 210–211.
3. Tiffany scrapbooks.
4. This sum, which was widely reported in the press of the time, was probably high. A bill from Tiffany for the major part of the service (1,080 pieces), dated April 26, 1879, totaled $57,978. This four-page detailed bill listed the cost for each piece as follows: "Patterns and Dies" in one column and the cost of "Making" in the next column. For example, the Pattern and Die column for the 22-inch meat dish in Figure 58 was $35.38 and the Making was $429.75 for a total cost of $465.13. We would guess the whole service in its boxes was delivered to Paris for somewhere around seventy-five or eighty thousand dollars. The half ton of silver required to make the 14,718 ounces of sterling which was furnished by Mr. Mackay had a value in 1878 of about $16,000.

5. The Sumptuous Table—2: Flatware

1. Florence Howe Hall, *Social Customs* (Boston: Estes and Lauriat, 1887), pp. 76–80.
2. [Tiffany & Co.] *Tiffany Table Settings* (New York: Thomas Y. Crowell, 1960).
3. Oscar Lewis, *The Big Four* (New York: Alfred A. Knopf, 1938), p. 150.
4. Correspondence with J. Carter Brown, Director of the National Gallery in Washington, D.C., and his father, John Nicholas Brown, indicates that the pattern was made for John Carter Brown who was the present J. Carter Brown's great-grandfather. The Brown family coat of arms appears on the pattern.
5. "Coppers" are plant records of flatware patterns stamped from the original dies in an inexpensive material, copper.
6. A detailed account of Tiffany's souvenir spoons can be found in Anton Hardt, *Adventuring Further in Souvenir Spoons with a First Glimpse of the Tiffany Souvenir Spoons* (New York: Greenwich Press, 1971).

7. Presentation Silver

1. Margaret Brown Klapthor, *Presentation Pieces in the Museum of History and Technology* (Washington, D.C.: Smithsonian Institution, 1965), p. 83.
2. *The Travels of Marco Polo* (Garden City, N.Y.: Garden City Publishing Co., 1941), p. 123.

8. Presentation Swords and Guns

1. We have been able to find very little on swords of the Civil War period in the Tiffany plant records. It has always been Tiffany's policy not to include most custom-made items in their regular plant journals and this would apply to many of the great Civil War presentation swords. The plant journal No. 1 covering the period 1851 to 1870 contains, near the end, two pages of references to swords. There are ten swords listed, two of which are silver, the others being gilt brass. The first entry reads:

No. 1 Silver-straight—grip fig of America—scroll guard
                Eagle and shield

P
                scroll and leaf plate—first mtg-group of flags and
                arm and head of medusa, 2nd reversed leaf

first one
                and laurel toe, scroll and leaves—with laurel vine

Aug. 13, 61

$250—31.08 oz.   charge in future   200—

There is another reference to the same sword in the regular chronological (1861) listing of objects:

No. 1168   Sword Crawford America
                      7836 first one $250
                                  31.08

Another entry reads:

No. 1411   Mt's Sword Case. Gen. Grant
                      Jan. 11, 64

Since references to swords in the regular plant journals are limited to these few items, we assume there was a separate plant record book for swords, but so far none has been located.

2. Jay P. Altmayer, *American Presentation Swords* (Mobile, Ala.: The Rankin Press, 1958), p. 45.

3. Ibid., p. 27.

4. The descriptions of the swords, in this chapter, belonging to the Smithsonian Institution were largely taken from: Theodore T. Belote, *American and European Swords in the Historical Collections of the United States National Museum* (Washington, D.C.: Government Printing Office, 1932).

5. Robert T. Sutherland and R. L. Wilson, *The Book of Colt Firearms* (Kansas City, Mo.: privately printed, 1971), pp. 577–578.

6. Ibid., p. 577.

7. Roy C. Jinks and R. L. Wilson, "Tiffany Stocked Firearms" in *Antique Arms Annual* (published by S. P. Stevens, 1971), p. 198.

8. Ibid., p. 200.

9. Yachting and Other Sporting Trophies

1. John Parkinson, Jr., *The History of the New York Yacht Club,* ed. Robert W. Carrick (New York, 1975), pp. 5–6. According to Parkinson, the Knickerbocker Boat Club of New York was founded in 1811, the New York Boat Club in 1830, and the Boston Boat Club in 1835, but all of these were short lived. The Detroit Boat Club was founded in 1839 and still exists.

2. Ibid., p. 16.

3. Charles H. Carpenter, Jr. "Nineteenth-century Silver in the New York Yacht Club," *The Magazine Antiques,* September 1977, pp. 496–505.

4. *The Jewelers' Weekly,* August 23, 1888.

5. From a letter from Robert G. Goelet, Jr., dated January 24, 1978.

10. The Japanese and Other Exotic Influences

1. George Frederic Heydt, *Charles L. Tiffany and the House of Tiffany &*

Co. (New York: Tiffany & Co., 1893), p. 13.

2. Christopher Dresser, "The Art Manufacturers of Japan, from Personal Observation," *Journal of the Society of Arts,* XXVI (February 1, 1878), pp. 174–175.

3. L. Falize (writing under the pseudonym of M. Josse), "L'Art Japonais," *Revue des Arts Décoratifs,* III (1883), p. 359.

4. G. deLeris, *Revue des Arts Décoratifs,* IV (1883), p. 119.

5. Samuel Bing, *Artistic America, Tiffany Glass, and Art Nouveau.* Introduction by Robert Koch (Cambridge, Massachusetts: The MIT Press, 1970), p. 156.

6. An unidentified clipping from the Tiffany scrapbooks.

11. Electroplated Silver

1. We do not feel that a discussion of the technical aspects of electroplating is relevant to this book. Readers are referred to: Dorothy T. and H. Ivan Rainwater, *American Silverplate* (Hanover, Pa.: Thomas Nelson, Inc. and Everybodys Press, 1968).

12. The Making of Tiffany Silver

1. "A Walk Through Tiffany's," *National Repository,* July 1878, pp. 11–28; "The Manufacture of Silverware," *Scientific American,* Vol. 26, New Series, No. 19, May 12, 1877.

2. Millicent Stow, *American Silver* (New York: Gramercy Publishing Co., 1950), p. 92.

3. Seymour B. Wyler, *The Book of Old Silver* (New York: Crown Publishers, 1937), p. 105.

4. Bernard and Therle Hughes, *Three Centuries of English Domestic Silver* (New York: Wilfred Funk, 1952). See Chapter 1 in particular.

5. Eric Delieb and Michael Roberts, *Matthew Boulton: Master Silversmith* (New York: Clarkson Potter, 1971), pp. 126, 127.

6. Allison Butts, ed., *Silver: Economics, Metallurgy and Uses* (New York: Van Nostrand & Co., 1967), p. 331.

7. Joseph Purtell, *The Tiffany Touch* (New York: Random House, 1972), pp. 226, 227.

8. Nancy A. Goyne, "Britannia in America. The introduction of a new alloy and a new industry," *Winterthur Portfolio II,* H. F. du Pont Winterthur Museum (1965), pp. 160–196.

9. Fine silver is the pure metal itself. For practical purposes it is defined as silver metal containing a minimum of 99.9 percent silver.

10. R. H. Leach and C. H. Chatfield, Tech. Pub. No. 60, American Institute of Mining and Metallurgical Engineers (1928), p. 1.

11. Karen Papouchado, unpublished research paper, "Quality Marked Silver," The Henry Francis du Pont Winterthur Museum, 1975.

12. Located near New York's present-day Chinatown. Part of the old Tiffany building is still standing on Prince Street.

13. *The Statistical History of the United States* (Stamford, Conn.: Fairfield Publishers, 1947), p. 91.

14. "How Skilled Work Remunerates Women in Silversmith Shops," *Harper's Bazaar,* August 18, 1883.

15. *The Jewelers' Weekly,* 1878, p. 3019.

16. *National Repository,* July 1878, p. 24.

17. Henry J. Kauffman, *The Colonial Silversmith* (Nashville, Tenn.: Thomas Nelson, Inc., 1969) describes eighteenth-century silvermaking processes.
18. *New York Tribune,* April 1, 1870.
19. Douglas Ash, *Dictionary of British Antique Silver* (London: Pelham Books, 1972), p. 90.
20. *Appleton's Journal,* December, 1878, p. 489.
21. Samuel Bing, *Artistic America, Tiffany Glass, and Art Nouveau* (Cambridge, Mass.: The MIT Press, 1970), p. 156.
22. Courtesy of Mrs. C. E. Galston.

13. Tiffany Marks

1. Montague Howard, *Old London Silver* (New York: Charles Scribner's Sons, 1903), p. 201.
2. The English system of marking silver is well documented. See, for example: Bernard and Therle Hughes, *Three Centuries of English Domestic Silver* (New York: Wilfred Funk, 1952) and Seymour B. Wyler, *The Book of Old Silver* (New York: Crown Publishers, 1937).

14. The Twentieth Century—A Postscript

1. James D. Van Trump, "Art Deco," *Carnegie Magazine,* May 1977, pp. 198–219.
2. Ibid., p. 203.

Tiffany Source Material

A. Source Material at Tiffany & Co. in New York

SCRAPBOOKS   In the Tiffany files there are about fifty large scrapbooks with material roughly in chronological order from the 1840s to the present containing Tiffany advertisements from newspapers and magazines, articles on the store and its activities, pamphlets, accounts of sporting trophies and other presentation pieces, as well as stories of people associated with the company. There are descriptions of Tiffany exhibits at fairs and expositions and material on their competitors and their suppliers, along with handwritten notes, letters, and bills of sale.

TIFFANY CATALOGS   The first catalog was issued in 1845 (see p. 7). It was not until 1878 that another was issued, but from that date onward the catalogs, or "Blue Books," were published annually. Although the nineteenth-century catalogs were not illustrated, they included lists of articles for sale and prices (pp. 131–139).

B. Source material at the Tiffany Plant

(Because of the nature of the plant operations none of the source material listed below is available to the general public or the casual researcher.)

The Tiffany plant has extensive holdings of nineteenth-century business records, drawings, dies and models, and books, which together constitute a great and important storehouse of American design. It would take a trained art librarian many months to catalog the various materials. Although we spent hundreds of hours going through these files, and made what we think are a number of fascinating discoveries, we are quite aware that an in-depth study of all of this material would be a major undertaking. We think the importance of the material warrants such a study and would like to see it done at some future time.

We made the greatest use of the following:

PLANT JOURNALS   There are three large plant journals or pattern books covering the period 1851 to 1903. The entries in the plant journals are chronological, based on pattern numbers. At the beginning, the plant journal listed only pattern numbers, the name of the object, the plant cost, and weight. Almost all of the entries are for hollow-ware pieces. There is a separate Spoon Book covering flatware of the 1870–1910 period.

After 1870 the plant records are more detailed. Order numbers, breakdown of plant costs, dates, and the number of different pieces made from the same pattern are indicated for many items. Thus it is often possible to obtain quite accurate data on individual pieces of Tiffany silver, when it was made and how much it cost.

There is one major omission from all of the plant journals that is troublesome for the researcher: special orders were never entered. There are no journal records for such items as the Mackay service or for any of the private flatware patterns. These objects must be identified in other ways. In the case of the Mackay service the records are available elsewhere* and there are many published accounts of it. The private flatware patterns were identified from "coppers" mentioned below and from patent records.

There does not appear to have been a journal or pattern book for special orders. Even in the twentieth century special orders are not recorded with the regular production items.

WORKING DRAWINGS   There are thousands of full-scale working drawings arranged by form (i.e., candlesticks, etc.) in approximate chronological order. We have illustrated a number of these drawings. The working drawings show the form and the construction of an object, but no engraving or chasing details (see Figs. 72 and 77).

SKETCHES FOR ENGRAVINGS AND CHASING DESIGNS   We were able to locate only a few sketches for engraving and chasing designs (see Fig. 93). On the other hand the working drawings for many of the objects in the book are still in the Tiffany files.

COPPERS   Models of flatware, hollow ware, medals, die-rolled borders, and casting details made in copper, pewter, or lead are scattered through the files. In some cases these "coppers" are the only available record of certain pieces (see Fig. 111).

HAMMERING DESIGNS   There are about two hundred hammering (and mounting and engraving) designs for Tiffany's silver in the Japanese style of the period 1873–1882 (see Figs. 258, 259, and 268).

THE DIE VAULT   The die vault contains thousands of dies for flatware, hollow ware, ornamental castings, decorative borders, and medals.

THE PLANT LIBRARY   There are several hundred books, scrapbooks, photographic albums, and boxes of photographs. We list volumes from the original Prince Street plant on page 230 and reproduce a number of photographs from the 1870s and 1880s throughout the book.

* The University Library, The University of Nevada, Reno.

Bibliography

BOOKS   Altmayer, Jay P., *American Presentation Swords* (Mobile, Alabama: The Rankin Press, 1958).

Ash, Douglas, *Dictionary of British Antique Silver* (London: Pelham Books, 1972).

Avery, C. Louise, *Early American Silver* (New York: Russell and Russell, 1968).

Barber, Edwin Atlee; Lockwood, Luke Vincent; and French, Hollis, *The Ceramic, Furniture, and Silver Collectors' Glossary* (New York: Dacapo Press, 1976).

Belote, Theodore T., *American and European Swords in the Historical Collections of the United States National Museum* (Washington: United States Government Printing Office, 1932).

Berlin, Ellin, *Silver Platter* (Garden City, New York: Doubleday & Co., Inc., 1957).

Bigelow, Frances Hill, *Historic Silver of the Colonies and its Makers* (New York: Tudor Publishing Company, 1948).

Bing, Samuel, *Artistic America, Tiffany Glass, and Art Nouveau*, Introduction by Robert Koch (Cambridge, Mass.: The MIT Press, 1970).

Bohan, Peter, and Hammerslough, Philip, *Early Connecticut Silver, 1700–1840* (Middletown, Connecticut: Wesleyan University Press, 1970).

Buhler, Katherine C., *American Silver* (New York: The World Publishing Co., 1950).

Burgess, Fred W., *Silver: Pewter: Sheffield Plate* (New York: Tudor Publishing Co., 1937).

Butler, Joseph T., *American Antiques 1800–1900, A Collector's History and Guide* (New York: The Odyssey Press, 1965).

Butts, Allison, ed., *Silver: Economics, Metallurgy and Uses* (New York: Van Nostrand & Co., 1967).

Byron, Joseph, and Lancaster, Clay, *New York Interiors at the Turn of the Century* (New York: Dover Publications, 1976).

Came, Richard, *Silver* (New York: G. P. Putnam's Sons, 1961).

Council of the British Society of Arts, *Report of Artisans Selected by a Committee Appointed by the Council of the British Society of Arts to Visit the Paris Universal Exposition, 1867* (London: no date).

Culme, John, and Strang, John G., *Antique Silver and Silver Collecting* (London: The Hamlyn Publishing Group Limited, 1973).

Davidson, Marshall B., ed., *The American Heritage History of Antiques from the Civil War to World War I* (New York: American Heritage Publishing Co., 1969).

Delieb, Eric, *Investing in Silver* (New York: Clarkson N. Potter, 1967).

Delieb, Eric, and Roberts, Michael, *Matthew Boulton: Master Silversmith* (New York: Clarkson N. Potter, 1971).

Dewing, Maria Richards, *Beauty in the Household* (New York: Harper & Bros., 1882).

Dictionary of American Biography (New York: Charles Scribner's Sons, 1936).

Fales, Martha Gandy, *Early American Silver for the Cautious Collector* (New York: E. P. Dutton, 1973).

Hall, Florence Howe, *Social Customs* (Boston: Estes and Lauriat, 1887).

Hardt, Anton, *Adventuring Further in Souvenir Spoons with a First Glimpse of the Tiffany Souvenir Spoons* (New York: Greenwich Press, 1971).

Hayden, Arthur, *Chats on Old Silver* (New York: Dover Publications, 1969).

Heydt, George Frederick, *Charles L. Tiffany and the House of Tiffany & Co.* (New York: Tiffany & Co., 1893).

Hoehling, A. A., *Thunder at Hampton Roads* (Englewood Cliffs, N.J.: Prentice-Hall, 1976).

Holland, Margaret, *Silver, An Illustrated Guide to American and British Silver* (New York: Derby Books, 1973).

Honour, Hugh, *Goldsmiths and Silversmiths* (New York: G. P. Putnam's Sons, 1971).

Hood, Graham, *American Silver: A History of Style 1650–1900* (New York: Praeger Publishers, 1971).

Howard, Montague, *Old London Silver, Its History, Its Makers and Its Marks* (New York: Charles Scribner's Sons, 1903).

Hughes, Bernard, and Hughes, Therle, *Three Centuries of English Domestic Silver 1500–1820* (New York: Wilfred Funk, 1952).

Hughes, G. Bernard, *Small Antique Silverware* (New York: Bramhall House, 1957).

Hughes, Graham, *Modern Silver Throughout the World 1880–1967* (New York: Crown Publishers, 1967).

Kauffman, Henry J., *The Colonial Silversmith, His Techniques and His Products* (New York: Galahad Books, 1969).

Koch, Robert, *Louis C. Tiffany, Rebel in Glass* (New York: Crown Publishers, 1964).

Lancaster, Clay, *The Japanese Influence in America* (New York: Walter H. Rawls, 1963).

Lewis, Oscar, *The Big Four* (New York: Alfred A. Knopf, 1938).

Link, Eva M., *The Book of Silver,* Translated from German by Francisca Garvie (New York: Praeger Publishers, 1973).

McClinton, Katherine Morrison, *Collecting American 19th Century Silver* (New York: Charles Scribner's Sons, 1968).

Miller, V. Isabelle, *Silver by New York Makers, Late Seventeenth Century to 1900* (New York: Museum of the City of New York, 1937).

Parkinson, John, Jr., *The History of the New York Yacht Club* (New York: New York Yacht Club, 1975).

Okie, Howard Pitcher, *Old Silver and Old Sheffield Plate* (New York: Doubleday & Co., 1928).

Peterson, Harold L., *The American Sword 1775–1945* (New Hope, Pa.: Robert Halter, The River House, 1954).

Purtell, Joseph, *The Tiffany Touch* (New York: Random House, 1971).

Rainwater, Dorothy T., ed., *Sterling Silver Holloware* (Princeton, New Jersey: The Pyne Press, 1973).

Rainwater, Dorothy T., *Encyclopedia of American Silver Manufacturers* (New York: Crown Publishers, 1975).

Rainwater, Dorothy T., and Rainwater, H. Ivan, *American Silverplate* (Nashville, Tennessee: Thomas Nelson and Hanover, Pennsylvania: Everybody's Press, 1968).

Rose, Barbara, *Art-as-Art, The Selected Writings of Ad Reinhardt* (New York: The Viking Press, 1975).

Savage, George, *A Concise History of Interior Decoration* (London: Thames and Hudson, 1966).

Schwartz, Marvin D., *Collectors' Guide to Antique American Silver* (New York: Doubleday & Co., 1975).

Seale, William, *The Tasteful Interlude, American Interiors Through the Camera's Eye, 1860–1917* (New York: Praeger Publishers, 1975).

Smith, Howard R. *Economic History of the United States* (New York: The Ronald Press Company, 1955).

The Statistical History of the United States from Colonial Times to the Present (Stamford, Connecticut: Fairfield Publishers, 1962).

Stow, Millicent, *American Silver* (New York: Gramercy Publishing Co., 1950).

Sutherland, Robert Q., and Wilson, R. L., *The Book of Colt Firearms* (Kansas City, Missouri: Published by Robert Q. Sutherland, 1971).

Taylor, Gerald, *Art in Silver and Gold* (New York: E. P. Dutton, 1964).

Tiffany Table Settings (New York: Thomas Y. Crowell, 1960).

Townsend, Horace, *A Touchstone for Silver* (New York: The Gorham Co., 1917).

The Travels of Marco Polo (Garden City: Garden City Publishing Co., 1941).

Turner, Noel D. *American Silver Flatware 1837–1910* (New York: A. S. Barnes and Co., 1972).

Wardle, Patricia, *Victorian Silver and Silver-Plate* (New York: Thomas Nelson and Sons, 1963).

Wenham, Edward, *The Practical Book of American Silver* (Philadelphia and New York: J. B. Lippincott, 1949).

White, W. C., and White, Ruth, *Tin Can on a Shingle* (New York: E. P. Dutton, 1957).

Wyler, Seymour B., *The Book of Old Silver* (New York: Crown Publishers, 1937).

MUSEUM PUBLICATIONS   *Cathay Invoked, Chinoiserie, A Celestial Empire in the West* (San Francisco: The California Palace of the Legion of Honor, 1966).

Classical America, 1815–1845 (Newark, New Jersey: The Newark Museum, 1963).

Ettinghausen, Richard, *Islamic Art* (New York: The Metropolitan Museum of Art, no date).

Hawley, Henry H., "Tiffany's Silver in the Japanese Taste," *The Bulletin of The Cleveland Museum of Art*, October, 1976, pp. 236–245.

Klapthor, Margaret Brown, *Presentation Pieces in the Museum of History and Technology, Smithsonian Institution* (Washington, D.C.: Smithsonian Institution, 1965).

Koch, Robert, "The Tiffany Exhibition Punch Bowl," *Arts In Virginia*, Vol. 16, No. 5, Winter and Spring, 1976, pp. 32–39.

Le Grand Lockwood (Norwalk, Connecticut: Published by the Lockwood-Mathews Mansion Museum, 1969).

Maryland Silver in the Collection of the Baltimore Museum of Art (Baltimore: Baltimore Museum of Art, 1975).

McLanathan, Richard B. K., ed., *Colonial Silversmiths, Masters and Apprentices* (Boston: Museum of Fine Arts, 1956).

19th-Century America, Furniture and Other Decorative Arts (New York: The Metropolitan Museum, 1970).

Tracy, Berry B., *A Bicentennial Treasury: American Masterpieces from the Metropolitan* (New York: The Metropolitan Museum, 1976).

Weisberg, Gabriel; Cate, Phillip D.; Needham, Gerald; Eidelberg, Martin; and Johnston, William R., *Japonisme, Japanese Influence on French Art 1854–1910,* Published jointly by The Cleveland Museum of Art, The Rutgers University Art Gallery, and The Walters Art Gallery, 1975.

Index

*Page numbers in italics indicate
illustrations*

Adams, C. C., 214
Adams, Edward Dean, 146
Adams & Shaw, 214, *215*, 218, *258*
Adams Gold Vase, 4, 83, 146, *147,*
148
Ailanthus pattern, *see Atlantas*
pattern
Ailantus pattern, *see Atlantas*
pattern
Altmayer, Jay P., 154, 155
American Automobile Association,
178
American Indian designs, 41,
American Cotton Oil Company, 146
205–210, *206, 207, 208, 209, 211*
America's Cup, 170, 173, 174
Ames Manufacturing Company, 166
Ames Sword Company, 165
Anderson, Peter B., coffee and tea
service presented to, 144, 145,
145
Annealing process, 231–232, *233*
Antique (flatware pattern), 97, 99,
107, 110, *111, 117,* 220
Antique Engraved No. 4 pattern,
107, *108*
Antique Engraved No. 20 pattern,
see Antique Ivy
Antique Ivy (flatware pattern), 77,
107, *108*
mark on, *256*
Apple Shape pattern, 78
Architecture, 1, 2–3, 15, 52–56, 268
Army and Navy Journal, 164
Art Deco, *116,* 263, 266, 268, 269,
270
Art Moderne, 268
Art Nouveau, 27, 31, 44–46, 49, 59,
79, 86, 105, 110, 120, 149, 172,
173, 178, *179,* 193, 263, 264, 266

Artistic America (Bing), 199
Ash receivers, 135
Assembling, 237
Atlantic cable items, 14, *14,* 15, *15*
Atlantas pattern, 99, *114,* 118
Audubon (flatware pattern), 27, 44,
97, 110, 111, see *Japanese*
pattern
Auto racing trophy, *see* Vanderbilt
Cup
Avery, M. S. P., 32
"Aztec" silver, 209

B. Lorillard Style, 78
B. Tiffany pattern, see *Atlantas*
pattern
Backgammon trophy, University
Club, 3, 3–4
Ball, Black & Co., 10
Ball, Tompkins and Black, 20
Baltimore Museum of Art, 193
Baltimore silver, 63, 244
Bamboo (flatware pattern), *119*
Banks, Robert Lenox, *83*
Banks, Thomas Crane, 8
Barney, A. L., 3, 150, 268
Barnum, P. T., 9, 22
dining room in house of, 54–55,
55
house of, 54–56
Battleship silver services, 150–151,
151, 152
Bauhaus, 3
Beauty in the Household
(Dewing), 95, *95*
Beekman (flatware pattern), 110,
110
Beer mugs, 135
Bells, 37, *37,* 135, 138
call, 132
Japanese style, 190
spring, 188–189, *189*
Belmont, August

Memorial Cup, 176–177, *177*
tray presented to, 149, *149*
Belmont, Perry, 40
Belmont Cup, 176–177, *177*
Belts, 132
Bennett, James Gordon, Jr., 170, 207
Berlin, Ellin, 58
Bicycles, 42–43
silver, designed for Lillian
Russell, 42, *42*
Bierstadt, Albert, 2
Bing, Samuel, 31, 199, 201, 240
Birch, Frank Stevens, 20
Birch, James E., *19*–21
Birch service, 20, *20*–21, *21,* 22
Bits, horses', 136
Black, Starr & Frost, 33
Blackberry dish, 80, *81*
Blue Book, 7, 42, 113, 120, 121, 124,
125, 131, 138, 167, 195
Bogert, *15,* 249
Boggs, Lindy, 127
Book of Colt Firearms, The, 165
Boston Museum of Fine Arts, 37
Bottle handle, 135
Bottle wagons, 65
Mackay service, 65, *67*
Bottles
glass toilet, 133, 135
Japanese style, 190
odor, 133
Boulton, Matthew, 224
Boulton & Fathergill, 16
Bouquet holders, 132
Boutet, Nicholas Noel, 155
Bowls
Brasher, reproduction of, 267, 268
finger, with stand, 46, *46*
Indian design, 210, *211*
Japanese style, 190
See also Flower bowl; Punch
bowls; Sugar bowls; Waste
bowls

Boxes, 7, 127, *127*, 132, 133, 134, 135, 137
  cigar, Art Deco, 268, *269*
  gold, 15, *15*, 141
  match, 127, *128*, 136, 137
  snuff, 7, 137
Brady, Diamond Jim, 42
Brady, Mathew, 162
Braque, 49
Brasher, Ephraim, 263, 267, 268
Briggs, Allan Lindsay, 49
British Museum, 235
Brooklyn Navy Yard, 150
Broom Corn pattern, 99, 114
Brown, Daisy Beard, *81*
Brown, J. Carter, private flatware pattern, 98, 104, *104*
Brown, John, 272
Brush holder, Bronze Japanese, 185, *185*
Brushes, 134
  hair, 133
Bryan, William Jennings, 51
Bryant, Edmund Cullen, 57
Bryant, William Cullen, 32–35, 57
Bryant Vase, 4, 27, 31, 32–36, *33*, 141
Buck Cup, 171–172, *173*, 199
Buckler, T. H., *198*
Buffalo Bill, 60
Butter dishes, Japanese style, 190
Buttons, 134

Cake plates, 80, *81*
Cake server, 106, *106*
California, University of, Birch service at, 19–21, *20*, *21*
Calculators, electronic, 271–272, *272*
Calling cards, 124–125
Cambon, Jules, cup presented to, 148, *148*
Candelabras, 80, *81*, 100
  electroplated, 217, *217*
  "Indian," 205–207, *207*
Candlesticks, 79, 80, *81*, 82, 131, 137, 266, *267*
Candy dish, 128, *128*
Canes, 135
Canister, 190, *190*
Cape May Challenge Cup, 171, *171*
Capitol, U. S., safe in, 126–127
Card cases, 7, 125, *125*, 133, 135, 253, *253*
Card trays, *see* Trays, card
Caskets, 139
Casters with three bottles, 135
Castilian (flatware pattern), *116*
Casting, 237

Catlin, George, 209, *211*
Centerpieces, 37, 79–80, *80*, 100
  "Four Seasons," 17, *18*, 37, 80, 141
Century (flatware pattern), *116*, 268, 270
Chafing dishes, 44–45, *45*, 49, 79
  yachting trophy, 172, *172*, 173
Chalice, 209
Chamberpot, gold, 42
Chariot (Tom Thumb's), 22, *23*, 141
Chartran, Theobald, 149
Chasing, 237, *238*
Chatelaines, 133, 134
  Japanese style, 190
Cheese scoop, 110, *113*
Chemical dips, use of, 275
Chests, silver, 55–56, *56*, 61–62
Children's silver, 17, *18*, 43, *44*, 88, *88*, 107, *107*, *112*, 137–138
Chinoiserie decoration, 9, 10, *10*, 180, 181, *181*
Chocolate pot, 77
Chrysanthemum pattern, 56, *56*, 77–79, 80, *81*, 98, 107, 113, *113*, 118, 119, 128, *129*
Cigar, *see* Segar cases; Segar lighters
Cigar box, Art Deco, 268, *269*
Cigarette cases, 135
City mark, *244*
Civil War, 21, 142, 143, 145, 154–166, 182
Clasps, belt and cloak, 132, 134
Classical design, 16
Classical Revival style, 15, 17, 62, 68, 170
Claverley, Charles, 32, *32*
Clearwater, A. T., 267
Cleveland Museum, 197
Clinton (flatware pattern), *116*, 117
Clinton Engraved (flatware pattern), 116
Clocks, traveling, 138
Cocktail mixers, 138
Cocktail strainers, 138
Cody, William F., *see* Buffalo Bill
Coffee services, *see* Tea and coffee services
Coffeepots, 48, 68, 69, 70, 72, 73, 76, 77, *77*, *78*, 79, *144*, 145, 266, *266*
  Art Deco, 269
  electroplated, 216, *216*
  Islamic, *194*, 195, 201, 202, *203*, 217
  Japanese style, 192, *194*, 195, 196, 197, *197*
  working drawing for, 189, *189*
  See also Tea and coffee services
Collars, dog, 133

Collecting American 19th Century Silver (McClinton), 4
Collins & Co., 160, 162
Colonial (flatware pattern), *114*, 118
Colonial revival style, 77, *77*, 262, 263, 266
Colt pistols with "Tiffany" grips, 165, *166*
Columbian Exhibition (Chicago, 1893), 4, 41, 42, 46, 146, *147*, 168, 201, 202
  Tiffany mark used for, 252, 257
Combs, 133, 134
  back, 128, 130, *130*
Compasses, 135, 137
Compotes, 79–80, *80*, 100
Comstock Bonanza, 57–58
Coney Island Jockey Club, silver trophy, 2
Congressional Medal of Honor, 153, *153*
Connoisseur, The, 1
Continental Congress, 154
Cook, Charles T., mark of, 252, 256, *256*
Cook (Saratoga) pattern, 97, *111*
Copper and silver objects, 57, 151, *152*, 192, *194*, 195, 197, *197*, *198*, 200–201, 210, *211*, 212, 225, 240
  marks used on, 253–254
Cordis (flatware pattern), *117*
Corks, silver-mounted, 136
Corning, Edwin Weld, 83
Corning, Mary de Camp, *83*
Coster, John B., sword presented to, *155*, 155–156
Creamers, *48*, 49, 72, 73, 79, *144*, *194*, 195
  Art Deco, 269
  electroplated, 216
  Islamic, 202, *203*
  Japanese style, 190–192, *191*, *194*, 195, *197*
  "Mooresque," 25, 28, 70, *71*
  niello work, 202, *203*
  Paul Revere, reproduction of, 267, 268, *268*
  See also Tea and coffee services
"Cross of Gold" speech (Bryan), 51
Crumbers, 90, *90*, 109, *109*, 255, *255*
Crystal Palace, 19
"Cuban" (flatware pattern), *104*
Cupids and Flowers pattern, 131
Cups, 88
  Adams Gold, *see* Adams Gold Vase
  children's, 88, *88*, 89, 138
  drinking, 135
  inlaid wood, 202, *203*

Japanese style, 190
loving, *see* Loving cups
shaving, 136
three-handled, 47, *47*, 128, *129*,
   146, *147*, 148, 148–149, *149*, *211*
Curran, John T., 41, *41*, 46, 99
Currier and Ives, 144, *145*
Curtis, Edward S., 205
Cushing, F. B., 127, *127*
Custer, George Armstrong, 205

Date letter, *244*
Davies, Arthur B., 266
Davis, Dwight F., 178
Davis Cup, 178
Decanters, 135
Decorating processes, 237–241
Degas, Edgar, 181
Deihm, Mrs. Charles F., 126–127
Delano, Franklin H., 32
Delmonico, Lorenzo, 37
Deringer guns, 164–165
Designing Room, Tiffany's,
   228–229, *242*
Dewey, George, 83
Dewey Medal, 153, *153*
Dewing, Maria Richards, 95, *95*
Diamonds, 8
Die, marking, 246, 256, 257
Dinner parties, Victorian, descrip-
   tion of, 93–96
Dippers, 92
Dips, chemical, use of, 275
Dish washing, 95
Dixon, M. B., 245
Dog collars, 133
Domestically produced silver, mark
   used for, 252
Dresser, Christopher, 184
Dressing cases, **135**
Dressing table silver, 130–131, *131*
   132
Drinking cups, 135
du Pont, Henry Algernon, 72
du Pont, Henry Francis, 3
du Pont, Samuel Francis, 17, 19, 141
du Pont service, 13, 17, *19*, 62, 72,
   72, 73, *76*, *77*, 141
Duryea, I. A., pitcher presented to,
   140, 141, 142
Dutch silver, 138, 226
Dwight, Jeannette A., *87*

*Early American Silver for the
   Cautious Collector* (Fales), 273
Ecclesiastical silver, 138
Electroplate marks, 257–259,
   258–259

Electroplated silver, 212–220,
   216–221
Elephant tusk, 173–174, *175*
Elkington, G. R. & H. (silverware
   firm), 25–26, 213, 214
Ellis, J. L., 7
Embossing, 238
Enameling, 240
Engine-turning, 239
English King (flatware pattern),
   114, 118, 220
English silver, marks on, 243–244,
   243–244, 254
Engraving, 238–239
Eoff, Garrett, 245
Eoff & Moore, 245
Ericsson, John, 143–145
Etching, 239–240
Etiquette, 93–96, 124–125
Ewers, *see* Pitchers
Exhibition of the Industry of All
   Nations, 17, 19
Exposition des Arts Décoratifs et
   Industriels Modernes (Paris,
   1925), 268
Exposition Universelle (Paris,
   1900), 42, 47, 202
   Tiffany mark used for, *252*

Factory, Tiffany, 226–237
Fales, Martha Gandy, 273
Falize, L., 198–199, 201
Fan holders, 133
Faneuil (flatware pattern), *115*
Faneuil Engraved (flatware
   pattern), *115*
Faneuil #95, see Feather Edge
Faneuil #225, see Reeded Edge
Farnham, George P., 41
Farnham, Paulding, 83, *84*, *123*,
   146, *147*, 162, 164
Farnham, Sallie, 83
Farragut, David Glasgow, swords
   presented to, 157, *157*, 159
Favrile glass, 46, 47, 50, 263
Feather Edge (flatware pattern),
   115
Federal style, 69
Fiddle and Thread pattern, 90, 254,
   254
Field, Cyrus, 14, *14*, 15, *15*, 141
Finger bowl with stand, 46, *46*
Finishing, silver, 241–242
Fish, Latham A., 173
Fish dishes, 82
Fish platters, 79, 82
Flasks, 128, 130, *130*
Flatware, 52, 55, 56, 90–123, 137

eighteenth-century, reproduction
   of, 267
electroplated, 212–220
handworked patterns, 107–110
making of, *232*, 232–234, *233*
marks, 245, 254–257, *254–257*, 259
patents, 97–99, 103, 104, 186, 188,
   207, 219, 220
pattern numbers and dates of
   issue (Table), 261
private patterns, 99–105
serving pieces, *105*, 105–107, *106*
standard Tiffany sterling patterns,
   110–113, *114–117*, 118, *119*
Flemish (flatware pattern), *116*
Fletcher, Thomas, 154
Fletcher and Gardiner, 154
Floral (flatware pattern), 98, 219,
   220, *220*
Florentine (flatware pattern), *114*,
   118
Flower bowl, USS *New York*, 151
Forbes, J. Malcolm, 173
Ford, Gerald, 125
Forks, 92
   fish serving, 91, *91*, 92
   serving, 105
   sterling silver, weight of, 113, 118
   See also Flatware
Foster, Mary Pauline, 71, *72*
"Four Seasons" centerpiece, 17, *18*,
   37, 80, 141
Fox Head (flatware pattern), *117*
Frames, picture, 134
Frank Leslie's Weekly, 14, 21, 159
French, Daniel Chester, 153, *153*
Fuller, A. J., private flatware
   pattern, *104*
Funnels, 135

Gadgets, 263
Gale, William, mark of, *249*
Gale & Hughes, 9
Garfield, James A., 158
Garrard, Robert, Jr., 170
Garters, 133
Gazette des Beaux Arts, 206
Gebhard, Fred, 2
Gentlemen, presents for, 135–137
George IV pattern, 79
German silver, 212, 226
Gilbert, Fred E., 127, *127*
Gilding, 241
Gladstone, William, 39–41
Gladstone, Mrs. William, 40
Gladstone Testimonial, *38–39*,
   39–41, 141
Goblets, USS *New Jersey*, 150
Goelet Cup for schooners, 173, *174*

Goelet Cup for sloops, 174–175, *176*
Goelet Prize for sloops, *45, 45–46*
Gold marks, 253
Gorham Manufacturing Co., 33, 44,
    91, 96, *131*, 214
Governor (flatware pattern), *117*
Gramercy (flatware pattern), *116*,
    117
Grant, Ulysses S., 60
    sword presented to, 159–161, *160*,
    161
Grant, Mrs. Ulysses S., 60
Grape Vine pattern, 98, 105, *105*,
    110
Gravy boats, 79
Great Seal of the United States on
    Lincoln ewer, 142, *142*
Grosjean, Charles T., 77, 98, 207
    death of, 98–99
    flatware patterns patented by, 98,
        102, 103, 105, 207, 219, 220
Grosjean & Woodward, 80, *81*,
    98–99
    mark used by, *248*, 259
Guns, 21, 164–168, *166, 167, 168*

Haggerty Silver Foam, 274
Hair brushes, 133
Hair ornaments, 133
Half Moon (Hudson's ship), 151,
    152
Hall, Florence Howe, 93–95, 124
Hall, Valentine G., *179*
Halleck, H. W., 156
Hallmarks, *see* Marks
Hallowell, Roger H., 224
Hamilton (flatware pattern), *116*,
    117
Hammering and mounting design
    number, 254, *254*
Hampton (flatware pattern), *116*
Hancock, Winfield Scott, sword
    presented to, 157–159, *158*
Handle parts, casting, 237
Harlequin (flatware pattern), *117*
Harper's Bazaar, 228
Harper's Weekly, 145, *176*
Hattersly, W., mark of, *243*
Hayden & Whilden, 9
Hayes, Rutherford B., 127
Heade, Martin Johnson, 2
Hearst, William Randolph, 208
Hearst service, *208*, 208–209
Hebbard, Henry, 9, 90, 245
    mark of, *255*
Heckscher, John B., 37
Heinz, H. J., loving cup given to,
    266, *267*
Herter, Gustav, 8

Herter & Company, 103
Heydt, George Frederic, 8, 180
Hiroshige, Ando, 181
Hobart, Clarence, *179*
Hokusai, Katsushika, 181
Hollow ware, 51–89, 187
    American Indian designs on,
        209–210, *211*
    electroplated, 212–220, *216–219*
    Japanese style, 189–198, *190–199*
    making of, 234–242, *235, 238*
    marks of, 244–245, 246, *246–254*,
        250, 252–254, 259–261
    pattern numbers and dates of
        issue (Table), 260–261
Holly pattern, 105, *105*
Hopkins, Mark, 102, 103
Horses' bits, 136
Hot milk pots, 69, *72, 73, 73*, 76, 79
Howard & Co., *131*
Hudson, Henry, 151
Hundred Guinea Cup, *see* Amer-
    ica's Cup
Hyde and Goodrich (silversmithing
    firm), 69

Ice cream dish, Mackay service,
    64–65, *66*
Indian design, 62
    See also American Indian designs
Indian spoons, 98, 120, 205, *206*,
    207–208, *208*, 210, 256
Infants, presents for, 137–138
Ingots, silver, rolling of, 231,
    231–232
Inkstands, 41, 53, *125*, 125–127, *126*,
    136
    traveling, 134
Inkwells, *125*, 125, *126*, 127
    favrile-glass, 47, *47*
International style (architecture), 3
Ionic pattern, 91
Ireland, National Museum of, 38
Islamic influence, 201–202
Italian (flatware pattern), 97, 110,
    110
Ivy Chased service, *73, 73–77, 74*,
    75, 250

Jackson, Frank J., 25
Japanese (Audubon) flatware
    pattern, 27, 44, 97, 110, *111*,
    186, *186*, 187, 190, 234, 242
Japanese influence, 27, 29, 37, 44, 47,
    59, 64, *64*, 109, 171–173, 180–201
Japanese style, 110, 171–172, *172*,
    180–198, 241, 266, 272
    mark used with, 253

Jelly glass with sterling lid, 263, *264*
Jelly server, 105, *105*, 106
Jensen, Georg, 268
Jeweler's Circular, 98, 119, 201
Jewelry, silver, 134, 136
Josse, M., 198
Jugs, 17, *17*, 195
    claret, 44, *44*
    Persian brass, 28, *28*, 86, 202

Kettle stands, 48, *48, 75*
Kettles
    hot water, 9, 20, 20 *48, 48*–49, *49*,
        55, 69, *72, 73, 73*, 75, *76*, 79
    toddy, 137
Kiddle, Henry, 202
King (flatware pattern), 98, 219,
    219–220
King, Mrs. Edward, *124*
King William (flatware pattern),
    111
Kirk repoussé work, 63
Klapthor, Margaret, 140
Klots, Allen Trafford, cup presented
    to, 146, *147*
Knives
    crumber, 90, *90*
    fish serving, 91, *91*, 92
    table, *91*
    See also Flatware
Kunstgewerbemuseum, 45
Kuzmichev, A., 139

Ladies, presents for, 132–135
Ladles, 92, 105, *105*, 106, *106*, 136,
    186, 186–187, 254, *254, 255, 257*
La Farge, John, 31
Laforme Brothers, 9
Lamont, C. A., 37
Lamps, 187
Lampstand, teapot on, 9, *10*
Lane, Fitz Hugh, 2
Langley, W. H., 171
Lantern, traveling candlestick, 137
Lap Over Edge (flatware pattern),
    27, 44, 98, 99, 107, *108*, 109, *109*,
    110
    mark on, 256
Lathe, spinning, 224, 234, 235, 236
Laurelton Hall, 50
Lawson, Edward Watkins, cup
    presented to, *149*
Le Corbusier, 3
Lefferts, Marshall, 20
Leris, G. de, 199
*Leslie's Weekly, see Frank Leslie's
    Weekly*
Library, Tiffany's Prince Street,
    229–230

Lienau, Detlef, 52
Life (magazine), 93
Lincoln, Abraham, 22, 125, 153*,*
    silver gilt pitcher presented to,
        141, *141*, 142, *142*
Lincoln Memorial (Washington,
    D. C.), 153
Lind, Jenny, 9
Linear marks, 253, *253*
Linenfold (flatware pattern), *117*
Liquor stand, Mackay service, 65, 67
Lockwood, Le Grand, 52–54
    inkstand of, 125, *125*
    silver medallion portrait of, 53, *53*
Lockwood, Mrs. Le Grand, 37,
    53–54
    silver medallion portrait of, 53, *53*
Lockwood, William B. E., *81*
Lockwood & Co., 53
Lockwood Mansion, 52–54
    dining room, 53, *54*
London Art Journal, 25
London Times, 40
Londros & Co. (London), 184
Loos, Adolf, 3
Loving cups, 137, 203, 204, 205, 267
Lusk, William T., 3, 4, 43, *44*
    mark of, 252, 256
Lyle, Dr. and Mrs. William Jones,
    69

Mackay (private flatware pattern),
    97
Mackay, John W., 56–60
Mackay, Marie Louise, 56–62, *100*
Mackay service, 37, 56–67, *63–67*,
    80, 82
    album containing photographs of,
        60, *60*
    flatware, *100*, 100–101, *101*
Magnolia Vase, 4, 5, 41, *41*, 42, 47,
    202
Maker's mark, 243, *243*, 244, 254,
    255
Manet, Edouard, 181
Manis, Maria Catherine, *81*
Marks, 243–261
    applying, 246
    English silver, 243–244, *243–244*,
        254
    Tiffany, 244–261, *245–261*
Marquise (flatware pattern), *114*,
    118
Marquise Engraved #226 (flatware
    pattern), *115*
Martelé silver, 44, 188
Mat finishes, 241–242
Match boxes, 127, *128*, 136, 137
Match stands, 136

McClinton, Katharine Morrison, 4
McCorkle, Francis D., 150
McKinley, William, 148
Meat dishes, 52
    Mackay service, 64, *65*
Medallion pattern, 91, *91*
Medallions, 53, *53*
Medals, 151, 153, *153*
Melting, silver, 230–231, *231*
Mentmore sale (England), 193, 195,
    254
Merrimack (ship), 143–145
Metal workers, Japanese, at
    Tiffany's, 198–201
Metals, mixed, 240
Metropolitan Museum of Art
    Bryant Vase, 34
    Clearwater silver collection, 267
    exhibition of *Nineteenth Century
        America* (1970), 4, 20, 34
    Moore's Oriental art collection,
        27–28, 182–184
    Nast Vase, 145–146
    Tiffany & Co. and, 4–5
Metropolitan Sanitary Fair (New
    York, 1864), 159, *159*
Mexican War, 155
Milk pots, hot, *see* Hot milk pots
Milk white finish, 242
Mirrors, hand, 41, 268, *269*
Mississippi Valley Sanitary Fair
    (1864), 158, 159
"Modern" silver, 266
Modernistic style, 268
Monitor (warship), 143–145
Moore, Corinne deBebian, 86
Moore, Edward C., 5, *11*, 11–12, 14,
    23, 24, 26, 31, 46, 48, 50, 62, 65,
    83, 90, 96, 97, 98, 100, 154, 155,
    196, 272
    Bing's opinion of, 31
    bronze bust of, 32, *32*
    death of, 201
    experiments with metal mixtures,
        240
    flatware patterns patented by, 97,
        100, 105, 186, 187, 188, 190, 220
    marks of, 246, *251*, 256
    Oriental art collection, 27–28, 86,
        182–184, 202, 229
    sketchbooks, 12, *12–13*, 13, 28–29,
        70, *71*, 182, *183*, 201, 205, 206
    tributes to, 31–32
Moore, John (Edward's grandson),
    86
    mark of, 252
Moore, John C. (Edward's father),
    3, 9, 10–11, 20, 69, 140, 141,
    224, 225, 226

marks used by, 245, *245*, 247, 248,
    249, 250, 256
Moore, John C., & Son, 246
Moore, John C., Co., 245
    mark used by, *246*, 247
Moore, Louis deBebian, mark of,
    252, 256
Moore & Dixon, 245
Moore & Hebbard, 9, 245
"Mooresque" service, 25, 28, 70, *71*
Morgan, J. P., 32, 82, *82*, 99, 164,
    175
    flatware pattern, 97, 104, *104*
Morgan Cup, 28, 173–174, *175*
Morgan service, 99–100
Mt. Vernon (flatware pattern), 98,
    219, 220, *221*
Mounting, 237
Mugs, 88, *88*, 138
    ale, electroplated, 216
    beer, 135
    Japanese, 182
Museum of the City of New York,
    253
Mustards, Japanese style, 190

"Napkin Clips," 65
Napkin rings, 138
Nast, Thomas, 145
Nast Vase, *145*, 145–146
National Repository, 193, 200
New Jersey (battleship) service,
    150–151, *151*
New York (battleship) service, 150,
    151, *152*
New York *Daily Tribune*, 59
New York Herald, 25, 99
New York Sun, 52
New York University Club, *see*
    University Club
New York World, 41
New York Yacht Club, 169–170,
    170, 172
"New Zealand Love Cup," *204*, 205
Niello work, 202, *203*, 240
Nimscke, L. D., 165
Norman (flatware pattern), 220,
    221
Nutmeg graters, 136

Old Dominion Steamship Co., *144*
Old French (flatware pattern), 97,
    220, *221*
Olympian (flatware pattern), 27, 97,
    107, 110, *112*, 113, 118, *119*
    Greek myths of the, 112–113
Order number, 254, *254*, 259, 260

Oriental art, Moore's collection of, 27–28, 86, 182–184, 202, 229
Orr, John W., 161
Osgood, Samuel, 34
Oxidizing, 240

Paine, Charles J., 173, 174, *176*
Pall Mall Gazette, 41
Palm (flatware pattern), 97, 111, 118
Palmette (flatware pattern), *117*
Pan-American Exposition (Buffalo, 1901), 42, 202, 205
    Tiffany mark used for, 252
Panic of 1837, 7
Paper cutters, 133, *136*
Paris Expositions: (1855), 12, 24; (1867), 25–26, 28, 182; (1878), 28, 31, 37–41, 58–59, 63, 188, 192, 193, 195, 196, 205; (1889), 31, 41, 201, 240
Patent date mark, 256, 257, *257*
Patents, flatware, 97–99, 103, 104, 186, 188, 207, 219, 220
Pattern number, 254, *254*, 256, 259–261
Penholders, 136
Pepper shakers, 88, *89*
    Japanese style, 190, *191*
    USS *New Jersey*, 150
Perry, Matthew C., 181
Persian (flatware pattern), 97, 110, *111*
Personal silver, 128, 130, 131, 132–138
Philadelphia Centennial Exposition (1876), 17, 34, 35, 36–37, 65, 77, 126, 171, 214
Philadelphia Museum of Art, 25
Philadelphia service, 70, 75
Philip, John W., sword presented to, 164, *164*
Picasso, Pablo, 49
Pile, William A., sword presented to, 162, *163*
Pitchers, 37
    Art Nouveau, 263, *265*
    chinoiserie, 9–10, *181*
    claret, 135
    Durea, *140*, 141, 142
    hot milk, 69
    hot water, 69
    Japanese style, 190, 192–193, *192*, *193*, *194*, 195–196, *196*
    Lincoln, 141, *141*, 142, *142*
    Mackay service, 65, *66*
    making, 234–237, *235*
    Tiffany, 28, *86*, 235

Tiffany, Young & Ellis, 17, *18*
    water, 27, 72, *72*, 79, *84*, 85, *85*, 86, *86*, 106, 137, *140*, 141
    See also Creamers
Plantation (flatware pattern), *111*
Plateau, 209, *209*
Plates, 82, *82*, 137
    cake, 80, *81*
    square, Art Deco, 268, *270*
    USS *New Jersey*, 150
Polhemus (Polhamus), John, 90, 91, *91*, 106
    mark of, 255, *255*
Polish, silver, 274
Polishing, silver, 241
Polo, Marco, 140
Porringers, 138, 190
Presentation pieces, 10, 27, 36–37, 39, 42, 44, 128, 140–153, *140*–*149*, *151*–*153*
    Field, Cyrus, 15, *15*
    "Four Seasons" centerpiece, 17, *18*, 37, 80, 141
    Gladstone Testimonial, *38*–*39*, 39–41, 141
    Heinz, Henry J., 266, *267*
Prince Albert's Exposition (London, 1851), 24
Prince Street building, 222, 227, 227–237, 231–234
Princess Hatzfeldt pattern, 131
Provence (flatware pattern), *119*
Pseudo-hallmark, 255
Pulitzer, Joseph, 40
Punch bowls, 86, *87*, 88, 136
    Japanese style, 197–198, *199*
    Mackay service, 65, *67*
    USS *New Jersey*, 150, *151*
    Viking, 5, 42, 202, 204, 205
    yachting trophy, *172*, 172
Purses, silver link, 134
Purtell, Joseph, 42

Queen Ann pattern, 97, 110, *111*, 115

Rat Tail (flatware pattern), *119*
Reed, G. T., 31
Reeded Edge (flatware pattern), *115*
Regent (flatware pattern), 98, 219, 220, *220*
Renaissance (flatware pattern), *115*
Renaissance style, 83
Ranaissance-type decoration, 17
Repoussé work, 237–238, *238*, *239*
Reproductions, early silver, 267–268, *268*

Revere, Paul, 263, *267*, *268*, *269*, 273
Revolutionary War, 154
Revue des Arts Décoratifs, 198, 199
Reynal, Jules, *178*
Richelieu (flatware pattern), *114* 118
Rivers, Ella, *124*
Riverside & Fort Lee Ferry Company, *149*
Robinson, Ethel Agnes, *106*
Robinson, John Cleveland, sword presented to, 161–162, *163*
Rococo style, 17, 20, *20*, 68, 69, 80, 85, 106, 130, 141, 217, *217*, 262
Rogers, Archibald, private flatware pattern, *104*
Rogers Brothers, 218
Rolling of silver ingots, *231*, 231–232
Roman silver, 225
Roosevelt, Eleanor, *116*
Roosevelt, Franklin Delano, *116*
Roosevelt, Theodore, 32
Rothschild, Gustav de, 37
Rothschild, Hannah, 195
Rules, silver, 136
Russell, A. D., private flatware pattern, *104*
Russell, Lillian, 42
Russian silver, 138–139, 226

Safety pins, 138
St. Dunstan (flatware pattern), *115*
St. James (flatware pattern), *114*, 118
Salem (flatware pattern), *117*
Salt and pepper, Russian, 139, *139*
Salt shakers, USS *New Jersey*, 150
Salts, 79, 92
    du Pont service, *19*
    Japanese style, 190
Salvers, *see* Trays; Waiters
San Francisco *Call*, 103
San Lorenzo (flatware pattern), *116*
Saracenic style, 41
Saratoga (flatware pattern), 97, *111*
Satin Finish, 241
Satterlee, Mr. and Mrs. Herbert L., 82
Sauce boats, 15–16, *16*, 79
    du Pont service, *19*
Sauce tureen, 16, *17*
Schofield, John McAllister, sword presented to, 161, *162*
Schuyler, Hartley & Graham, 165
Scissors, 136
Searles, Edward T., 102–103
Searles, Mary Frances Hopkins, 101–103, *102*

Searles service, private flatware pattern, 98, 101–102, *102*, 103, 257
Segar cases, 136
Segar lighters, 136
Serving dishes, 52
  du Pont service, *19*
Serving pieces (flatware), special designs for, *105*, 105–107, *106*
Sharp (Japanese firm), 272
Shaw, Frank, 214–216, *215*
Shaw, Thomas, 213–214, *215*, 216
Shaw, Thomas & Company, 213, 214
Sheffield plate, 212–213
Shell and Thread (flatware pattern), 115
Sherman, William Tecumseh, sword presented to, *156*, 156–157
Sherman, William Watts, *18*
Shopping bags, 134
Silver
  care of, 273–275
  domestically produced mark used for, 252
  out of the dining room, 124–139
  production of, 51
  Tiffany, making of, 222–242
Silver Platter (Berlin), 58
Silver polish, 274
Siphons, 137
Sloan, Samuel, gold tea service presented to, 253
Slop bowls, *see* Waste bowls
Smith, Willard A., 146, *147*
Smith & Wesson, 164, *167*, 167–168, *168*
Smithsonian Institution, bicentennial show (1976), 34
Smoking set, USS *New York*, 151, *152*
Snarling, 238, *238*
Snarling iron, 238, *238*
Snuff boxes, 7, 137
Social Customs (Hall), 93–95, 124
"Society for the Encouragement of Arts, Manufactures and Commerce," 25
Soup tureen, Birch service, 20, *21*
Southside Sportsmen's Club, 177–178
Southwick, Albert A., 150
Souvenir spoons, *see* Spoons, souvenir
Spanish-American War, 148, 149, 153, 162, 164
Specialization of silvermaking processes, 223–224
Spinning, 224, 234, *235*, 236

Spoons, 92, 105, 138, 150
  berry, 106, *106*
  Indian, 98, 120, 205, *206*, 207–208, *208*, 210, 256
  serving, *91*, 92, 105, *105*
  souvenir, 99, 119–122, *121*, *122*, *123*, 257, 268, 270, 271
  sterling silver, weight of, 113, 118
  Tiffany Building, 47, *123*
  Vine pattern, *187*
  See also Flatware
Stamp, marking, 246, 256, 257
Stands
  kettle, 48, *48*, 69, 72, 73, 75, 76
  liquor, Mackay service, 65, 67
  match, 136
  wine, 137
  See also Tea and coffee services
Stanton, E. M., 156
Starr & Marcus, 33
Steins, 174, *175*
Sterling, 225–226
Stetson, A. M., 156
Stevens, Frank S., 19, 20
Stimers, Alban C., 143, *143*, 144–145
Stokes, Edward C., 150
Stove, electroplated portable, 218, *218*
Stuyvesant (flatware pattern), 220, *221*
Sugar bowls, 15, *15*, 48, 63, 64, 70, *70*, 72, 73, 79
  Art Deco, 269
  electroplated, 216, *216*
  Islamic, 202, *203*
  Japanese style, 190–192, *191*, 194, 195, *197*
  niello work, 202, *203*
  Paul Revere, 267
  presentation pieces, 143, *143*, 144
  See also Tea and coffee services
Sugar tongs, *203*
Sullivan, Louis, 146, *147*
Superbowl trophy, 176
Suspender mountings, 137
Sutton, Sir Richard, 171
Swords, 21, 22, 37, 83, 154–164, *155–164*, 166

Table setting, 93–96
Tankards, 137
  Paul Revere, 273
  silver, made for Jenny Lind, 9
Tantalus, *see* Liquor stand
Tape measures, 134
Tarni-Shield, 274
Taylor, Edwin C., 193, 200
Tea and coffee services, 25, 27, 41,

47, 48, *48*, 49, 52, 55, 56, *56*, 68, 68–79, 70, 72, 73, 131, 143, *143*, 264, *265*, 266
  Anderson, Peter B., *144*, 145, *145*
  Art Deco, 268, 269
  Chrysanthemum pattern, 78–79
  electroplated, 216
  gold, 253
  Japanese style, 194, 195, 197, *197*
  marks on, 245, 259
  niello work, 202, *203*
Tea caddies, 77, *77*, 190, *190*, 254
Tea trays, *see* Trays, tea
Teapots, 9, *10*, *48*, 69, 70, *70*, 72, 37, 79, *144*, 239
  electroplated, 216, 217, *217*
  Islamic, 202, *203*
  sketch for, by Frank Shaw, *215*, 215–216
  See also Tea and coffee services
Tennis trophies, 178, *179*
Tête-à-tête service, 63, *64*
  Islamic, 202, *203*
Thermometers, 137, *137*
Thimbles, 7, 134
Thompson, Mrs. Elizabeth, 127
Thread pattern, 90, *90*, 91
Thumb, Tom, 22, 141
Tiffany (flatware pattern), 13, 26, 97, 98, 110, *110*, 118
Tiffany, Burnett Y. (son of Charles Louis), 99
Tiffany, Charles Louis (son of Comfort),
  biographical sketch, 6
  Bryant Vase and, 34
  death of, 1, 43
  honors bestowed upon, 38, 196
  international expositions and, 24
  mark of, *251*, 256, 257
  Metropolitan Museum of Art and, 4
  Moore, Edward C., and, 11, 154
  Moore, John C., and, 10–11
  president, Tiffany & Co., 26
  publicist, 14, 22
  Robinson sword and, 162
  treasurer, Thomas Shaw & Co., 214
Tiffany, Comfort (father of Charles Louis), 6
Tiffany, Louis Comfort (son of Charles Louis), 31, 32, 46–50, 88, 121, *123*, 187, 263, 264, *265*
Tiffany & Co.
  Adams & Shaw firm absorbed by, 214
  Bryant Vase, *see* Bryant Vase

Tiffany & Co. (*continued*)
  founding of, 1
  Heydt's history of, 180
  incorporation, 26
  international expansion, 24
  international expositions and, 24–42, 182, 202, 252, 252
  Japanese metal workers at, 198–201
  marks, 244–261, 245–261
  Moore Company merges with, 26, 246
  silvermaking processes, 222–242
  training program, 31
Tiffany & Reed (Paris), 12, 31
Tiffany & Young, 6–7
  printed label, 7
Tiffany, Young and Ellis, 7–14, 17, 18, 69, 88, 90, 91, 181
  marks used by, 246, 247, 254, 254
Tiffany Studios, 47–50, 122, 263, 264
Tiffany style, 86
Tiffany Table Settings, 96
Toaster holder, 55
Tobacco boxes, 137
Toddy kettles, 137
Tom Thumb, 22, 141
Tomato Vine pattern, 98, 105, 105, 106, 106, 110, 257
Tongs, sugar, 203
Touch mark, *see* Maker's mark
Toulouse-Lautrec, Henri de, 181
Trays, 55, 79, 82–83, 83, 131
  Art Deco, 268, 269
  bell, 135
  Belmont, 149, 149
  Birch service, 20–21, 21, 22
  card, 124, 124, 125, 258
  circular "Aztec," 209, 209
  cloverleaf, 63, 64
  electroplated, 216, 217
  feeding, 138
  Japanese style, 197, 198
  Mackay service, 63, 64, 64
  oval, 17, 18, 82, 83, 83
  tea, 49, 50, 82, 83, 84
  USS *New Jersey*, 150
  See also Waiters
Trenton (light cruiser), 150
Trophies, 42, 169–179
  Coney Island Jockey Club, 2
  Japanese style, 190, 199
  University Club, 3, 3–4
  yachting, 29, 169–176, 170–176, 263, 271, 271
Trowels, silver, 136

Trumpet, speaking, 146, 146
TS1-701 (silver polish), 274
Tureens, 55, 79
  duPont service, 19
  sauce, 16, 17
  soup, Birch service, 20, 21
Tweed, Boss, 145
Twentieth-century silver, 262–275, 264–266, 268–272
Twinkle, 274

Umbrellas, 134–135
Union League Club
  gilt dinner plate presented to, 82
  sword presented to Admiral Farragut by, 157, 157
  vase presented to Thomas Nast by, 145, 145–146
University Club, silver backgammon trophy, 3, 3–4
Urn, coffee or hot water, electroplated, 218, 218, 258

Van Cott, Albert H., 91
Vanderbilt, Cornelius, private flatware pattern, 98, 101, 102
Vanderbilt, William K., private flatware pattern, 98, 101, 102
Vanderbilt, William K., Jr., 178, 179
Vanderbilt Cup, 178, 179
Vanderbilt Mansion, 128
Vases, 41, 45, 45, 47, 128, 129, 173, 174
  flower, 79, 128, 129
  Japanese, 182, 185, 185–186, 190, 193, 193, 195
  presentation, 146, 147
  working drawing for mounting design on, 188, 188
  See also Adams Gold Vase; Bryant Vase; Magnolia Vase; Nast Vase
Veblen, Thorstein, 93
Vegetable dishes, 15, 16, 16, 55, 79
  Birch service, 20, 21
  du Pont service, 19, 62
  Mackay service, 62, 63, 63
  yachting trophy, 170, 170
Victory, Queen, 1, 40, 43, 103, 244
Victorian Society in America, 4
Victorianism, changing views on, 1–5
Viking Punch Bowl, 5, 42, 202, 204, 205
Vine (flatware pattern), 27, 44, 98, 105, 110, 111, 186, 187, 187, 195

Wainwright, Richard, sword presented to, 164, 164
Waiters, 49, 79, 82, 263–264, 265
  electroplated, 216
  Mackay service, 64, 65
  See also Trays
Wall Street Journal, 272
Ward, John Quincy Adams, 165
Warren, George William, 34
Waste (slop) bowls, 48, 68, 70, 72, 73, 74, 76, 79, 144
  electroplated, 216
  See also Tea and coffee services
Wave Edge (flatware pattern), 98, 114, 118
Wave pattern, 78, 79
Wax-taper case, silver, 136
Weights of silver spoons and forks, 113, 118
Whistler, James Abbott McNeill, 181
Whistles, 137
Whitehouse, James H., 31, 33
Whitney, Emily Frances, 48, 49, 264, 265
Whitney, Gertrude Vanderbilt, 49
Whitney, Harry Payne, 49
Whitney Museum of American Art, 49
Whittier (flatware pattern), 220, 221
Wilkinson, George, 91
Windham (flatware pattern), 116
Wine coolers, 86, 87, 137
Wine labels, 137
Wine stands, 137
Winterthur Museum, 3, 77, 226, 273, 274
Winthrop (flatware pattern), 115
Women, status of, in Tiffany's, 228
Wood & Hughes, 9, 88
  mark, 247
Wood-block prints, Japanese, 181
Worder, John, 145
World's Columbian Exposition, *see* Columbian Exposition
World's Fair, New York: (1853), 19, 141; (1939), 263, 268
Worshipful Company of Goldsmiths (London), 243
Wright, Frank Lloyd, 3

Yachting trophies, 29, 169–176, 170–176, 263, 271, 271
Young, John B., 6, 7, 8